The Dreamer and Renaissance Man

— DIALOGUE WITH MY FATHER —

TERRY STONE

Fulton Books
Meadville, PA

Published by Fulton Books 2022

ISBN 978-1-63985-829-3 (paperback)
ISBN 978-1-63985-830-9 (digital)

Printed in the United States of America

The Dreamer and Renaissance Man is dedicated to the memory of my father, who indeed embodied these qualities. From reading his memoir and writing this response, I have learned about him and how his and my fraught relationship informed me as a person. This has been cathartic and transformative. Thank you, Daddy, for clearing things up.

It is also dedicated to the memory of my wonderful editor, Nancy Addison, writer, editor, and harpist extraordinaire. Sadly, she passed before seeing the book published and in finished form. No doubt she is playing her harp in heaven with the rest of the angels.

CONTENTS

Introduction..7

Chapter 1: Early Boyhood 9
Chapter 2: Stone Family Beginnings 16
Chapter 3: S. J. Stone, Merchandise........................23
Chapter 4: Country School Days................................28
Chapter 5: A Country Wake 36
Chapter 6: Samuel Jackson Stone Jr. 39
Chapter 7: Growing up on Lynches River 43
Chapter 8: Civilian Conservation Corps 52
Chapter 9: The Anvil Rings 59
Chapter 10: Social Life in Georgetown 65
Chapter 11: Life in Camp...70
Chapter 12: Myrtle Beach State Park 74
Chapter 13: Myrtle Beach Work and Play.................83
Chapter 14: Days in Old Gotham...............................92
Chapter 15: Job Hunting...108
Chapter 16: Facing Life's Realities...........................112
Chapter 17: 1946, Passing of an Era 122
Chapter 18: 1946–1948: Building a Home................126
Chapter 19: 1948–1956: Domestic Struggles............133
Chapter 20: 1971: Nobody's Perfect.........................144
Chapter 21: 1950s, '60s, and '70s: Thirty Years of Shipbuilding 149
Chapter 22: Strange Pastures.....................................183
Chapter 23: Camera and Typewriter 211

Chapter 24: Adventures Here:...225

    Miami, Florida 225
    Outer Banks, North Carolina................................230
    Brown Mountain Lights, North Carolina.............237
    Jamestown, Virginia 240
    Everglades, Florida 242
    Southwestern United States 267

Chapter 25: Adventures There: 269

    Canada...269
    Scotland 273
    Yucatan 283
    Cayman Island 296
    Jamaica..298

Chapter 26: Rubbing Shoulders and Noteworthy Encounters....303

Afterword..319
Acknowledgments 323

INTRODUCTION

My relationship with my father was fraught with tension, discord, and unpleasantness. I guess I was a sensitive child, but my dad's gruff personality was off-putting, and his energy conveyed that I was a nuisance. He lived his real life apart from mine. The only way I could interact with him was in his world, which was in printing black-and-white photos in his darkroom or building a boat in our garage. As I grew up, and after I was out on my own, we connected somewhat. But I had no knowledge of how remarkable his life had been. When he was about seventy years old, he wrote an autobiographical memoir, and it unlocked the door into his extraordinary life. I carried around his manuscript for thirty years, trying to figure out how I could get it published. Finally, I joined a writer's group, the Cornelia Company of Writers, and this book resulted. I very much want others to get to know this man, who was a dreamer and Renaissance man. I now feel I know his heart, and I love him dearly!

He dedicated his book to me: "For Terry, with whom I wish I had spent more time." His stories drew me into his world of a South Carolina country boy growing up on a river, loving his life yet dreaming of the world beyond. They revealed that he had a difficult time expressing love for the people closest to him, including me. But I came away with the idea that perhaps his dedication to me was only part of the book's purpose. The title, *Too Many Walls to Climb*, actually conveyed that his ultimate goals were thwarted by others. Nevertheless, in the first section, entitled "Observations," he recalls a time with me.

> I remember Terry, as a little tot on a brief trek of make-believe; a trek through the wild, green myrtle bushes and sand dunes of eastern Folly [Beach]. A pretense of a stranger frontier and suddenly the sea. I'll always regret not creating more of such situations with and for her. Life passes so fast. Little ones grow up so soon. Before you know it…the chance is gone.

I have no recollection of that day. I wish I did. It was obviously a special day for a dad and his little girl.

My father wanted to be a motion picture photographer. That goal was thwarted by external forces—namely the Great Depression, family pressures, and World War II. He subsequently felt his life wasn't successful or quite fulfilled. However, the memoir revealed that the life he actually did live was rich and fascinating. He related stories of his growing up in early twentieth century rural South Carolina, two-year commitment with the Civilian Conservation Corp, and experiences in New York studying motion picture photography. Unable to find a job in the motion picture industry, he returned to South Carolina and met and married my mother. His story continued with his building a cottage on the marsh of James Island and his struggles as he described a life and career as a shipbuilder. Emotional challenges sent him into a mysterious world of mystical experiences, followed by a second career in photojournalism and art. Finally, his travels and exploration in various parts of the world developed his talents as an archeologist. Quite a diversity of experiences made him the man I knew several years before his death in 1998.

The events he experienced and the people he encountered deserve to be known by people other than me. I want to let him tell his own truly amazing story, through me sometimes, but mostly in his own words. I will interact with him along the way.

Early Boyhood

Daddy's earliest recollections, beginning in his infancy around 1913–1914, are a treasure trove of wonderful stories, told as only he can tell them:

> I have a faint recollection of the old log trains that passed through the big pasture back of our house on their way to the big saw mill down by the river. This view, I believe, was from my basket by the kitchen window. And much later, there were the soldier trains that passed on the main railroad that ran in front of our house. I was impressed by the khaki-clad arms, waving from the train windows, boys, like I would later be, on their way to kill "Kaizer Bill" (William II of Germany). I recall finding along the railroad track a steel battlefield helmet that had fallen from a train. I proudly wore it on my small head, though it hid my eyes and ears as I strutted around with a stick gun on my shoulder and my asafetida ball on a string around my neck. I too was off to war to kill that bogeyman, the Kaiser.
>
> On Armistice Day (November 11, 1918), my father loaded all of us in the car, and we went to town to share in the cheering and to have our

pictures made. Bands marched in the streets and made a lot of noise. I was dressed in my little white suit with knee-length pants and held a small American flag. My knee-length white stockings had more wrinkles than the flag had bars. The big eyes under my cowlick were the result of my search for the birdie the man with the black rag over his head said I would see but didn't.

This picture of him is adorable. I remember seeing it many times during my lifetime, but it is only now that I can see a little five-year-old girl who looks amazingly like him in pictures he took of me when I was that age. I, too, have a vague memory of lying in my crib under a sunny window. I also remember the night my pacifier broke—a real calamity! I remember Mother setting me on the worktop of the Hoosier cabinet in the kitchen of our second-story apartment on Cleveland Street in Charleston, near Hampton Park. I was wailing to beat the band. God only knows where he found a pacifier in 1947, when there weren't so many twenty-four-hour drug stores. Yet he went out in the middle of the night and came home with a new one, which I wouldn't have anything to do with because it didn't feel like the old one. I don't think I ever used a pacifier again.

I had two experiences when I was four years old that stand tall in my mind. I got lost in the deep woods, and while climbing a peach tree in our backyard to get one of the pretty pink peaches, I fell out into bamboo cane stubble that had been recently chopped off and required my first trip to a hospital to have it removed. I remember fighting the black thing they held over my face as they gave me gas to knock me out. My mother kept the joint of cane stalk in her jewelry box for years. I still have the scar.

The "lost" incident happened one late evening when my parents and older sister and brother were walking a winding road through the big forest that lay to the east of our home. We were coming home from an afternoon visit to the Taylor farm. My siblings were far ahead of my parents and me, and I wanted to run ahead, catch up, and walk with them. Permission granted, I dashed off, rounded the next bend in the road, and out of vision of everyone. I took a wrong fork somewhere in the road that led me farther and farther from the main trail into a vast, swampy bog, where I got all mired up and my shoes came off in the sticky mud.

My parents arrived at the house and inquired about me. Brother and sister hadn't seen me. Night was approaching and they all hurried back toward the big forest, enlisting the aid of old "Uncle" Wash McIver and his wife, who lived in a cabin in the first clearing by the branch, where the kids caught crawdads to use as fish bait. Before the search party got to the big forest they saw Tom, the older Taylor boy, coming toward them leading by the hand the muddiest little boy they had ever seen. He had heard me bawling like a young calf down in the swamp and found me. He said the first words I had spoken as he approached were, "Hey, Mister, put on me this shoe!"

I can see the image of that little boy now: The tears well up in my eyes, thinking about how precious he was to his family and community. Life must have been delightful in that country place near the river where he grew up. His earliest experiences informed his personality without a doubt.

By the time I was five years old, I had already established two awe-striking objects in my trinity—the motorcycle and the tractor. They were sacred idols in this growing boy's mind. Remove all other things from the face of the earth, but not the motorcycle and the tractor. Their looks beguiled the lad's young soul; their sounds sent thrills up his spine. Their tracks in the sand were symbols showing that these magnificent creations had passed that way. After World War I, my infinite triangle was completed—the "aeroplane" was added.

Its coming completed my trinity. Little girls had their dollhouses, tiny tea sets, and frilly little things with which to putter—blah! Not me! With my visions of the motorcycle, the tractor, with its "clacky" wheels, and the airplane with broad yellow wings and gulping engine, let me retreat into the recesses of the childhood mind where dreams are born.

The first airplane I ever saw was on the ground. My pa (I never called him Dad—somehow it sounded silly) had loaded us all in the car (a 1916 model Dort) and drove to the Fair Grounds on the north side of the nearest town where the two World War I flyers had started some early day barnstorming. The big yellow thing, all smutty around the nose, sat there on the racetrack on its two wheels and tail. One of the fellows wearing a leather coat and cap crawled up to one of the holes on top and slipped down into it with only his head sticking out and hollered, "Contact!" The other man took hold of the shiny board fastened into the front, called a propeller, with both hands, threw one leg up in the air like he was trying to split his breeches, and snatched down so hard it made him grunt. Instant hell broke loose. Black smoke and fire belched from the engine as it roared into life, blowing my hat off and filling my eyes full of trash. I regained my eyesight in time to see the big yellow bird lift off the ground at the end of the field and "wabble" into the sky. That was the clincher! The noise, the trash, and the hat—all was forgiven!

The aircraft of the early years were so slow and so noisy you could hear one coming when it was five miles away, if the wind was right, and you can imagine what a hole that put in Miss Hortense's reading class at the community school house. When some sharp ear picked up the first exciting drone of an oncoming airplane, the whole school went into pandemonium. Doors burst open, screaming kids poured out, all eyes to the distant sky to be the first to see.

A railroad ran through my community, and in those days, aviators usually followed the tracks leading from one place to the other. That gave our school kids the frequent treat of watching an aircraft flying over. Everyone searched the horizon until the oncoming plane was spotted, a distinction that made the spotter hero of the day. Also, everyone watched until the passing plane was a vanishing speck in the distance, some claiming to see it long after it had vanished. With much wild shouting, Miss Hortense would finally get us all back in our desks, but the airplane was the general topic for the rest of the day.

I had a swing under the limbs of a big maple tree in the cow pasture behind our house. It was my aeroplane! I would put on a pair of old miner's goggles, which had no glass in them, and in that old swing, I would fly, fly, fly! I visited the old home site not long ago, some forty-five years after I had left there. The old buildings were gone, fire removed them years before; new buildings stood here and there. But back in the thicket that had been the cow pasture of my boyhood, I found the old maple tree. It was dead, a still-standing ghost of yesterday, and still clinging to the big limb were rusted fragments of the cables of my swing.

I remember the many Sunday afternoons Daddy drove my mother and me to the municipal airport in Charleston, South Carolina, where he parked the car across the road from the airstrip. We would watch for a couple of hours as airplanes took off and landed. Airplanes varied from small, privately owned planes to large commercial airliners. They were much smaller and all propeller-run unlike the passenger jet airliner of today. We watched them take off and land, wondering where they were going and from where they were coming. Little did I know that Daddy's first experiences as a tiny boy had instilled a passion in him for these planes that would accompany him through most of his life.

A token from his childhood fascination with tractors still survives. I still have the little iron tractor with the "farmer" riding it. That tractor used to be black, as I recall. But somewhere along the

way it got sprayed with gold-colored paint. He never got a real tractor, nor did he get an airplane or a motorcycle.

Before we continue with his stories, let's see exactly where and
when those stories occurred. Of course, he has covered even this in
his memoir.

Stone Family Beginnings

I was born in the small farming community of Effingham, South Carolina, at 10:00 p.m. the winter night of December 21, 1913, under the sign of Sagittarius, just two hours out of Capricorn. This cusp situation has caused no problems though because the two are so much the same. I was delivered by a country doctor named Dr. O. W. Purvis, the father of the FBI agent, Melvin Purvis, noted for his role in the G-men/John Dillinger affair. My father was Samuel J. Stone, and my mother was Ellen Lenore Turner Stone. They spent their adult life in the retail mercantile business. I have two living siblings, William Golden, brother, and Jewell Cowart, sister, both older than me. With my entry into this cycle of materiality I brought numerous attributes, many which were good and were definitely not acquired in the Victorian era. A few bad ones were.

The records I have on my father's side of the family show the purchase from one James Keith one hundred acres of land on Lynches Creek in which is now Florence County on January 14, 1775, by one Austin Stone, my great-great grandfather, for the sum of 250 pounds. This tract was granted to James Keith by King George III through the Lord Proprietor Lord Charles Grenville Montague. I have the original land grant. On November 1, 1802 (after the colonies gained independence), Austin Stone enlarged this holding by a grant of 435 acres adjoining from the Honorable John Drayton, Governor of South Carolina.

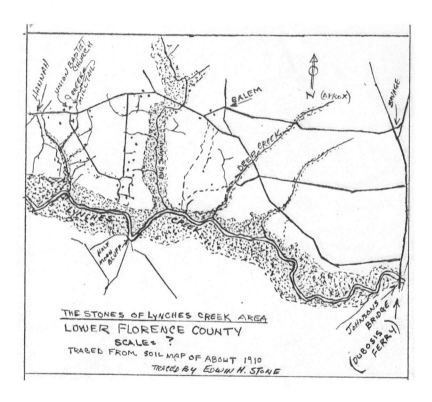

THE STONES OF LYNCHES CREEK AREA
LOWER FLORENCE COUNTY
SCALE: ?
TRACED FROM SOIL MAP OF ABOUT 1910
TRACED BY EDWIN H. STONE

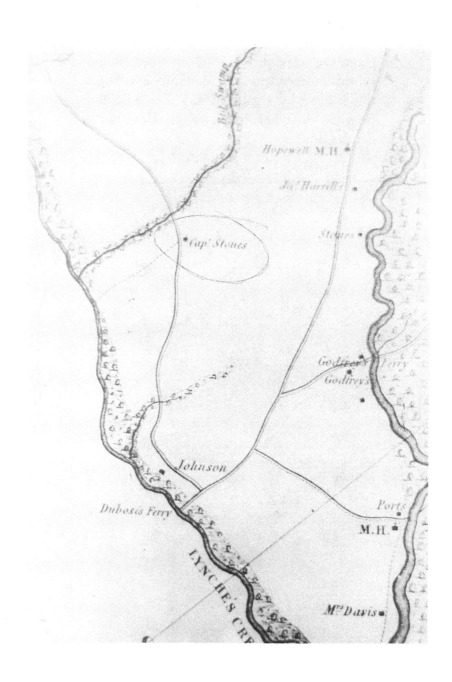

Later an additional grant added eight hundred acres across Lynches Creek to Austin Stone's estate. Austin Stone was the patriarch of the large family of Stones that developed in the eastern part of the state and was involved in the early development of the state's waterways. He was involved in the war of independence, both in the military and as a civilian supporter of the army with foodstuff and other supplies. Austin Stone immigrated into South Carolina from North Carolina and Virginia. This migration and the family lineage are traceable through records compiled by descendants who have devoted much time, effort, and money to it.

There are but few void spaces in the lineage that leads back through North Carolina, mid-state, and the tidewater area of Virginia. The earliest Stone traceable goes back to the year 1644. This was one William Stone. It is known that no less than twenty-one William Stones came to Virginia in the founding period of the colony of Virginia so within that group the lineage is lost. Carolyn P. Ward, a researcher of note, has developed this lineage to its ultimate loss in infinity. To her, credit for the following list falls. I'm also indebted to James Allen Poston for his aid in my earlier search and for referring me to Mrs. Ward.

The beautiful Lynches River is a large part of my dad's boyhood. Here he describes what the river meant to him:

The river: nothing is so dear to the heart of a country boy as the river. Cheated is the boy who does not have a river. If he knows the river, he has the fundamental requirements for a boy's outdoor life. He is a cane pole expert. On the river, he is a coon-skinned wilderness explorer. On the river, he is a reincarnated Huckleberry Finn.

I grew up by the river, and all of these things were mine. The river is an ever-changing thing, with the seasons like the fields and forest through which it flows. In winter, its waters are cold and dark in the depths and is seemingly motionless. It is brownish over the sandbars where its tannic acid shows through. With spring comes the freshets from upcountry rains, and it becomes a surging, yellow serpentine thing rushing to the lowlands, then on to the sea. Then back to normal and the warmth of summer—back to swimming days, fishing days, a gentle, flowing thing. The river has a soothing, magical quality. It is a gathering place, if not to swim or fish, just to sit and dream and watch a leaf float by.

This river has always been a part of the Stone family. Years before the country boy's idyllic river life, patriarch Austin Stone and his father loaded their crops onto barges to journey further down to Georgetown, where they were collected into ships to take them across the Atlantic to England until the Revolution and then Europe later on. The Lynches River not only provided the means of transportation but also made the crops themselves possible by watering the rich soil in which grew tobacco, cotton, vegetables, peaches, and other fruit.

For around 250 years, our relatives have inhabited and dominated that part of South Carolina. Stone descendants saturate the towns around the area, starting with the main city, Florence, and including Pamplico, Lake City, Johnsonville, Effingham, and Hemmingway. But the river runs far beyond our family's lands.

This photo by an unknown author is licensed under CC BY-SA.

The Lynches River meanders from Union County, North Carolina, southeast through Chesterfield, Kershaw, Lee, Darlington, Sumter, Florence, and Williamsburg counties in South Carolina. It eventually joins the Pee Dee River to flow into the Atlantic Ocean at Georgetown, South Carolina. In 1828, gold was discovered along tributaries of the river in the Pageland and Jefferson area, and no less than fifty-eight gold mines were worked over the next century.

When Austin Stone Sr. died, he left his property to his children and so on down the line until my great-grandfather's passing. My grandfather, Samuel Jackson Stone Jr., chose not to settle on the family land. I have heard it told that he was disinherited because he moved away from the home place and settled in Effingham to live out his life and become quite the center of the community with his big country store. I'll let Daddy describe S. J. Stone, Merchandise, the store he grew up in.

CHAPTER 3

S. J. Stone, Merchandise

My father's country store deserves a good bit of exposure. It was the turn-of-the-century type, where the merchant established his business and his family in one building. The big store occupied the larger area with rooms for the family at the back and upstairs. It was the big general store, where anything that would sell was sold. Often, the medium of exchange [currency] was the lowly egg. Sometimes corn. Frequently, the "jot 'em down" system was used. Familiar phrases were, "Three egg worth of sugar," "five egg worth of kerosene." Eggs were a good exchange. The hotels and restaurants in town were ready markets. But no guinea eggs! You could not sell guinea eggs for use as breakfast food. Besides, my father bitterly hated guineas, hated the noisy "chanty-chant" of the little round speckled fowl!

Merchandise was a diversified inventory. You could buy in his store a baby carriage or a two-horse wagon; a horse collar or a lady's corset. Shoes, rack dresses, ready-made shirts, pants, bolt by-the-yard cloth, parcels, chambrays, and homespuns. Also, green coffee beans, barrels of flour, oil sausage, nutmeg, shotgun shells, and bile pills. The list would be endless. Before the influx of the automobile and good roads, the store was literally an institution. Three times a year, my father made buying trips to Baltimore and New York to the big wholesale houses and bought three carloads (railroad boxcars), have it shipped by coastal steamer to Charleston, then by rail upstate where wagons completed the transit to the store.

Unpacking was a big task, which my mother always supervised. She was probably more efficient than my father and was generally considered the store's manager. The store was my father's life. However, not a great believer in change, he failed to follow merchandising trends as the automobile and highways led the rural populous to the big chain stores going up in the cities, and I saw him sit in his country store as the era of the country merchant declined and faded away, and so did he.

Perhaps there were a couple of things relative to the era that he passed on into the next. There were names for his children, two of us anyway. He picked names for his children from the products sold in his store. He got my sister's name, Jewell, from a lard tub. Swifts Pure Jewell Lard. On the tub was a picture of a very wholesome-looking girl. I suppose that has some implication in his choice for her. As for my name, I never understood it. I was named after a very pungent perfume, popular in those days—"Hoyt's Nickel Cologne." The five-cent bottle of fragrance was guaranteed to squelch any and all body odors. Just a dash or two and people could tell where you had been for a week after. The manufacturer of this potent stuff was Edwin W. Hoyt. I got his first and last name.

The domestic element of my father's building where I grew up spilled over into the business part of it. We actually lived all over the place, especially in winter. The store was heated by a big flat top, two-eyed, cast-iron, wood-burning stove, located near the rear of the store. It was never without a pan of roasting peanuts (five cents a bag) on its top. We kids studied our lessons on the counters closer to the stove by kerosene oil lamplight. Papa chewed his chewing tobacco and spit toward the cardboard cuspidor, sometimes hitting it. Mama stirred the peanuts and did the many things mothers do. On a box stood a scratchy gramophone and a few records, mostly classics. There were two or three I remember—*Ballet Egyptian* part 1 and 2, and *The Owl and the Pussycat*. I always liked the first one. The gramophone survived until the battery-powered radio was moved in.

The cast-iron stove was efficient but not without its problems. The stovepipe extended up from the stove, high enough to clear one's head. Then it elbowed across toward the side of the room. Finally, it turned up again into an open bottomed brick flue through which the rain came sometimes when the wind was out of the north. When it rained, black soot would fall into the rice barrel below. To relocate the rice barrel was not desirable because the only other spot available would make it necessary to reach over it to get to the nail kegs. We tried covering the rice barrel with a burlap sheet, but that formed a pitfall on the cat's route from the cheese box to the salt herring barrel. I don't think it was necessary for the cat to scatter that much rice every time he fell in, but that was the way it was, and the burlap was soon discarded.

*****

Old Santa Claus lost his mystique very early in my childhood. In my neck of the woods, Christmas stocking stuffing was indeed a broken-record thing. Each year, always the same: one apple, one orange, a web of raisins dried on the stem, the box of sparklers, a pack of little "fizzlers" (Chinese fire crackers), and if you were old enough, a roman candle and one or two big-bang pyrotechnics. Anything more was, for many kids, nonexistent. But for those who did get a toy, there was the doll for the girl, the pocket-knife for the boy. One thing that brought about my early understanding of Santa Claus was my father's country store. It didn't take much, even for a dumb kid, to see that Pa's store was really Santa's supply house and not some workshop up near the North Pole.

Although my grandparents still lived in the old store and home place when I was born in 1945, I don't recall it at all. My parents told the story about my first birthday, when they took me up to Effingham to visit my grandparents for the day. Even though I have no conscious recollection of the day, it was marred with something that has lurked deep in my subconscious ever since.

On June 20, 1946, dawned a beautiful, sunny day. Mama spread a blanket out on the grass by my grandparents' house, put me down on it, and gave me some saltine crackers to try out my few teeth on while everybody enjoyed the sunshine. Apparently, I was left unsupervised for a few minutes. The old rooster was also left unsupervised. The story went that the rooster just walked right onto my blanket and pecked a cracker out of my hand. It was said I howled and screamed bloody murder. To this day I have an aversion to things with beaks.

Another event occurred that marked the memory of the day as bittersweet. My parents and I had traveled back to Charleston the afternoon of my birthday. The following month, July 21, 1946, my grandfather went into the outhouse for his "daily constitutional" and died from a heart attack right then and there. My mother has always said that my dad changed that day, and he never really recovered from losing his father. How sad for everyone. I don't remember my grandfather at all. They say he absolutely loved me to pieces. My cousin Bill and I were recently going through an old photo album my dad had put together decades ago. In it are photographs of our grandmother and grandfather that my dad apparently had taken that same summer birthday we had visited them. Amazingly, his great-grandsons Sammy (named for him) and Tommy look just like he did. He was in his late seventies when the photo in the album was taken (the day of my first birthday). Although it is one of only a couple of pictures I have ever seen of him, I have a glimpse of him through my younger cousins, now in their early sixties.

Before continuing with Daddy's recollections, I must talk a bit about how I came to call my grandmother Ma 'Tone. Cousin Billy (we are the only first cousins on our fathers' side) was born about eleven years before I was.

As the firstborn grandchild, Billy got to name our grandparents before I came along. I suppose Billy was a bit tongue-tied as a little fellow. He just could not say Grandma Stone or Grandma Coker (his maternal grandmother) to save his neck. So, he called our paternal grandparents Ma 'Tone and Pa 'Tone and his maternal ones Ma 'Tokey and Pa 'Tokey. I called Ma 'Tone (pronounced with short *a*) by that name for the rest of her life, and so did Billy.

Country School Days

A s early twentieth-century general stores differ from our shopping experiences of today, the little country schools also offered a different experience from our modern mega-schools. The intimacy of small classes and small teacher-to-student ratio created an atmosphere of learning far different from current schools. Modern schools with a large student body in a more formal setting have the advantage of many teaching strategies that broaden the students' lives. But these tiny country schools, while challenging students in a number of ways, provided priceless opportunities for bonding with their classmates, as well as learning certain "housekeeping" skills. Daddy writes about one of these, as well as other school day traditions.

The most memorable thing about the closing of our country school year was an event that took place on the last day—the traditional turning over of the boys' outdoor toilet. It was really a kind of ritual. Although the meaning may be hidden somewhere in the recesses of my boyhood mind, I cannot recall what it was. It was an annual occasion; five or six of the bigger boys— we had some seventeen and eighteen-year-olds still in fifth grade—would put their farm-built muscle to the little three-hole, slanted roof shack and amid the squeals and cheers of all the students gathered there to watch, a big heave-ho and the little backyard establishment went up and over on its back. Looking through the three holes from the bottom was an unusual experience, but no one got too close because the pit was still there.

Probably the most memorable thing about school opening each September was the pain of walking on the stubbles of freshly mowed stink weed with bare feet. The yellow stinkweed stubble was like walking on an Allahabad Hindu holy man's spike board.

The school building was not far from my home, in sight across an eighty-acre field, about five minutes fast walking. School buses hadn't found their way into our neck of the woods yet, and some kids had to walk four or five miles. The building was a box-like, two-story thing with two classrooms downstairs and a big auditorium upstairs where school assembly, playacting, and after school affairs were held. The home demonstration lady met the women of the community there once a month to tell them they had been doing things wrong all their lives and to teach them how much better baked yeast loaf was for them than the starchy flour dough biscuits.

This was the beginning of the sandwich revolution and the ending of the lowly biscuit in the kid's lunch pail. I always carried my biscuits in a brown paper bag because my pop owned a store and plenty of paper bags were handy on the counter by the scales where coffee, rice, dried beans, and other dry vittles were weighed. It always embarrassed me to take lunch in a paper bag because the stain of my oil sausage went clean through and everybody knew what I was having for lunch. Most kids carried lunch in the traditional little bright tin pail with the string for the finger on the top of the lid. These little round pails turned brown spotted with rust in time. There also was a transition about that time. The pails began to disappear and were replaced by a square tin box with a hinged top and a ball for a handle. They were painted gay colors and had little white lambs holding hands and dancing painted all around the sides. It always puzzled me how lambs could hold hands.

But by bag or by box, the country biscuit was an institution! Until one thinks about it, he doesn't appreciate how far reaching in character a country biscuit was. The ways to alter the basic biscuit were many: there was the ham biscuit, the sausage biscuit, the fried egg biscuit, the jelly biscuit, the molasses biscuit, the butter biscuit, the sugar biscuit; and some combination of these. My mother frequently made a butter-sugar biscuit. Splitting a biscuit in half, she would spread butter on one half, usually the bottom half—of course biscuits have a top and a bottom half— and on the butter she sprinkled sugar until it looked like frosting. Then she put the two halves back together. It was very tasty, but I always had the feeling of chewing sand.

There was another aspect to a biscuit. The variation of size, shape, texture, color, and taste. There was the normal biscuit—average size, brown on top and bottom, firm—real good for butter, egg, sausage patty, and that kind of stuff. Some country gals liked to be dainty and bake little things about the size of half dollars. I always called them tonsil teasers. You could throw in a hand full and *gulp*! They were gone!

Then there were the big, pale, fat softies—these made fine molasses biscuits. You bored a hole into its interior from the side with a stiff little finger and poured in the molasses, corn syrup if store-bought, and packed the soft white dough into the hole to keep it from running back out. By lunchtime, the sweet stuff had filtered much of the biscuit's fluffy interior and...oh! What a treat. I think this it was probably the forerunner of the jelly doughnut.

Biscuit-grown school kids had many complexes. Some forward and bubbling, some shy and reserved. I remember little seven-year-old Mary C, who never got up the nerve to raise her hand until after she had wee-weed in her pants. Modern psychologists would call this delayed infantile attention-wish syndrome. I would call it delayed bladder revenge! Some had wild things to tell. One eager little red-headed boy was concerned and dead serious as he told his teacher that his daddy had had a fit on top of his mamma that morning before they got out of bed.

I had nice teachers for the most part but not old lady Hodges. I hated her and her big black Essex that she drove out from town each morning. She flunked me once, adding another year to my lower grade schooling. Miss Gant was a honey pie, and I stole apples from my father's store many times, slyly leaving them in her desk drawer. She knew I did it and would give me a little touch on my shoulder as she passed by my desk. All that came to an end, though, when she opened her drawer one morning and found a dead sand hill crane stuffed in it. After ordering one of the bigger boys to remove the bird, she ordered everyone to never, never open her desk drawer again! There went her candy.

Snows of winter would bank snowdrifts up to the window level, and the little wood-burning stove didn't keep down the chill. Kids had head colds and wiped their noses on their woolen sweater sleeves, which in time became crusty. Boys took turns bringing wood from the woodpile down in the thicket, and we liked that because it was an opportunity to grab a few puffs on a rabbit tobacco cigarette.

Every Friday afternoon there was a program upstairs in the big hall. There were speeches, songs, and prayers. It was a break from routine and also an opportunity for little talents to be heard. Once, I decided I should be on the program; so I memorized a little poem from one of our books and told my teacher I was ready for the next Friday's program. "You're sure you know it," she had insisted. I was sure. Friday came, and in time, I was announced and the name of my rendition. To this day, I cannot remember the title of the poem, but I will remember forever the line on which the teacher had to cue me when my mind went blank toward the end. I stood on one leg like a stork, rubbing the side of it with a dirty foot and muttering, "I forgot the rest of it." After an eternity, the teacher said, "our thrushes..." Oh yeah, I grabbed the line, red-faced and trembling, "Our thrushes now are silent, our swallows flown away..." I finished the poem and ran from the stage.

I got into another situation that turned sour at school a year or two later. The school's bully, Woodrow, a big-eared, owl-headed fellow, who had overstayed his time in grade school by a couple of years, had riled me and another diminutive boy named Charlie, and we planned to fight him after school. Word passed fast, and all the kids gathered in the cornfield down the road to see us beat the bully. It was planned that Charlie would tackle him from the front, and while he had him occupied, I would come in from the rear for the kill. Charlie flew into him like a mosquito hawk on a fence post, and I—equally small—climbed him from the rear. He lunged forward to the ground, squishing Charlie under him and pitch-

ing me over his head. By the time Charlie and I
got to our feet again, he had taken real defensive
action. Pulling up a cornstalk, roots heavy with
dirt, Woodrow swung it around and around like
a club. I thought of Goliath and that little fellow on the mountain. Charlie dived through his
defensive gyrations and locked arms around his
legs. I tried to dive in also, but the swinging club
walloped me against the head. The stars flew, and
my eyes and mouth were filled with dirt. I was
out of it—the action. I decided that fighting was
as defeating as poetry.

Romance began to play a role in Daddy's development before
he even went into puberty. Many boys want nothing to do with girls
when they are in elementary school, but I have known one or two
myself who always liked the girls and whom the girls always liked.
My dad was definitely one of these.

I was beginning to discover girls in the later
years of grade school and soon learned that this
interest also held hidden hazards. This was in the
transition period from flapper girl to bloomer girl,
the middle of the Roaring Twenties. My first girl
frustration was a little dark-head, slightly freck-
led gal in my class. All little girls and some bigger
ones were wearing the black pongee bloomers
under abbreviated skirts. The full-cut bloomers
had elastic in the legs just above the knee that
allowed them to blouse and bounce sassily as the
girl walked. I don't think she cared too much
for me, although I wasted a lot of time looking
moon-eyed at her instead of paying attention
in class—probably the reason old lady Hodges
flunked me. She was too old to remember young
love. I do remember that a few years later in

high school, when the young girl and I were old enough to know a bird from a bee, I walked her home from church. We decided to kiss and see if there was really anything there. After two or three kisses from which no bells rang, no stars twinkled, and no steam arose, we concluded there wasn't anything, so we just let it be and remained good friends.

CHAPTER 5

A Country Wake

In the small town of early twentieth-century Effingham, deaths were not observed in quite the same way as they are now. No funeral home viewings. No funeral homes, period! Daddy religiously followed the customs associated with the passing of family and friends. He tells of one occasion in his earliest recollections.

It wasn't a spreading chestnut tree, but it was a spreading oak. On a little rise by the county road stood the village blacksmith shop. On the north side of the smutty little building stood the oak, its spreading limbs reaching over the chimney through which the smoke from the forge passed. To the east, only a bit farther than you could spit, were the railroad tracks, and southward beyond a dog fennel patch was the cotton gin—one of them. At times, depending on the ebb and flow of prosperity in the farming community, a second one operated. The community also had a sawmill, a gristmill, and four or five stores, depending on when you counted them. There were only two big general stores where you could buy anything. One was my father's S. J. Stone, Merchandise. Other stores were small limited-stock things that opened and closed intermittently like bullfrogs catching flies down in the cattail pond.

Old Mr. Hudson's blacksmith's shop was the place my mother knew to look for me when I was missing. The old man, big and hairy with a walrus-like mustache and a voice so soft you'd think his whole diet was marshmallows, had a voluntary helper—*me*! The country boy with the cowlick was probably more in the way than he was help, but the old man never failed to let me do that which I could do. I turned the crank that made the forge blow and kept the tools in the wooden water tub so they would not come off the handle. He tried to explain everything he was doing to me, and it was from this humble shop that certain things later in life became relative.

The old man died when I was twelve or thirteen, and I was one of several males to sit at his wake. A country wake—this was before mortuaries and embalming was popular in our neck of the woods—was not always like the name implies. Everyone usually didn't stay awake. To sit up all night where the corpse lies on a table grows tiresome, and most if not all people present sometimes fall asleep. This happened at Mr. Hudson's wake. The object, other than ritualistic respect, is to keep the house open, all windows and doors, to see that the body stays as cool as possible, keep flies away, and that the half dollars over his eyes stay in place. The first half of the night usually goes well—serious conversation is livelier in an effort to stall off fatigue. But by two or three in the morning, most sitters are snoring in their chairs. This was the case at my old friend's wake. I alone succeeded in staying alert all night. I would have felt unfaithful if I had not.

My dad was always respectful of the passing of people in his life. He was faithful to go to funerals, as long as he was able. This early experience with Mr. Hudson embedded in Daddy a loyalty he never failed to demonstrate in later years.

CHAPTER 6

Samuel Jackson Stone Jr.

W hile we are talking about my grandfather's store and as we travel through my father's life, I certainly want to call attention to my grandfather—Samuel Jackson Stone Jr. Since I never had the privilege of knowing him, and my dad never talked much about him, Daddy's memoir opens the door to my Pa 'Tone's life. Like his father, my dad, Pa 'Tone was a man of many interests and talents, himself.

My father's life was diversified—farming in his boyhood in summer, rafting logs down the river. He had been store clerk, later opening his own store. He owned three stores at one time, which didn't last because he trusted people. He also, in earlier years, owned a turpentine still, made wooden barrels, owned a sawmill, cruised timber, had a bicycle shop, was a watch and clock-maker, was a photographer, postmaster, gunsmith, had a real estate mortgage business, and started an early car dealership that failed. Some of these ventures ran concurrently with some degree of success. However, his main string was his big mercantile business, of which my mother was perhaps the unofficial manager. I think his brief venture in the auto dealership had the most interesting twist.

His first car, a copperhead Model T. Ford, was replaced with a new car just out in 1916 called the Dort, an assembly car put together in Flint, Michigan. There was an assembly plant where all components were contracted. Fisher built the body, Lycoming built the engine, Tempkin built the gears, wheels, and all the rolling parts. My dad took one Dort for himself—a touring car with fabric top and side curtains and red Kelly Springfield tires. He sold four cars and, went out of business. Two years later, Dort Motorcar Company in Flint went out of business also. In those days, cars were not traded in. When a person got a new car, the old one was dragged out by the barn where hens nested in it and weeds grew through it. My father's Dort didn't suffer that fate. With the failure of the Dort company, parts were no longer available, but my dad went out and found the four cars he had sold—some were junked—and bought them back, had them dragged to our back yard. By cannibalizing them, he kept his touring car running for fifteen years.

The Dort played a role in an incident of nature's fury when a tornado swept through Effingham in the early 1920s. My dad writes about it, describing the storm and its aftermath:

A tornado swept through my home community on April 30, 1924. I didn't see the actual funnel but experienced the rain and wind. It was about 4:00 p.m. We were in the old square, wooden school building, and the rain and wind were something terrible. School turned out about the time it all ended, and I ran the path through the broom straw bottom to our house over by the oak grove about a quarter mile away.

My father was getting the Dort touring car out to go up to where the storm had passed. He had seen the funnel passing to the north of us, with treetops and parts of buildings whirling in the air. He said, "There was destruction that thing!" We traveled the sandy road up as far as the railroad and turned north into the old Florence road that went past Java and Bannockburn. At the Booty Ward place, we saw where the tornado had passed. Trees were twisted up and houses and barns scattered like matchwood. Dead and injured people lay all around.

My father flagged a passing freight train, and some of the injured were put into the caboose to be taken to the hospital in Florence. The homes of some of my school chums were destroyed, and their people injured. One boy's mother was killed. The next day, my father made pictures of some of the destruction, which I kept for many years. Old timers who remembered other tornados said our community was in the "storm path."

Two brothers, Dory and Frank Waddell, who lived by the river, soon dug themselves a "storm cellar" in the red clay bank and fitted it out with bed clothes, bottles of water, etc., and every time the skies darkened thereafter, they rushed their families into the cave. After a number of years, this practice was abandoned, though. Then one night a small tornado passed through, twisted Dory's house off the foundation, and dropped it with the front door, looking the other way with Dory in it. No one was injured.

I'm impressed that Pa 'Tone took the lead to help the injured and be a calm but strong force in the community.

Growing up on Lynches River

A kid growing up by a waterway lived an idyllic life. At least it seems that way to me since I grew up on salt marsh creeks on James Island, outside of Charleston, South Carolina, in the 1950s and 1960s. For my dad, the freshwater Lynches River provided the resources for a kid to learn self-sufficiency at a young age. He tells of several adventures, typical of country boys in the early part of the twentieth century:

> My friends and I had a camp on the river (who doesn't if they are a country boy?). It was a wooden lean-to covered with bowers to turn the summer night's dampness or a winter night's wind. Trotline fishing was our specialty, mainly because it was done at night and was also almost effortless. Stubby poles with a short line attached and a hook, baited usually with "mudpuppies" (salamanders found under decaying logs), were distributed from the leaky bateau, stuck above the water at intervals of about a hundred feet. Up one side of the river until half of the poles were out (about twenty), then down the other side of the river the remaining poles. Back at camp again, the bait can was rinsed out and the coffee put on. Our coffee was so strong you never tasted

the mudpuppies. By the light of a big campfire
we played cards for a couple of hours. Then two
guys would take the boat and the smoky lantern
and pick up the lines and the fish. Mostly, everything went great, but I do remember one night
when we caught no fish.

That was far from normal, but it did happen. There simply were not any fish. The skil-
let was hot and ready; the flour dough was
mixed. But without any meat what did we have?
Hoecakes and coffee was not a country boy's idea
of a meal—not even a camping meal, which at
best is often a diversified menu. One country
boy's eyes brightened; he had worked on the Lee
farm, which was up the hill a ways and he knew
where the hen house was. Eggs would be nice,
especially since we had nothing else. We always
carried flour, lard, and coffee on our overnight
camps and relied on the land and our skills for
the main course. Eggs, a big fluffy, yellow omelet,
would be great; it was midnight and we were
hungry!

Roy picked up his big straw hat and headed
off into the dark woods. We soon heard the barking of a dog in the distance and hoped it was
not interfering with Roy's mission. We waited,
stirred up the fire, and made the pan ready again.
In time Roy returned with his hat in his hands.
At least a dozen eggs lay therein. Down on his
knees before the pan Roy began cracking eggs
and lopping the yellow yokes into it. Tom stirred
them with a large spoon. They actually developed
a kind of rhythm. Pop-sizzle, pop-sizzle. As the
last egg went in both boys staggered backward
grabbing their noses. God! The awful stench of
rotten egg enveloped the camp. The last egg had

been rotten. The whole thing was ruined. They threw the conglomeration into the river and tried to scrub the scent out of the pan...finally putting the pan in the fire upside down and letting it burn out. Hoecake and coffee seemed to be our midnight fare!

Then, I had an illumination. I had heard earlier in the evening the "thrump-thrump" of bullfrogs from somewhere across the river, perhaps in the old pond that had been created when the Sand Hill road had been built many years before. I had my 22 Remington rifle (I always carried it on camps). Another boy had a flashlight. That was the combination for night hunting bullfrogs. Frog legs were a delectable dish, and we would surely eat tonight! Taking the old bateau, we crossed the river and beat our way by flashlight through the big cane breaks that lay beyond. Arriving at the pond, which was over half a mile away, we prepared for the hunt.

The process was not ideal, but then what was? We shed our shoes and rolled our overall legs up above our knees and waded out through the reeds. Shining the frog's eyes was a simple matter, and my friend held the light on the dark head with its two bulges that glowed like red coals of fire while I took aim and made the kill. Shortly, we had eight or ten of the large amphibians and were on our way back to camp. About three o'clock a.m. our meal was ready and consumed. We rolled in our blankets and let the crickets and an obstinate hoot owl lull us to sleep.

Sometimes, in winter, squirrels were our object for a camping meal, shot in the late afternoon while there was still light. Sometimes we dined on rabbit. These camping trips on our sacred river often involved other activities.

A couple of bootleggers had a whiskey still not far from a camp we had once. It was in an especially dense part of the swamp, and we river-wise boys knew how to get to it. We never went there (to the still) while the moonshiners were there. We didn't want whiskey anyway; but we sure did enjoy the "beer." The beer was obtained by skimming the scum off the top of the mash barrels and dipping out the cool, clear liquid that glistened in the moonlight as we poured it into our bucket. Eight or ten quarts of the fragrant mash, if it wasn't too "green," would last us throughout one camping night. If the mash was too green, it would give you a belly ache and make your bowels run off.

Needless to say, we were not "L. L. Bean" campers. Our equipment was as basic as a blanket or two to roll up in. Leaves and straw made good ground cover. I always used one or both of my shoes covered with straw as a pillow.

It was about this time that the country boy began to see changes on the river. This was perhaps the first time that events in the outside world would dash his hopes of a career even if it was just a fleeting wish.

I saw the demise of the river steamboat in the Carolina Lowcountry. I saw this passing of the small side-wheelers and sternwheelers, small compared with the Mississippi boats because the Carolina rivers were and are small. The Waccamaw, the two Pee Dees, the Black and the Lynches were the main rivers, although the Lynches saw little steamboat traffic, not because the river was not large enough once one was in the river but because of its several, narrow, crooked, delta-like water courses through which it flowed into the Big Pee Dee, of which it was a tributary.

My father recalled one sternwheeler coming up the Lynches when he was a boy, as far as Half Moon Bluff—a river configuration just down the river from the old Austin Stone's (my great, great grandfather's) plantation. I saw the riverboats at Allison's Landing on the Pee Dee just east of the little railroad junction town of Poston, S. C. What a thrill it was to the country boy to watch them load bales of cotton on the boats and greater still was seeing the man poking long logs into the fire box under the boiler. That was for me! I would be a fireman on a steamboat! The last steamboat to see service between Georgetown, Smith's Mills, and Pee Dee (the river began shoaling badly above there) was the side-wheeler—*Ruth*. Then, she went the way of the others. Her last run was up the Little Pee Dee river to Galivant's Ferry, where, during a spring freshet when the river overflowed its banks, she was floated out on the shore and left high and dry to rot away with the passage of time. She was an attraction for years, sitting there by the river and the highway that ran from Florence to Conway. I drove there not long ago to make a photo of her, but she had burned. Only the rusting boiler, engine, and other iron parts remained.

My friends and I grew up swimming in Ellis Creek, the navigable waterway that joined James Island Creek and flowed out into Charleston Harbor. We didn't camp out, shoot bullfrogs and squirrels, or have the adventures my dad had grown up enjoying. Our life in the creek mostly involved swimming.

In the opening scene of the hit film, *The Prince of Tides*, based on the late, great Pat Conroy's novel of the same name, three little blond-haired children run down the dock and jump into the saltwater creek with total joy and abandon. That scene has always triggered precious memories of my dear friend Cynthia and her brothers, Kinsey and Randy. The four of us could be caught doing the same thing almost every summer day that dawned during our childhood, even up into our teens.

Often during low tide, we would "bog" down the creek bed to a sandbar that provided a more solid surface to stand on. Otherwise, soft, "pluff mud" began to sink us, pulling our feet and legs down. To pull our feet out from it, we experienced a sucking sound, "slll-lurrrpp," and we repeated the slow rhythm of stepping in, "slurrrr-rpp-ing" out down to the friendly sandy bank. If you haven't gotten a whiff of pluff mud, you've really never experienced the marsh as the locals do. A mixture of rotten eggs, sulfur, and rotting fish might begin to describe the aroma! However, I cannot think of those days without feeling a rush of nostalgia recollecting my growing up with such special friends and swimming off their dock in the salt marsh.

After the house burned where my cousin Billy and his family lived, they moved a couple of different times. Finally, they settled into a house farther up Ellis Creek from my friends. Billy told of a different pastime he shared with his young buddies. They learned that when they flushed the toilet, the waste went through a pipe that carried it straight into the creek without any treatment or any kind of filter. They used to find it fun to go to the bathroom, flush, and then rush out to the dock to see if they could get there before the refuse emptied into the creek! Eeewwwwwwww! Ugh! Yuck! No wonder our parents made us take typhoid shots every summer before swimming season started!

There is another story I had heard Daddy tell from his earlier childhood. Thankfully, he includes it in his memoir.

> My first and only childhood playmate was Erve T., the youngest of ten children of a tenant farmer who lived across the field from my father's store. Our relationship started in romper days and continued into our late teens. We played together with our tin can cars in the yards of our homes, in Stone's Grove, and his father's barnyard.

Together, we learned to forage through the nearby woods, to explore the world beyond the garden fence. We built corn stalk waterwheels on pasture streams, made our first slingshots, played pranks on our elders, smoked rabbit tobacco, and made blackberry wine in an old stone crock in the cotton house each spring.

Of the wine, I remember one year our wine was superb. We invited all who passed the cotton house to come in and gave them a sip. Using a tin cup that hung from a nail on the wall, we'd dip up the tasty liquid from the open-ended crock after skimming off the gnats and other flotsam from the surface. Yes, that year it was mighty fine wine! Everyone said so.

When the crock was empty, we dumped out the sediment to make ready for washing it and stowing away until next season. In the sludge we found a field mouse that must have fallen in during open fermentation. The chemicals of the wine had removed all of the mouse's hair and bleached its skin as white as snow. We decided it best not to tell anyone about the wine's unexpected ingredient. We gave each other our secret pledge of silence, "Gung Ho! Gung Ho! And Bad Bladder Blue!"

All things relative to the growing boy we learned and did together. We trapped snipes in the big ditch over by Old Lady Hicks' place, got our first 22 rifles, discussed the mysteries of girls, started to work in the fields with the adults, and hated school.

Erve's house burned up one hot summer day. Neighbors rushed in and saved everything but a pair of rubber boots that were behind the kitchen door. Ajax Movers never emptied a house of its entire contents that fast. My father, a kind old man, asked them to move into the big hall over his store, where they lived until their land-lord could build them another house on the site of the old one.

I still laugh out loud at the image of that white, hairless mouse. About my grandfather's kindness to Erve's family, no further comment is necessary, except to say that I have seen great kindness in his son too. Back in my youth, the United States Marine's program, "Toys for Tots," which provided toys for poor children, didn't ask for brand-new toys in the box like they do today. People didn't have that kind of money to spend anyway. My dad would find used toys at various secondhand shops, bring them home, repair and paint them as needed, and take them to designated pickup locations. At least one year, he fixed up an old bicycle. He did this quietly, never saying a word about what he was doing, just going about the business of showing compassion for those who had less than we did.

CHAPTER 8

Civilian Conservation Corps

In 1929, the stock market crashed, fueling the Great Depression of the 1930s. With the inauguration of President Franklin Delano Roosevelt in 1932, major programs, funded by federal government dollars, brought training and work to many unemployed United States citizens. People needed money, and many had lost their jobs and savings as well as their homes in the crash of the market. It was a desperate time. Some even committed suicide.

In 1933, Daddy graduated from high school. According to him, his senior year in school saw him taking three different years of English courses, which he had failed miserably before. How he became a writer is undoubtedly due to his being a dreamer rather than a student of grammar, spelling, and punctuation. I have handbooks he left behind when he passed away in 1998 on writing techniques and storytelling. I think the storytelling actually was innate. Based on editing his manuscript, I can well see why he had taken the three years of English simultaneously in order to graduate.

I do not know what he did during the immediate months afterward. He was twenty years old. But apparently, Daddy needed a job. The president was innovative in handling this national crisis, developing programs under the umbrella of the New Deal employing US citizens and improving, developing, and building the nation's infrastructure. I know just a little about the results of two of those programs, the Works Project Administration and another plan called the Civilian Conservation Corps.

The Works Project Administration (WPA) employed people to perform specific tasks. Although it might have seemed like "busy work" or even a "boondoggle" at the time, looking back on the 1930's program today reveals that documentation, recorded by these agents, contributed mightily to the recorded history of our culture. In graduate school at The Citadel during 2003, I used WPA research in one of my projects. One of the last courses I took that year was Lowcountry Literature. My research project involved a study of historic cemeteries in downtown Charleston, and the analysis of what the tombstones' inscriptions tell us about the early history of Charleston, South Carolina, and its citizenry.

I worked on this project in August. Now if you've never been in Charleston, South Carolina, during the summer, let me tell you that living there is like living in a steam bath. At least a sauna would be dry. But breathing the air in July, August, and September is like being water boarded using a hot, wet blanket. Stomping around the graveyards of historic churches in the scorching sun and humidity, trying to read the inscriptions with sweat running out of your hair and into your eyes, is one of the most miserable experiences you will ever know.

Another frustration is that, over time, pollution from factories and acid rain plus torrential rains and flooding from hurricanes have almost obliterated a lot of the texts on these historic grave markers. In order to discover some inscriptions that I could not make out on the stones themselves, I worked closely with the South Carolina Historical Society, housed in Charleston's Fireproof Building on Chalmers Street. That street was paved with cobblestones that had been used as ballast in the seventeenth, eighteenth, and nineteenth-century sailing ships that brought goods into the port of Charleston. The Historical Society houses a treasure trove of documentation on various topics, including one on historic gravestones—many of which have stood in the cemeteries since the late 1600s and early 1700s. It turns out that one WPA project included the visual inspection and recording of all of these headstones' texts and was done in the 1930s, prior to so much erosion in the late twentieth century. This documentation is important to genealogists and other researchers like me.

The other major program was the Civilian Conservation Corps, known as the CCC. President Roosevelt signed it into law on March 31, 1933. Three hundred thousand unemployed men, ages seventeen to twenty-eight, enrolled in the CCC. This organization extended into areas all over our country, providing work under the purview of the Department of Interior (National Parks Service and Forestry Service). Many units worked on state and federal recreational areas, including the development of state and national parks.

The US Army provided housing and uniforms for the CCC, made assignments, and supervised the projects. Although my dad had tried in vain to join the US Navy, he was repeatedly rejected due to his physical stature, which he will tell you about later in this chapter. But the CCC accepted any able-bodied, unemployed young man of the required ages. My dad's recollection of that time begins at Fort Moultrie on Sullivan's Island outside of Charleston, South Carolina.

Fort Moultrie was a regular Army Post then: A Quartermaster Corps, where reservists trained on the big Coast Artillery guns that squatted in their bunkers with long barrels pointed toward the distant rim of the sea. All military units within the district were outfitted here and so was the newly formed Civilian Conservation Corps in the (Charleston, SC) district. The Corps, called the CCC for short, was really a civilian relief program formed during the great depression of the 1930s by President Roosevelt, and many a country boy, as well as city boys and men, found themselves in it.

The Army handled the personnel end of it—the housing, feeding, clothing, health, discipline—and it was indeed Army. Drill and training in fighting was, of course, missing. Work was the element that took drill's place. Work was under the supervision of the particular project the Corps was assigned to and located in.

Some were on Forest Department projects, some Department of Interior projects. The company I was eventually assigned to worked for both departments but not at the same time, however. Fort Moultrie was the staging area.

Two weeks of indoctrination, getting shots, sleeping in tents, KP, guard duty, and some real work to fill in the time. I helped paint, using the army's red-lead paint, water tanks and the sheet-iron roofs of almost all the buildings on the Post. I also caught a couple of days of duty as a deck hand on the *Sprigg Carrol*, the Quartermaster Corps harbor work boat, which hauled barrels of flour, rice, and other staple grocery stock, and other provisions, including personnel, to Fort Sumter in the Charleston harbor and other places. It also carried the schoolchildren—kids of the army people—to Charleston and back each school day. I liked the duty because I liked boats.

The year before I joined the CCCs, I had tried to repeatedly join the navy, but there was always the same old runaround: filled up, too skinny—underweight. A friend of the family, Tom Taylor, who many years before had probably saved my life, was a recruiting officer in our district for a while, and he promised to "sneak" me in, but he never did.

Nightlife on the Post was a great, new world for the country boy. A far cry from the dark, silent vale of farmland, lying for miles in front of my father's store. How many lonely nights had I sat there? How many million stars in the western sky had I counted? How many fireflies have blinked along their busy way?

There, in my solitude, I smelled the mild stench of burning chicken feathers from someone's yard fire on the light night air, heard he plaintive barking of a dog somewhere in the distance. The Post was like turning a page. A marquee of the Post Theater was brightly lit. It featured current hits, such as *Hollywood Hotel* and *Gold Diggers* of 1933. These were the days of the big musical extravaganzas that filled you with dreams and joy, not crime and gore that warped minds with names you can't pronounce or want us to pay four bucks to see. Admission at the post then was a dime. And a dime was hard to come by. The Post Exchange across the street provided candy, pop, ice cream, and a scratchy jukebox. Down the street, just outside the military line but still policed by military police, were a couple of bars, and in the bars, a few girls— ladies of the evening—could always be found chewing gum and were available for one dollar. Some of the CCC recruits stayed broke all the time, but [Queen] Victoria would never let me partake of it. [Queen Victoria of England reigned from 1876 until 1901. The period toward the end of her reign is known as the Victorian Age, and the culture of the day, marked by a prudishness, spilled over into the early twentieth century. Thus, my dad's morals were rooted in the shadow of that age.]

The old Puritan Hotel operated then, the clientele being mostly wives and girlfriends visiting a soldier boy at the Post. The colorful little hotel stood, a sagging derelict, for years after Fort Moultrie was closed as a military post, to be finally torn down to make way for modern buildings. Now and then, I had a visitor—an uncle or a boyhood friend or two from Charleston come to see me. We recruits could not leave the Post, except on work details. We were quarantined for the two-week period, waiting for shots to take, to see if anyone would come down with some bad disease. But I was never lonely or homesick. Far from it. The country boy was busy with the world at hand. There was the beach by our tenting area, the sounds of the surf to lull me to sleep, the shades of Edgar Allen Poe to explore, and then it ended.

My father always had the habit of investigating and discovering something unique and of historical interest everywhere he went. He was attracted to the idea that nineteenth-century poet and storyteller Edgar Allan Poe had spent a brief year and a month as a soldier stationed at Fort Moultrie on Sullivan's Island prior to the Civil War. When I was a child, Daddy would point out Gold Bug Island whenever we crossed the Ben Sawyer Bridge to Sullivan's Island or Isle of Palms. These two islands are just north of Charleston, South Carolina, and are accessible from the town of Mount Pleasant. They feature two of the local beaches that tourists and residents have enjoyed for at least two centuries or more.

Poe was certainly famous. Thus, Daddy was on it like white on rice—and with good reason. Poe was an interesting person. After having been expelled from the University of Virginia for gambling debts, Poe had enlisted in the Army for a five-year stint under the name of Edgar A. Perry. It was during this period that he wrote three of his stories, "The Gold Bug," "The Oblong Box," and "The Balloon Hoax." Somehow, his Army service was cut short, and afterward, he was enrolled in the United States Military Academy. Of course, he washed out there too after about a year.

Gold Bug Island remains a small island, which lies under the Ben Sawyer Bridge linking Mount Pleasant and Sullivan's island. Today, it holds a venue used for weddings and other events, but it was made famous by Mr. Poe.

Fort Moultrie was built by Col. William Moultrie as a bastion against British invasion during the Revolutionary War. He thought that area was most prone to the English warships coming in and the outlying sandbars and other obstructions would prevent the ships from sending soldiers ashore. Indeed, between the barriers off shore and the well-enforced fortress, the British avoided that part of the coast. It is still a tourist site and a memorial to the American patriots who succeeded in gaining the colonies' independence.

The Anvil Rings

Remember Mr. Hudson, the kind blacksmith who taught a young boy everything he knew about the craft? He returns in a special appearance during the time my dad was stationed near Georgetown during his CCC days. I don't know much about the technical aspects of blacksmithing. Frankly, I don't know what the hell Daddy's talking about in technical parts of this section of his work with the CCC! But what does come through reveals a lot about his life in his early twenties.

It's obvious that my dad had never experienced the climate and accompanying pests that will ruin your life in the Lowcountry. He gives an impression of not having had to deal with heat, humidity, and insects all at one time. His beloved Lynches River's tannic acid component is a deterrent to mosquitos that lay eggs and procreate in standing water. They may not have been prolific on the many nights he and his friends camped out and got up to their boyhood hijinks. But welcome to the Lowcountry with all its beauty and horrors! He quickly figured out there was a major shock awaiting him.

A sunburned, mosquito-bitten, dehydrated country boy emerged from the mess hall in response to the bugle call that meant return to work. I had spent my first half-day with the Forestry Fire Fighters detail, cutting fire breaks in the steamy depths of Georgetown's Black Mingo.

There no air moved except the wash from insect wings.

Sweat flowed like mountain brooks sapping the frail bodies of their strength-giving salt. This was the Civilian Conservation Corps. Two weeks at Fort Moultrie had passed. *This* was the real thing. Why couldn't I have been a cook and work in relative cool and shelter of the kitchen? Why couldn't I have been a truck mechanic and work in the truck shed? No. I had to say I was the outdoor type. "Gimme the outdoors." I got the black flies, whose bites instantly turn into whelps filled with water, as well as the mosquitos that sing around your head and jab you repeatedly. We had come back into the campground, had lunch, and now we climbed painfully back into the awaiting trucks to be carried back into the infernal swamps where a million insects would have theirs.

The Forestry Office door opened, and the superintendent stepped out, raising his hands to stop the truck. He said, "Any of you recruits know anything about blacksmithing?"

Oh! God! Mr. Hudson, you are looking down on me. I suddenly remembered staying awake all night at the old man's wake!

"I have," I said in my typically timid voice that could not be heard beyond the truck.

"Hell, boy!" a redneck recruit next to me with mosquito welts all over his face said. "Jump off! Jump off! Don't go back into them damned woods."

I jumped. The regular blacksmith was being discharged next month, and the country boy with the cowlick became the company blacksmith.

Georgetown, South Carolina, is a quaint coastal town located north of Charleston and south of Myrtle Beach. It is the second oldest city in South Carolina, but its population is still pretty small—in 2016 estimated at 9,024. It's antebellum buildings and plantations set it aside as another delightful tourist destination.

Georgetown was one of the sites for CCC boys to live and work in the Francis Marion National Forest. The Civilian Conservation Corps' mission was to build national parks and the state parks. The "dust bowl days" marked a period when lands had been abused. The dirt was dead basically and needed to be renewed through crop rotation and other means of conservation. The CCC implemented the state and national park systems to help recover the health of our lands and water systems.

Apparently, always searching for relief from the heat and humidity of the summer climate, Daddy continues extolling the virtues of the Georgetown CCC Camp and the perks it offered.

> Georgetown CCC Camp had advantages over many other camps around the state in respect to location. Located on the site of the old Kensington Gardens Spa, there was a mammoth swimming pool. It was high on a hill to catch the breeze. The hill was studded with giant spreading oaks existent from Plantation Days. From the pool sweeping views over green wetlands lay that were former rice fields and the broad convergence of the Black and Pee Dee Rivers. The far shore to the east was Waccamaw Neck where Spaniards are supposed to have started a settlement before St. Augustine. I used to look out my blacksmith shop window over this wide, green land and feel that I could see forever. It was like the effect of the expanse of farmland, fields of grain back home to the west from the old store— only different—exchanging sunset and twilight for twilight and sunrise.

Thomas Wolff said, "You can't go home again." But you can in mind. But as he meant, not physically, not in reality; it's all different, but go anytime you wish—in dreams.

The smell and the feel of salt air on this hill were always present. It was only three miles to town. Walk it if you can't hitch a ride. Your girl is waiting. If only Ruby Keller at the Front Street theatre, lounge, and sip cokes on the porch of the Gladstone Hotel. They have no guests, anyway. Smell the bounties of the sea as you walk past the Fish and Oyster House mixed with the tang of coal tar and pine lumber from the big mill.

Blacksmithing at Company 1408, our Company ID, entailed more than just anvil forging of steel in repairing tools and making things. An old machine shop foreman, Captain Scott, thought all steel work should pass our way, and it usually did. Captain Scott maintained a saw shop in connection with the blacksmith shop, where wooden signs depicting CCC boys fighting fires were made for distribution on roadsides throughout the state.

To the blacksmith shop also fell the task of handling, fitting, sorting and labeling the steel parts and pieces for the numerous fire lookout towers that were erected around the Lowcountry by the Forestry people. We would take two or three trucks to Florence (always stopping by my home in Effingham to say hello to my father and mother), where the tower material came by rail. At Florence, a distribution point for the towers and trucks from other Forestry Districts picked up their towers also.

Back at the blacksmith shop in Georgetown, I assorted all the materials for the different towers to be erected in our Forestry District. Company 1408 CCC also built the largest tree seedling nursery in the southeastern United States. It was a fourteen-plus acre seedling bed farm growing yellow, loblolly, and slash pine, sweet gum, poplar (Lowcountry variety), and black locust. All were fast-growing trees to be used in the land erosion prevention projects. This size and type nursery required an irrigation system. Guess who? The blacksmith!

We dammed up a small creek. I pushed a wheelbarrow on the project for a time and also created a water source. We poured the foundation and built a pump house for the big gasoline-powered water pump. Back at the shop, Captain Scott, who was actually a die and pattern maker, set up a device for cutting, threading, and tapping the thousands of feet of pipe that went into the sprinkler system. I learned a lot from this meticulous person, and he was generous with his vast knowledge of machinery. I wish he could have stayed with us longer. Machinery is an interesting subject, but of course, blacksmithing was my first love in the mechanical trades. Give me the heat and smell of a coke forge, the ring of the anvil under the blows of a sixteen-pound sledge hammer, the spattering glow of molten steel. Never in my blacksmithing experience, had I made shoes for a horse. But I could do it. I'd seen Mr. Hudson do it and anything Mr. Hudson could do, I could do. I'd have to. He was watching me!

TERRY STONE

CHAPTER 10

Social Life in Georgetown

My dad's experiences in the Georgetown CCC Camp weren't limited to work. He talks about his social life too. And I have a lot to say on the subject of the society of these historic coastal cities—after he tells you this.

Regardless of my extreme fascination with the little out-of-the-way seaport town of Georgetown, I never seemed to fit in with its society. I soon had a girl there, several in fact. But each didn't last long. Victoria again, perhaps. Of course, no one had any money. These were depression years. It was a laughable joke but true. The girls of the town—Southern Belles of the magnolia-shaded streets—told one joke about a group of boys standing around on the corner of Highmarket and Mills Streets, "One was a CCC boy, and the others didn't have any money either."

Georgetown had the most parties of any town I've ever seen. Some girl gave a party every Friday night. I guess there was not much else to do in the place. Most parties were in town, but at times they were at plantation houses down on the North Santee River, where we CCC boys went when the company commander would turn his back so we could steal a truck. Since the CCC boys, though void of cash, were new faces and perhaps new challenges, the parties were unusually heavy with khaki colors. By khaki, I mean the dress of the CCC boy. Our dress uniforms were army uniforms left over from World War I in supply depots. Of course, we modernized them by splitting the pegged legs and sewing in wedges giving them a bell-bottom look. The smell of mothballs was perhaps the worst thing. So long and so well had the brownish wool clothes been packed away and preserved the odor was with them to stay. Absolutely nothing removed it. There was but one hope. Please, God, let the girl not be allergic to naphthalene!

The old homes of the town—many antebellum—had high ceilings, archways, and balconies overlooking gardens with flagstone walks and wrought iron gates. Most of the girls—the world "belles," always came to mind when I saw one of them—were enticing. One I liked a lot, but she didn't care much for me and broke it off after a few dates. Another—a little ash blonde—I'll remember forever. I only dated her once, in a flower garden on Highmarket Street.

I was not comfortable with her. She was blue-blooded and definitely "programmed" for situations I would be awkward in. A country boy is a country boy no matter how much icing you smear on him. I felt inferior—the CCC thing, which really translated to a relief program, embarrassed me. Not with most girls but with her. She didn't frown on me or anything like that. In fact, she seemed to be aware of my discomfort and went the extra mile. But I could not help it. I didn't ask for another date and spent many sleepless nights trying to figure it out. I don't think Victoria had anything to do with this one.

I lost my CCC complex after I got wise, as did other boys, and wore civilian clothes on dates. But I never really got off the ground with meaningful girl relationships in Georgetown. I guess the thin, light-complexioned belles of this moonlight-and-magnolia-town were too much of a contrast to the tan, firmly built country girls I grew up with.

We had our own parties at camp too. The mess sergeant would cut corners on the ration allowance until there was enough money to hire a small band, usually from Charleston, and we would have a big dance in the recreation hall by the big swimming pool. The hall was named Brogdon Hall, named for a former CCC boy from our camp who had been killed. These dances were well attended by the "Magnolia girls" from in town and also the officers' wives, who were very popular and knew their way around and didn't look down their noses at CCC boys.

The girls Daddy met in Georgetown did indeed go out of their way to make the boys feel comfortable. The "magnolia girls" were reared to have impeccable manners and were taught the fine arts of conversation and entertaining. Of course, no one should ever mistake their politeness as an invitation into their select society.

There is and was a "blue blood" sector in both Georgetown and Charleston's elite. They were, in general, descendants of plantation owners or other wealthy old families and founding fathers. Outsiders could marry into it, but otherwise, you had to be born into it. In addition, you had to be accepted, if not embraced, when marrying into it. From my reading of eighteenth- and early nineteenth-century English literature, such as Jane Austen's novels, the manners of society in New World across the Atlantic Ocean traveled with those who migrated to American coastal areas.

Americans forged vast and important plantations and companies, which made their money largely through trade. Other professions were acceptable too, such as law, medicine, and architecture. Working in a carpentry or blacksmith shop or retail store was not. Yet many lost everything when the South lost the Civil War. The citizenry had converted all their money into Confederate dollars, which were worth absolutely nothing—not even the paper they were printed on—when the South lost the war and rejoined the Union.

My personal knowledge of this part of society comes from growing up and living in the Charleston area. Poverty didn't deter the aristocrats' image of themselves. They may have become even prouder than before. The preservation of all the old antebellum, Greek Revival homes in Charleston was simply due to the fact that the owners didn't have the money to tear them down and build the newer Victorian-era homes. The old saying, "too proud to whitewash and too poor to paint," resulted in the decay and decline of many old homes in historic Charleston. In early twentieth century, many elderly owners sold their homes for a pittance to people who could afford to bring them back to their former glory. Today, most of the homes are owned by people from "off."

"Off" had a significant meaning to the old blue-blood citizenry in Charleston. When you came to Charleston to live, especially if you were involved in anything in the downtown Charleston area, your ancestors were either from Charleston or from "off." That signified that you were a person who did not belong in Charleston's "polite society." If you were from "off," you were from nowhere.

In Charleston, there were a few elite clubs. Someone from "off" may be liked very well by the people they interacted with on a daily basis. But those from "off" were not included in the most private social clubs, such as the St. Cecilia Society, which held a ball every season, at which time young ladies would be introduced to society. They made their social debut on this occasion and were called *debutantes* until they were engaged or married. Other exclusive clubs were the Charleston Yacht Club and the Hibernian Society. Today, the "blue blood" in Charleston has been watered down significantly since the late twentieth century. The old families are in decline. But if you want to become one of them, it won't happen, unless you marry one.

In Jane Austen's famous novel, *Pride and Prejudice,* the protagonist Lizzie meets the upper-class Mr. Darcy, who eventually falls in love with her and, despite her lower social status, wants to marry her. His aunt, Lady Catherine DeBourgh, does not feel it is a good match. When she meets Lizzie and converses with her, she is concerned about Lizzie's heritage and asks her, among many other questions, what had been her mother's maiden name. Lady Catherine feels the need to assess Mr. Darcy's marriage choice and wants to evaluate Lizzie's suitability. The society of this era very much showed itself across the Atlantic Ocean in Charleston.

My first husband was born into this society. At our wedding in 1963, his grandmother told my mother that she must be happy that I had married into their family. Family name is everything. Indeed, the first time I met Grey's grandmother, she asked me what had been my mother's maiden name. I'm sure she did not deem me suitable for her grandson. Little did any of us know then that my ancestry had a long, noble history, directly back to the Middle Ages in England. A descendent had come to America in the early 1600s and one of his progeny had established a big dynasty in the middle of South Carolina. But that was still "off" to old Charlestonians.

So in comment on my dad's failure to feel comfortable with the "magnolia girls" of Georgetown, I confess that I never felt comfortable in the presence of that blue-blood society in Charleston. Bob and I volunteered with various festivals and historic house tours but were never invited to the after parties. Although I had been born in Charleston, my current husband, Bob, was born in Georgia. We clearly were not part of them. And we wouldn't have felt that we fit in had we received an invitation.

Life in Camp

D addy recounts one awful event in Georgetown's CCC camp that I remember him telling about many years ago.

All of my recollections of life in days gone by are not pleasant, not amusing, not productive. Some are very disturbing to even think about now. I probably came close to losing my life in the Georgetown camp. There, I, through inexcusable carelessness, took a gulp of carbolic acid. The experience was not pleasant! Since childhood I had been plagued with sore throat. How well do I remember those days when all the other kids were out playing in the whirling snow, and I sat inside by the window looking out, stuffed up with a snotty cold and sore throat.

For days, my throat had been scratchy; the blanching effect of coke smoke from the forge aggravated it. I went over to the dispensary for something to relieve it. I presented my problem. The corpsman, without looking up from the book he was reading, reached up to a shelf, fumbled for a bottle, and said, "Go into the laboratory and gargle with this." At the sink I tipped my head, placed the bottle to my lips and took a sizeable

70

swig into my mouth. The sweetish taste hit me first—then the fire! I spit it out, grabbed a glass and rinsed my mouth over and over with water, but it kept burning. The inside of my mouth, tongue, and lips shriveled up like a prune, growing slick and clammy. I tried to spit. White curdy flesh came out. I could tell where the acid had stopped in my throat. A spastic reaction had kept it from going further down. Things around me began to whirl; I was blacking out. I do remember going down the back steps of the building; I came to sometime later, lying in the grass. There is no way of describing how my mouth felt, but I had presence of mind to know I needed help. Brogdon Hall was close by. I wondered if they would name something after me!

Through the window of the hall I could see the medical officer, Lt. Holliday, shooting pool. I dragged myself to my feet and went to him. I could not talk. I pointed to my mouth. He walked me to the dispensary, saw the bottle and exclaimed, "My God! Full-strength carbolic acid!" The corpsman was demoted in rank and assigned to the work crew in the woods. Something should have been done to me for not reading the label, but then I guess the butter was enough punishment. I had to keep a stick of butter in my mouth day and night for several weeks. I could only take liquids through a straw. Speech was impossible for several days. But ugh! That butter! I wouldn't eat butter again for years. Six months after, the burned imprint of the round bottleneck was still on my lips. In that mishap, another branded impression was made upon me—upon my brain. Never take anything without reading the label!

I remember hearing that story several times as I grew up. My dad never did drink anything without reading the label to be sure of what it was. Apparently, the aftereffects were few. Yet he still had sore throats and colds for decades. He also had an aversion to butter and would never spread it on bread.

*****

His lifelong love of photography continued during his years in the CCC.

> My Georgetown interval renewed my activity in photography. I had developed and printed photographs as a child on my father's equipment and had become quite proficient. Three boys were taking a correspondence course in photography and had set up a small darkroom in the back of the Education Building. They asked me to join them. In time, the others dropped out. I canceled the course but kept the darkroom open as a hobby throughout my two years in the CCC, both in Georgetown and Myrtle Beach. I maintained a photographic darkroom with others joining me from time to time.
>
> My interest in archeology began to develop in Georgetown. I, with the aid of a sidekick, dug into the ruins of an old fort behind an old abandoned plantation house, finding lead musket balls and a badly rusted Navy Colt revolver. The plantation house was of interest also. It was built of cypress with inner walls plastered with rice straw plaster. It was surprising how well preserved the plaster was considering the roof of the building was almost gone. It had experienced the great earthquake of 1886. There had been a rice mill—the tall brick chimney still stood—

and the marshes were trenched with canals and rice banks. My friend and I discovered this old home site one Sunday afternoon when a north-easter blew our rowboat up a rice channel while crossing the upper reaches of Winyah Bay. I don't know the name of the fort or plantation site. One of the failings I had in my earlier days of writing and photography was getting names.

There are several forts and plantation sites along the area named "Winyah." One is a civil war site, and another dates back to the Spanish settlement days. I cannot pin down, in today's online information, which one my dad discovered. However, the one of Spanish settlement days was restored since my dad's time in the CCC, c. 1934.

Interesting to note is the preservation of the cypress structure. Cypress was (and I guess still is) a preferred wood in the coastal south. It holds up against the constant insect onslaught, as well as frequent salty water that blows onto them during hurricanes.

After a year at Georgetown, the company finished up and moved the entire camp to Myrtle Beach, where they would launch their next project.

Myrtle Beach State Park

The Civilian Conservation Corps seemed to do a little bit of every-thing. They planted soybeans on soil that had become infertile from depletion of essential nutrients, which restored nitrogen and other elements. They preserved woodlands. They built fire towers and began a railway to transport materials to the fire tower construction sites.

Throughout South Carolina, CCC chapters also built a total of sixteen state parks. One of them was at Myrtle Beach. Although one of the CCC chapters built Lee State Park, along Daddy's beloved Lynches River, his company built Myrtle Beach State Park, thirty miles north of Georgetown, on the Atlantic Ocean.

Myrtle Beach is a premier beach destination along the Eastern Seaboard of the United States. Before it was developed into the tour-ist mecca it is today, it was inhabited by the Waccamaw Indians. They grew corn, pumpkins, kidney beans, lima beans, squash, mel-ons, gourds, and tobacco. The Waccamaw also domesticated animals, including deer, and actually made cheese from doe's milk. They kept fowl, such as chickens, ducks, and geese. In addition to their pri-vate gardens, they kept communal gardens, which were attended by everyone, including the chiefs. They navigated and fished along the Little River. The town that settled by White Americans along that the river was eventually given the river's name.

My dad was about twenty-two or twenty-three years old then.

Company 1408 CCC, under the Forestry Department in Georgetown, was transferred to the Department of the Interior for the purpose of building a state park at Myrtle Beach, South Carolina. We knew the move was to be made. In fact, we had sent a cadre of forty men to the state park site to set up barracks and service buildings. Before the Myrtle Beach campsite was finished, a mix-up in orders brought ten big trucks from Company Post Headquarters at Fort Moultrie with instructions to move Company 1408 that day to the new camp. Captain "Squee" Wells, our commanding officer, whose mouth was always bigger than he was, screamed bloody murder. But what could he do? Orders were orders, even though screwed up by some nincompoop! Men were recalled from the woods. All camp personnel turned to in the breakdown of Camp Lafayette on the hill, under the spreading oaks that had once shaded the great French General himself. Much of the heavy work fell to my helpers and me.

The blacksmith shop, of course, was dismantled. We took down the kitchen stoves, sinks, and other equipment. The boiler room was dismantled. We took down the lavatories, showers, everything! Trucks shuttled back and forth between Myrtle Beach and Georgetown all day and into the night. The blacksmith shop was on the last load, and I was riding with it. The new campsite was a place of accelerated pandemonium. In the pinewoods, with no lights, barracks unfinished, open ditches, bunks and mattresses, duffel bags were scattered everywhere.

The cooks had managed to set up one stove out in the open and prepared a continuous meal.

Meal? It was elastic macaroni. The server slapped a ladle full on your mess kit. As one walked away it strung from the ladle to wherever you were going, around trees, people. It was life for the exhausted and near dead. The coffee was never blacker, never better. And there was bread. Store-bought bread. After filling of the starch, I found a pile of soft duffel bags that wasn't occupied and fell asleep before I even stretched out.

First of all, macaroni is not in and of itself stringy. Southern people often refer to mac and cheese as just macaroni. In the 1930s South, the idea of its being cooked with cheese was taken for granted. All those carbohydrates do contribute to a wonderful sleepy feeling. Coupled with the exhaustion of a hard day's work, I'm sure that sleep was deep and restorative to those poor boys in the CCC. The dismantling of the Georgetown camp was rushed and exhausting, but the setting up of Company 1408 in Myrtle Beach went much more smoothly. Daddy gives a technical but entertaining account of it.

Setting up camp in Myrtle Beach was much like taking it down in Georgetown but much, much more orderly and at a slower pace. Of course, much of the heavier work fell to the black-smith. Aside from setting up my shop, which was deferred to until last, I set up the kitchen, stoves, sinks, and that kind of thing. The smoke stack for the hot water boiler got mashed up and was beyond repair. We used regular seven-inch stove pipe available at any hardware store, so I went to the CO and got a voucher drawn on the Chapin Company in town and asked for a truck to go get it. No truck being available, the CO ordered the ambulance driver to take me and bring me back with the stovepipe.

After dropping me off at the hardware store, the driver suddenly remembered he had a personal errand to run (probably to the bootleggers on the old Sacostee Road) and would be back for me in twenty minutes. I got the seven joints of stovepipe, stood them outside on the sidewalk, and waited. A half hour passed, then an hour passed. People walked past me and smiled. I stood with my stovepipe for another hour. The camp phone had not been put in yet. I had no access to help from there. How would it look hitching the four miles along the highway with seven joints of stovepipe? I moved all the joints down to the corner of Highway 17 and began thumbing. People looked and laughed. Some shouted smart remarks, and I told them where they could stick it! A fishermen's truck came by and picked me up and delivered me and my pipe to camp. The ambulance was sitting by the First Aid Kit. The driver said he had forgotten me! I always figured he was some kind of a nut, anyway. I'm sure he got his whiskey.

My dad tells stories in a way that makes me feel I am present with him in real time. He breaks from his adventures to describe the Myrtle Beach site. Although Myrtle Beach is densely developed now, my dad's experience was in 1934. He writes his memory of it in 1984, fifty years later.

The site of the state park, SP 4, was unique—three hundred and twenty acres of woodland with a half-mile frontage on the beautiful Atlantic Ocean. (Most of the woodlands are not now part of the park. It was taken in during World War II and became part of Myrtle Beach Air Force Base.) Most of the original acreage was first designated and became a wildlife refuge. Large waterholes existed there. These were meteor holes caused by a meteoroid shower that hit the eastern USA sometime in the distant past. The projectile side, or entry side of the hole, made a sloping approach from which wild animals could reach the water that the holes collected.

Immediately behind the beachfront, which was a beautiful strand, was a level plateau of pinkish sand from clay. This area was dotted with lovely high, white dunes extending back to timberline. This plateau was dotted with clusters of myrtle brush, and several wrecked ships tossed up by countless hurricanes lay here and there, largely covered with sand. Rotting timbers contained long, rusting spikes and other iron scrap. This seashore plateau had also been an Indian encampment at one time. There were thousands of shards of pottery, arrowheads and spears lying around. On this plateau, the recreation part of the park was built. The big two-story pavilion with steps extending around three sides stood for several years before being destroyed by fire. I mention the steps because this was a feature I was personally involved with and regrettably so.

Being behind on their construction schedule, the boys on the carpenter detail were given a helping hand by other crafts in the camp—blacksmith included. My job was to saw out the 105 step stringers from ten- by fifteen-inch cypress boards. I cut them all out, and they were all cut out wrong! The pitch and width had to be changed in order to recut them and salvage the material. Captain Fitz cried for a week over my mistake. I firmly proclaimed, "I'm a blacksmith, not a carpenter."

We built the Park Superintendent's house too. (I only did the steel work.) The architect wanted the CCC boys to do as much of this building as possible, a project in creativity! We rented a sawmill, cut the logs, and sawed the boards. The sills were hand hewn with adzes. Shingles were made from red cypress. I made them in the blacksmith shop, as well as the large spear-headed hinges for the exterior shutters, the HL hinges for interior doors, and cabinets. I even made the key escutcheons and doorknobs. The mortise locks were bought, also glass for the interior doors and windowpanes. I hand-forged boot scrapers to be mounted beside the entrance door and big-ringed doorknockers that mounted on the door's exterior surface. This was indeed a magnificent building and all hand made by the CCC chapter. The building stands today by Highway 17 at the Park entrance [1984].

The park in those days was teeming with wildlife. Alligators inhabited the ponds, and fish hawks nested in the tall cypress of the swampland. The lonely stretch of beach had once been a rumrunner's landing point back in the days of prohibition. Captain Charlie, foreman of the mechanical crafts, claimed he had been forced once to help unload a "rummy" boat on the beach there. He had happened on the scene quite by accident, he said. They forced him to help and then gave him a fifty-dollar bill and told him to get lost! One wonders.

The Works Project Administration (WPA) operated a mullet fishery on the beach there. The operation was unique. A boat with several hundred yards of net lay on the beach. A lookout stationed about a mile up the beach signaled when

he saw a school of fish moving down the shore-
line a mile up the beach just outside the breakers,
their silvery glitter sometimes covering as much
as an acre of water. The boat put out through the
breakers, spilling the net overboard, and, when
the net was all out, the boat dropped anchor and
waited for the school of mullet to swim into it.
They then encircled the school and pulled toward
shore through the breakers again. A truck hooked
onto the net and dragged in the catch sometimes as much as five hundred pounds. Workers,
mostly women in the sheds, cleaned the fish, preserved them in salt brine, and packed them in
wooden barrels to be shipped to cities where the
Great Depression was most felt. The operation,
all WPA, provided jobs for the fishermen and the
packers, and provided "giveaway" food also.

*****

It was at Myrtle Beach that I first saw the
Atlantic Ocean. I was about ten years old. I will
never forget it. The road from Conway, a farming
town about twenty miles inland from the sea, led
through pinelands and black jack thickets (short,
scrubby oaks). Then, suddenly, it emerged from
the timber onto this wide plateau. The character-
istic shelf of the seashore is the area of Long Bay.
There were only a few houses at Myrtle Beach
then, and the street we entered was wide and
led straight ahead. Two or three stores bordered
the street, which led the eye to the phenomena
the country boy had seen only in pictures—the
broad, blue rim of the sea. It was beyond all my
expectations. It seemed that I was standing in a
hole and looking up at it. This was years before

our CCC project at Myrtle Beach, even before the church camps I used to attend each summer at Cherry Grove Beach, about ten miles up the coast.

By the time the CCC arrived at Myrtle Beach, quite a bit of a town was developed—several hotels, many cottages, and a mile-long boardwalk. The old and tilting Ocean Forest Hotel was there, the Strand Theatre, Chapin's business complex, a drugstore, a couple of liquor stores, a high school, a few churches, and more. The Cozy Corner Restaurant and Sandwich Shop kept little kids happy. The roadhouse south of town kept pretty girls, who relieved men of their problems and their money.

Much had changed since I first saw it back in 1924—all except the sea. An old man at a Conway hospital told me something one day that I found hard to believe. He had lived near there all his life and had never, ever seen the ocean! I insisted he was kidding. "No," he said, "I just never went down there." I figured there wasn't anything else for me to say. I always liked the beach better in winter and still do. The crowds of summer were okay and brought variety in the fair sex, but there were enough girls who lived there permanently to make long strolls on the winter beach enjoyable. There were the girls from Murrells Inlet down the road a ways, and Conway was in easy reach.

When I was young (can't remember exactly what age), Mama, Daddy, and I drove up to Myrtle Beach one Saturday or Sunday. We drove into the state park and got out at a rather large, one-story building. The black wrought-iron hinges, door handles, and other hardware stood out against the stark white wood and steel-gray skies.

Daddy pointed to the hardware and told us that he made those during his time at the CCC camp. It didn't mean much to me then. I was more interested in seeing the beach. After reading his account of the work and life he lived there, an overwhelming, bittersweet feeling invites me to look at this all more closely—from the perspective of a young man who would later marry my mother and become my father.

Working on this memoir has brought me close to him in a way that had been impossible while he was still alive.

CHAPTER 13

Myrtle Beach Work and Play

A new craft was added to my activity at the Myrtle Beach camp. A woodworking program was introduced into our training system and Company 1408 was to be the pioneer camp for the program. As usual, eyes turned to me and my blacksmith shop. Captain Charlie was probably responsible for directing it my way. He thought if the world needed something done to, I could do it. (I earned my extra $15.00 a month.)

Bathhouse furniture
Myrtle Beach State Park

Bench on trail to beach / made in blacksmith's shop
Myrtle Beach State Park

I already had added one "educational" appendage to the humble blacksmith shop by walling off a 6 × 10 foot corner of the interior for a photographic darkroom. There was no room inside for wood shop equipment. Not to be out-done by the lowly blacksmith, the CO ordered a new building joined onto the blacksmith shop, and in it I set up the woodworking machinery: lathe, ripsaw, drill, planers, and other things. With that, I became proprietor of the whole complex.

Two more boys were assigned to me to work the woodshop, and my first project was to manufacture fifty folding beach chairs to be used by the park. Before long, the district man-ager was detailing me to other CCC camps to set up woodworking machinery for them. The CCC also had a booth at the state fair in Columbia to show the public what the government was doing with their tax dollars.

I was sent up there, too, for the fair week to operate the woodworking machinery. All was not boring, though. A delightful girl, the sister-in-law of the superintendent of CCC vocational activities, was visiting her sister at the time and because the project required the sister and her husband's time most of each day, the girl was hanging loose. She chose to spend her time in the wood shop with me. I had a faint recollection of the girl when she was a child. At least, I knew her family because she was born and grew up in the neck of the woods I was from, and she was of the same breed of delightful country girls I had known and admired. Monetta was really a life-saver for me. I hated for the week to end.

In time, the boys in camp, who had an interest in photography, increased to the point that my small darkroom in the corner of the shop was outgrown. We needed the space anyway for blacksmith things. At my request, the CO gave us an old storage room at the end of the recreation hall, and we set up a big darkroom in there. Interest waned and flowed, and at the time, I was the only one that used it.

We had a minstrel group at camp organized and directed by the company architect named Wolff. I think his first name was Louie. There were some musically talented boys in camp; also some good at acting. I was in one of the skits. We were good and played in numerous small towns at high school auditoriums and made extra money, which was divided among the players. I made a little extra money developing and printing pictures for the boys.

Lots of guys had private projects. One sold belt buckles made to order with initials. One sold postage stamps at one cent above cost. His was the most convenient enterprise in camp. One boy, who dabbed in photography quite a bit, made pictures with his Kodak of scenes around the Park and Myrtle Beach and sold prints made in the darkroom. Sources of income were varied. I never tied on with an expensive girlfriend, and that saved a quarter here and there every Saturday night. Being a "leader" drawing $15.00 extra a month added to my "kitty" I had building up at home.

Much fun and amusement could be had at the park without cost. A favorite summer Sunday activity was a jaunt off shore in a big eighteen-foot sea boat, which belonged to the Corps of Army

Engineers who supervised the dredging of the
Inland Waterway Canal through the highland
between Little River and the Waccamaw River at
Bucks Port. Something had bashed in the boat's
bow, and they hauled it to the Park's blacksmith
for "fixing." It was a boat and I loved boats, so I
didn't scream too loud.

It lay by the shop a couple of months, and
some of the boys got an idea. They dragged it to
the beach with one of our Cletrac tractors and on
Sunday mornings we put to sea in it. Six or eight
of us, when supplied with sandwiches and a jug
of tea through the back door of the kitchen by a
cooperative cook, would get out the oars, launch
the big boat through the breakers and row out to
sea. Knowing that coastal currents ran southward
along Long Bay, we would set a course northeast-
ward and row bias across the current and into the
wind. Each person took turns at the oars—sixty
strokes and change, each man responsible for
his own count. Some of them you had to watch.
They would cut short. We went seaward until
the last bit of landfall dipped beneath the rim of
the sea. Then we stopped, secured the oars under
the seats and had lunch. Nature did the rest, the
return trip. We had approximately two hours of
free ride, if the wind was normal. The current
down the coast brought us southward, and the
wind carried us inland to the beach. We only
needed the oars again when we started through
the breakers to the beach. Oh! What a ride!

At other times we would take a truck, one
with plenty of gas in it, and go to Brookgreen
Gardens. It was free and privately owned. Anne
Hyatt Huntington lived there in winter then and
could often be seen in the Gardens. We visited

Atalaya, the Huntingtons' palatial home on the Atlantic Ocean to the east of the Gardens. The building was inhabited by the Huntingtons and their guests. Today, red ants and lizards occupy its ruins.

One could say that the CCC boy who was lucky enough to be assigned to SP4 was in for just one long, delightful holiday. We did our work, and we did it well, but come night and weekends the world of excitement was at our door. This was particularly true in summer. The Beach Spa was in full swing, and even with the CCC boys' lean budget there was something to fit every purse. I was often down to my last dollar, and once I was embarrassed to discover I didn't have *that*.

A dollar was enough for an evening with your girl. Hot dogs and Cokes were five cents each. That was only twenty cents, unless you had a fat girl, and then you cut her off with just one more. Movies were twenty cents, and there was no state tax in those days, so you really had change left over. One night in question I walked my girl up to the ticket booth at the Strand and, after inverting all my pockets, I realized I had lost my dollar. She didn't have any money either, so all I could do was walk her away.

Once a month we had a dance at the rechall in camp. I couldn't dance much in those days. Still can't. However, it was so nice to hold on and walk around. A WPA artist was sent to our camp to do local oils of camp life. He was a New Yorker. Few people liked him. He went home with me for a weekend, but I don't think either had much fun. He was a good painter. A scene of the tool shed in our camp, which he painted, was chosen by President Franklin D.

Roosevelt to hang in the White House. He was Polish. Cannot remember his name. I'll call him "Unknownski."

I went home on weekends about once a month. I had a stunningly pretty, long-legged, black-haired girl at home named Grace, who I often dated when at home. I liked her very much, and she liked me. But I think we were both just playing the field in a six-year void in my real heartthrob affairs. Not one meaningful relationship developed between high school and my relationship with the pretty country blond I married in 1938. I want to call those "void years" struggling years. But when I think about it, weren't they all?

I haven't been to Myrtle Beach State Park in decades. The beautiful main building had burned not many years after completion. I don't know whether any of those original CCC-built structures are even still standing. Quite a number of destructive hurricanes have come through Myrtle Beach since we were there that day looking at his handiwork. But I want to give you some interesting background on Brookgreen Gardens, which was built at the same time my dad lived and worked in the area.

As Daddy relates, the land on which Brookgreen Gardens was built was purchased by one of the richest men in the United States, Archer Milton Huntington, in 1930. His wife, Anna Hyatt Huntington, had contracted tuberculosis, a potentially terminal illness. They developed the Gardens as a summer retreat. Anna was a noted sculptor and wanted to place her work around the landscape at the home. In 1931, the Hyatts opened the property entitled "Brookgreen Gardens, a Society for Southeastern Flora and Fauna." In addition to showcasing the natural landscape, the garden houses the many exquisite sculptures of Anna Hyatt throughout. It was also to be a wildlife preserve—adding the third of a triple approach to developing the beautiful property. My parents and I visited there a number of times during my childhood and youth. The garden exists today, and I would love to see it again—especially now.

I have tried to find something online about the artist that painted the woodshed painting that graced the White House during the Roosevelt years. So far, I haven't had any luck. But Daddy has more to tell us about his time at Myrtle Beach.

> It was during this time I was beginning to think of photography as a career. I had dabbled in still photography since I was born almost. I cut my teeth on my father's tripod legs. But now, more and more, thoughts of motion picture photography kept bugging me, especially the field of news reel and travelogue. My father wanted me to become a watchmaker—offered to send me through the Kansas City School of Horology. I didn't want that. Watch repair was too tedious for me. I wanted to go to the New York Institute's Cinematographic School. My pop wouldn't budge. No! My mother was on my side and agreed to help me. She would keep all the money I could send her and when there was enough I would go to New York. I still wasn't sure if that was what I really wanted to do. I had always figured I was on the "low road," and on that road I enjoyed life most. I was a blacksmith with a sledgehammer in his hand. Watchmaker? It wouldn't be! But what else? I started saving my money although I had no idea what I would do with it.

> Actually, an incident with a girl sometime later brought an abrupt decision. It forced me to make a move, but I don't think it solved anything. I am what I am—newsreel cameraman or blacksmith. Call it "high" or "low;" I could orbit

in the "high," but I never lost a love for the "low." The result did not bridge the gap.

The night was balmy, and the girl I had a date with was the girl I had finished high school with. Not lovers. No. But we had been very close, shared our troubles, pooled our thoughts. She and some college chums were spending a weekend at the beach. She had notified me when and where she would be. We had corresponded frequently since high school. I had walked to town, found the cottage. She was, as always, the delightful Evelyn. At the Arcade Center, we had hot dogs and Coke, mingled with the crowd awhile, and eventually took a long stroll on the beach. I don't think there was a moon but that didn't matter. We were just snuggling friends, nothing more.

After a time, she asked of the time. I struck a match (I smoked in those days). "Eleven-thirty." She said she had to go back to the cottage. I protested. It was early for the beach. She should really stay out much later. "I know," she said. "I have another date at twelve o'clock mid-night." A ton of bricks couldn't have mashed my ego flatter. I don't know why. She wasn't my girl. I didn't care who she dated, but something about it hurt me terribly. Then came the coup de grace. As we reached the cottage, a long, shiny convert-ible purred up to the walk. The door opened and, with a quick peck on the cheek, she slid in beside the man, and the car eased off into the night. I walked the four miles back to the camp. The high road and the low road were no longer in conflict. My mind was made up.

This was the end of his time in Myrtle Beach, as well as the Civilian Conservation Corps. He received his official discharge papers on March 31, 1936. The Myrtle Beach State Park officially opened three months later on July 1, 1936. I can proudly say that my dad contributed greatly to the building of it.

Below is a picture postcard depicting the brand-new Myrtle Beach State Park's main structure, overlooking the ocean:

CHAPTER 14

Days in Old Gotham

Almost immediately upon leaving the CCC, my dad went to New York City and enrolled in the New York Institute of Photography (NYI). They still exist today, and they offer online courses. The program my dad was in apparently was a short-term course lasting about three months. This was a huge move for a young man twenty-three years old, who had never been out of the state of South Carolina. His ancestors had emerged from the Middle Ages in England to a New World in the 1600s. They had embodied the spirit of discovery. And my dad, some three hundred years later, was about to set off on yet another discovery. What an adventure, beginning with his journey by steamship.

For two days and nights the Clyde Mallery Line's coastal steamer *Seminole* corkscrewed her way up the east coast of the United States. The little steamer did this once a week, every week in the year. But this time was different—the country boy was on board! He was on his way to New York to make his mark in the world. The blacksmith with the cowlick had laid his hammer down! No more smut and smoke and fumes from the coke furnace. No more *clang, clang, clang* of steel on anvil. I had $200.00 in my pocket and a paid-up tuition at the New York Institute of

Photograpy's Motion Picture Arts and Sciences department. I had one Sears Roebuck suit and one pair of shoes, which I was wearing, a couple of shirts, socks, BVDs in a cardboard suitcase, and nothing under the sun was going to stop me! Look out, Hollywood, the boy is coming! No, I was not going as an actor. I would be behind the camera. Actually, to become a newsreel cameraman was my dream, and the time was to come when Pathe, Hearst, Fox-Movietone News, and others would offer me $100.00 a day plus all expenses to work for them. But not yet, boy, not just yet.

Right now, we were steaming up the narrows, the neck-like connection of New York's upper and lower bays. I missed the traditional welcome, the famous skyline. It was wrapped in fog. My first sight of Old Gotham was from its interior. No skyline, no Statue of Liberty, no nothing. Just the dense fog and the "burrumph, burrumph" of fog horns. The ship's speed seemed to be almost zero as she literally felt her way through the soup. We could hear the noises of the city—the rattle of the elevated trains, distant car horns, a siren wailing—all somewhere out there in front of us in the peasoup fog. Tugboats came from out of nowhere and nugged up against the ship, and after much bell clanging, whistle blowing, bumping, and tugging, we were secure in the Clyde-Mallory's old Hudson River terminal. The *Seminole* opened her huge doors and ejected a small, big-eyed boy with his cardboard suitcase out into a strange, mad, mad, world!

Daddy certainly absorbed everything he learned, as I can attest to by living with him for about twenty years. However, he also tells us about the sights, sounds, and people he encountered while there. Remember, this was 1936, a relatively peaceful time before gangs and crime had made traversing the city on foot rather dangerous.

Having visited New York only a couple of times myself and those fairly recently, I did some of the same things he did at the time he lived there. But let him tell us about what impressed him most.

> On the other side of the silver screen—or the stage, as the case may be—there are other names, people who made this country boy's list of who is who and added fuel to his eager ego. Most were Broadway's smaller people because I frequented mostly the matinees rather than evening shows.
>
> Erskine Caldwell, who had married the fascinating NYI student, Margaret Bourke-White, was achieving much acclaim for his hit, Tobacco Road, which was playing the Forest Theatre off Broadway and was destined to continue running to break all records (at that time) for a continuous run play. The play starred James Barton, a former homestate man (South Carolina). In this country boy's philosophy that made him a "relative" vs. relative. Also, another player in the show, though not from "home," did work a number of years later in the Public Relations Office at the Charleston Naval Shipyard. I worked at the shipyard during World War II, and, although I can't remember his name, I guess that makes him a relative too. And, of course, Caldwell was relative. He was from Augusta, Georgia, and the play was based on the real Tobacco Road, which exists just outside of the city.
>
> Gypsy Rose Lee was coming on big on the vaudeville circuit about that time too, but I always liked Marie Lavinski at Minsky's Burlesque

best. The "Bubble Girl," Martini Martin, was a joy to behold! She is also relative. Though not from "home" then, she did surface in Charleston years later. Two autographed photographs of this handsome redhead grace the first two pages of one of many photograph albums and a personal note on the back makes her definitely relative. It was on Broadway at the Paramount Theatre one afternoon that I saw a young band leader, Ozzie Nelson, introduce his new bride, Harriet Hilliard, and also introduce to American show business a chubby little big-mouth gal named Martha Raye.

The country boy was not totally out of place at the institute. I already had a general working knowledge of the photographic processes, having learned from my father who was a horse-and-buggy photographer among his many other sidelines. Also, a correspondence course in basic photography during the CCC days with three other boys had my skills up to par. The science of it had changed little, and the tools, cameras, etc., not at all. I found instructors looking twice at my work. Students, too, acknowledged my homegrown expertise. Ethel Dupont, of the gunpowder family, who later married Franklin Delano Roosevelt Jr., stayed close to me in the darkrooom much of the time, asking questions about this and that. I had numerous discussions with the institute director Benjamin Falk and photogaphic consultant Karl Barleban, Fellow of the Royal Photographic Society (FRPS) on a pet dream of mine—the possibility of coupling the photo-electric cell with the camera aperature on motion picture cameras so that the aperature would open and close automatically as the light increased or waned. A few years later, this was done.

I met a number of noted, impressive people at the school. Some were students, who went on to make a name in the industry. Margaret Bourke-White had already made her mark in commercial/industrial photography but was in NYI to study the new field of photography—*color*. On the cover of *Life Magazine*'s very first issue was one of Margaret's great industrial photographs. Margaret also became one of *Life*'s four original photographers. Elliot Elizofon and Carl Mydans also joined *Life* after NYI. Bob Capra worked assignments for *Life*—one in Indo-China years later. He was killed there. Technicians of top caliber visited and/or lectured at the school. I met Carl Luis Gregory, a pioneer in motion picture photography and a FRPS, and I think my most notable and influencial acquaitence was Edward Steichen, Carl Sandburg's brother-in-law. Basically a still photographer, his magnificent mood pictures set the standard for which I was to strive to reach all of my life. He once said to me, "Sometimes your worst pictures are your best if viewed from the art standpoint."

Color photography was just coming in if you overlook the old *National Geographic*'s Autochrome. The institute had just installed a color department under the guidance of a tall, lanky instructor named McDonnel. He was the King Boy (I don't remember his first name) from the great King Ranch in south Texas and was hired away from them when King quit school and opened a commercial photo processing laboratory in a second-floor flat up on 36th Street, just off of 6th Avenue.

The motion picture studios we studied in were those of Universal Photographers, who owned NYI and was located in the same building. Commercial films mostly were made there. This was where I learned to crank a camera at 16 frames per second and to process 35 mm film hundreds of feet long. People from the industry on the West Coast drifted through on occasion. Some of the people at NYI and Universal had worked in Hollywood, and friends stopped to see friends as they passed by. Also, some came over from Astoria, Long Island, the last-stand hangers on that remained in the old Astoria Studios after most producers had moved to sunny California.

James Montgomery Flagg, the noted illustrator (and a former NYI student) used to call. Also, John Craig, the globe-trotting, daredevil motion picture cameraman, who brought to the American screen many of the early travelogues that we enjoyed in those days. Craig did much to advance underwater photography—perhaps even more than Gregory (aforementioned). He and his lovely wife Gloria—equally the daredevil—worked side by side on many adventures. These people probably have no recognition outside the industry, and their names mean nothing to anyone who reads this today. However, to the country boy, then and now, they were pillars under the motion picture industry's structure. There are/were too many to mention, but three more I must. Ernie Crockett, once Craig's sidekick and head of Warner Brothers' special effects department in Hollywood, Doug Campbell, and Mel Charlton, formally with First National Picture Studios in Hollywood and my motion picture

instructor in New York at the New York Institute
of Photography.

I have Daddy's textbook *Motion Picture Photography* by Carl
Louis Gregory, FRPS. It was published by Falk Publishing Company,
Inc., in New York City. Copyright date is 1927. It is the second edi-
tion. The hardback book is covered with orange linen, frayed around
the edges and smudged with decades of being handled. The spine,
about two inches thick, is also ragged and mended with celophane
tape, brown and cracked from age.

The first chapter, "History of Cinematography," recommends
that the reader go back to his high school physics and chemistry
textbooks to review the basics of light itself. (I would be heading to
the airport for a return flight home, had I been in Daddy's shoes. I
didn't take physics, and chemistry and I weren't meant to be together,
either.) His textbook's pages are yellow with age and interspersed with
diagrams of light angles and refraction. Chapters are all titled and use
Roman numerals for labeling. There are also photographs borrowed
from various sources, illustrating the light patterns written of in the
text. This was before color photography became commonplace. The
course is rooted in black-and-white photography and film. Daddy
wrote on the flyleaf his name, the name of the institute, the address
where he stayed, and the title of the book from its cover—his pen-
manship a work of art in itself. The Institute sat in the shadow of
the newly built Empire State Building. He stayed there about three
months and received his diploma on the thirteenth day of July, 1936.

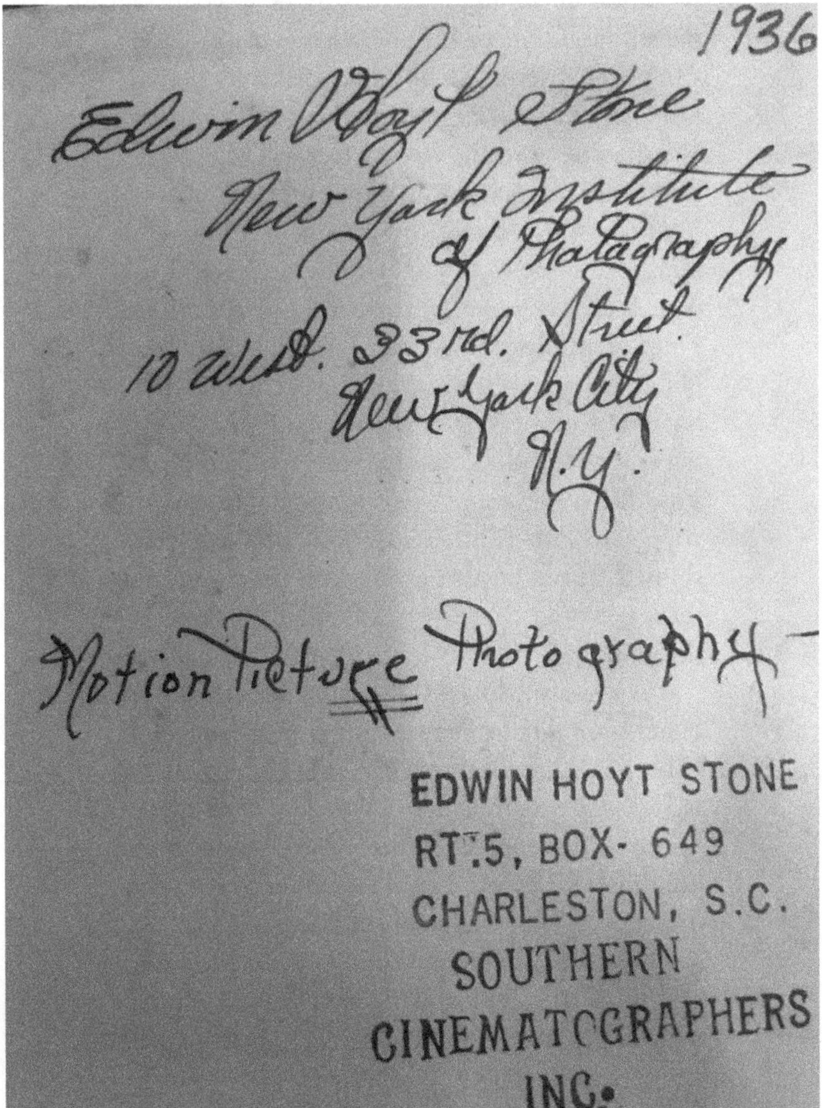
1936
Edwin Hoyt Stone
New York Institute
of Photography
10 West. 33rd. Street.
New York City
N.Y.
Motion Picture Photography
EDWIN HOYT STONE
RT.5, BOX- 649
CHARLESTON, S.C.
SOUTHERN
CINEMATOGRAPHERS
INC.

There are experiences and tasks he undertook within the framework of the course. They also made short field trips to satisfy their instructor.

Not all of my camera studies were inside the studio. On occasion the instructor would say, "Take the Eyemo (a portable Bell and Howell motion picture camera), go out on the street, and get a news scene. Twenty feet will be enough, unless the city is burning or something."

For still pictures the camera would be the Graflex, the newspaperman's favorite tool of the day. I always enjoyed these freelance outings. Once, I photographed the English ocean liner *Queen Mary* on her maiden voyage to America. She was a beautiful thing coming up New York's lower bay. I also filmed the French queen of the seas, the *Normandie*. This was on her second voyage to America. Seeing both of these great ships, I think, enhanced my love for ships, and the day would come that fashioned my career in shipbuilding.

I was also all set to film the German dirigible *Hindenburg* on her first flight over New York City, but I overslept in my St. George, Staten Island, flat that morning. I was awakened by the drone of her engines as she passed low over the building and before I could slide into my pants, dash down three flights of stairs to the street, the great airship had disappeared beyond the buldings on Totd Hill and headed for Lakehurst, where on a later flight to America, she exploded and burned.

In those days the old *Leviathan*, the German ocean liner acquired by the United States under the terms of World War I's 1918 armistice, lay rusting and forlorn, tied up to a Hoboken pier in the Hudson River. My love for ships drew me close to this grand old hulk as my ferry ride from Staten Island to Manhattan brought her into view each morning and evening. I always hoped that someday she would be refitted for some type of service so that once again she could return to her rightful place on the high seas. This never happened, however. Some years later, she was towed to a scrapyard and reduced to scrap iron.

Apparently, when Daddy lived there in the early 1930s, the Mafia was running rough shod over many of the industries there, but it was a time before crime heated up for the average citizen or tourist in New York or at least not in his area. He elaborates on that from a pre-World War II perspective.

I'm glad that I got to know old Gotham during the priceless period that justified the words so aptly composed and often sung about this great city: "New York, New York—a wonderful town!" Those were the days of New York's manifold charm. Whether one dwelt in one of its many boroughs, uptown, downtown, east side, west side, or on Washington Square, they were

caught up in the captivating magic of its many
individual cultures.

Friendly—an unbelievable description
today—was a solid truth in the early twentieth
century. The terror of neighborhood street gangs
was limited to their agility at handball against
a warehouse wall. Before the influx of grasping
minority groups with their animosity, lawlesss-
ness, and greed, ethnic neighborhoods were concerned first with the preservation of their culture
and honor, second with the welfare of neighbors, and third with the rights of mankind and
the qualities with which their forefathers made
America great. This is not to say that some bad
seed did not grow in the field of life, but those
that did were vastly overgrown by the good ones
therein. This potpourri of cultures in New York
was the substance of the city's intrinsic values.

The ethnic individuality of neighborhoods
of that era was so marked that if one were blind-
folded and dropped into a certain village, it would
be identified by the sounds and smells: the Italian
village would be alive with shouted greetings from
open windows along the streets. The tinkle-clang
of oriental music, delicate odor of oriental food
meant unmistakably "Chinatown." I might add
here that I have walked through Chinatown at
midnight with no fear of anything. The smells of
the Fulton Street Market, the strange mild stench
of the Bowery when the wind didn't blow, or the
rattle-clatter of the old Third Avenue el—all in
its own way made up by the sensuality of the
metroplitan town.

I think what I liked most about New York
was the fact that the whole world was just around
the corner. I spent a lot of time in the city's great

library on Fifth Avenue, where, if you should sneeze, a dozen peering eyes arose above the book tops and stared at you as if you had pulled the fire alarm.

In Central Park I liked to stand behind the Metropolitan Museum of Art and gaze in awe at the giant red syenite obelisk, an original Heliopolis sentinel that heralded the reign of Ramses II and Thutmose III in ancient Egypt.

I remember the automats. One who has not acquired lunch at an automat has missed a page in Metropolitan Americana, where you, if you have it, drop a dime in the slot and open the little door (like post office boxes) and take out a liverwurst sandwich...and so on for our coffee and a piece of pie. For one who did not have the dime, there was still hope. He looked twice over his shoulder, took a paper cup from the rack, filled it half-full from the hot water tap, moved to the "fixin' bar," and with a couple of slugs of catsup, a squirt of mustard, onions, relish, salt and pepper, and a quick stir, and behold! A hot cup of soup. New York's rivers had their own fascination. I liked to ride the old side wheel steamer *Clearmont* (not the one Fulton built) on Sunday morning with the picic crowd up the Hudson valley, past the Palisades, Ossinging, and Tarrytown to Bear Mounain, where the many families disembarked to spread their checkered tablecloths on the grass and from wicker baskets set a table fit for a king. Someone always adopted me, and I would return to my flat late that night happy, well-stuffed, and ant bitten.

New Yorkers of that period were heavy on holidays. Come the Fourth of July especially, the whole town emptied out! I have stood in the middle of Times Square on a Fourth of July at 10:00 in the morning and I, me, the country boy, was the only person to be seen. I used to do crazy things like standing on the George Washington Bridge and dropping a penny over the side. If you kept your eye on it as it fell the 250 feet, you could see it all the way down and see the small splash. If you took your eye off it on the way down you could not see it again. The 250 feet above water is the designed height. On hot days in July, the distance is more like 240 feet. With the heat it expands, stretches, and sags as much as ten feet. I have seen the Tri-Borough Railroad Bridge expand in July heat until it could not be opened for boat traffic on the East River until long after nightfall and the steel cooled.

Visits to the city now are not really nostalgic due to so much change—or should I say additions and moderations. I have ridden a jostling little yellow street car out from Brooklyn through brush patches, potato fields, past quaint little villages along the track to Huntington Station. But not anymore. This was yesterday. New York, New York. Where have you gone?

Let me interrupt here for a minute. The 1930s saw the beginning of the streetcar's decline, as more people bought automobiles and moved into the suburbs. This period ushered in the design and construction of intrastate highways, welcome to rural and suburban citizens since they offered an easier daily commute into the city. Design and building of the super highway stretched out between one city and another in the 1940s and 1950s. Easy driving to other parts of the United States opened up this great, expansive land for citizens to begin experiencing the beauty and differences of parts of the country into which they would otherwise have never been able to travel.

The auto industry also benefitted from these highways, since travel and commuting now demanded more and more vehicles for people to purchase. Other beneficiaries were the designers and construction companies who, mostly without consultation with citizens in the big cities, drew up the pathways for wide strips of concrete to wind through and intrude in, and in many ways, decimate their communities.

The neighborhoods chosen to be razed to make way for the superhighways were typically those of the ethnically powerless. In fact, some groups were singled out to "clean up" the part of town in which they made their homes. This had a devastating effect on the communities that Daddy so fondly talked about. Neighbors and even families were separated by these intrusive roads, usually four-lane, which nobody could (or should) cross on foot. You could no longer cross the narrow street from your home to the local butcher shop or vegetable market. The uniqueness of the Irish, Italian, Black, Hispanic, and other groups weakened. The intrastate system in New York City left a city fragmented and dreary in favor of those who were White, prosperous, successful, and in charge of businesses, banks, learning institutions, etc. They made a lot of money from it. Of course, it brought jobs, which was helpful following the Great Depression and World War II.

When looking back at the romantic version of New York in the 1930s, one must keep in mind the changes made later in the twentieth century. Daddy visited New York City again decades after the changes occurred, though, and appropriately mourned the loss. But at this point in his story, it was still 1936.

> One could get lonesome in New York. When I found myself lonely, I would leave my Staten Island flat on St. Mark's Place and walk over to the municipal pool (I was there the day they opened it and nearly broke my back showing off on the high diving board). If the girls at the pool didn't relieve my mood, I walked down the hill to Tomkinsville and Stapleton and sometimes Fort

Wadsworth. There was a graveyard of forgotten ships there. Most were old harbor tugs and river boats, side wheelers, etc. Their useful life gone, they were run aground on the flats and left to rot or rust away. It isn't there now. The Verrazano Narrows Bridge went through it. Sometimes you could read the name on those boats of yesteryear and wonder if their ghosts haunted the rivers and seas from which they came.

Still restless, I would catch a rickety little trolley and ride down the narrows through fields of straw, woods, and briar patches to South Beach and Great Kills Park. This area was kind of wild in those days, where swinging New Yorkers came to let their hair down. Several old mansions stood here and there; some were said to be haunted. This was an area Thorne Smith took as the setting for one of his fantasies. By the time I'd get back to my St. George flat, I was usually content to get on with life in Old Gotham across the bay.

If you search the Internet for *St. Mark's Place, St. George, Staten Island,* and select "images," you will find a collection of grand old houses and other structures linked to real estate sites. However, about halfway down the page is a collection of old photos, taken in the mid 1930s, which gives a thrilling view of where Daddy lived during his stay in New York. Wikipedia relates that St. George is a neighborhood along St. Mark's Place, a major road through Staten Island, easily accessed from the Staten Island Ferry. In this magnificent age of information easily found through various search engines, I can almost return to the streets and landmarks Daddy visited during his time there. Wow!

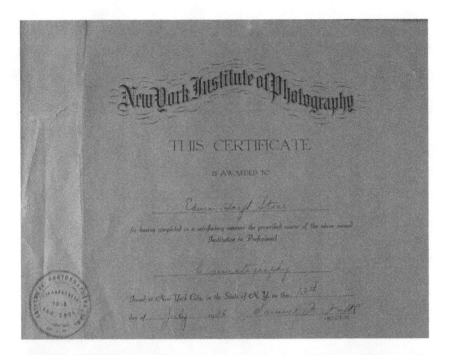

This photo by an unknown author is licensed under CC BY-SA.

CHAPTER 15

Job Hunting

Back to Daddy's next adventure: job hunting! In New York, mid 1930s, things didn't go well. The Great Depression had stymied development and productivity. Jobs went down the drain along with the chance to develop talent and skills. People suffered. Daddy vividly recalls one experience looking for work after learning everything one needed to know back then about motion picture photography.

It was a hot July day in Old Gotham. The year was 1936. I had graduated from "Falk College," our nickname for the institute. I was going out to offer my services to the world. I had an appointment at the photographic department of Columbia University's Medical Center in New York City. The city (as well as the whole country) had not yet struggled up from the Great Depression and photographers, *experienced* ones, were still in the soup lines. Competition was great.

I rode the ferry from my flat on Staten Island to lower Manhatten. From there, I took the 9th Avenue L up the city's teaming west side in the hot midday sun. It was the kind of summer day that newspapers dramatize by showing photos of eggs being fried on manhole covers. I really wasn't pleased with my apparence. The long ferry ride had been devasting—no breeze prevailed, and sooty cinders from the smokestack covered my face and hair. My old suit was a disgrace!

Somewhere near 39th Street I had an inspiration. I departed the train and hastened along the avenue until I found a press-while-you-wait shop. In a booth for the purpose, I stripped the humble rag from my skinny body and passed it over to waiting hands. I don't think air-conditioning had been invented then; at least One Lung Jum didn't have it. While the Chinaman worked with the hissing steam press, I sat in the booth where my sweat-drenched BVDs left their imprint on the seat. Hell had competition that day. I put on the hot, steam-pressed suit and climbed the stairs out to the elevated station. Water flowed out of me like a mountain brook by the time I arrived at the top of the granite steps of the University. Water puddled the carpet in the staff office during my brief interview; and it is needless to say I didn't get the job.

Those in business and prospering in New York City sent their wives and families to the suburbs and beaches during these hot months of the year. On weekends, the bankers, lawyers, oil barons, and others commuted out of town to join them. Exquisite summer homes dotted the shore line on Long Island and further down along the Hudson River. Mansions, really. Marks of wealth and success. Their heyday had been in the late nineteenth and early twentieth centuries, though, and some of them were no longer occupied by important people.

But poor, young country boys trying to make it big in the motion picture industry (or even make a living) didn't stand a chance. Not then, anyway.

My last weeks in Old Gotham were spent
job hunting. I had been feeling things out even
before that. On the heels of the Great Depression
jobs were few and far between. Dishwashers—
yes, these signs were all one saw. No thanks, that
was a bit too much on the low road. News reel
company cameramen were layed off and in the
souplines—experienced photographers. There
was no work.

The news reel companies, mostly in the
West 54th Street area, were a close-knit bunch.
You could knock on several doors and be turned
away in as many minutes. A kind of federation
existed there—had always been—and they had
a system that enabled all to survive. The companies, I mean.

When news, local or world events, was so
scarce, their daily or weekly issue would be so
short they would share their stories. All news reel
companies would run the same file story regardless of whose cameraman shot it. You would hear
Lowell Thomas's voice narrate a ship disaster
on the Fox-Movietone News; you would hear
another narrator on Hearst Metrotone News telling the same story and show the very same film.
Pathe and others would have it too.

Everyone in the offices of the abovemen-
tioned companies were in a kind mood the last
time I inquired about a job. They all said the
same thing, of course. "No, we have cameramen
with long experience laid off!" But all added
kindly, "You may submit an applicaton and it
will be kept on file." At least they had my name,
and they did intend to keep it.

Six or seven years were to pass. World War
II had covered two continents and three oceans.

The country boy began to get letters. "Are you available for foreign assignment? Can you join us immediately? Rates $100.00 a day and all expenses, and $100,000.00 life insurance." Photographers get shot too. I had a real decision to make. I was involved in war work—work I liked immensely; I was married; I had no desire to be shot at. The answer was, "No!"

CHAPTER 16

Facing Life's Realities

This is where the story gets tough to write. Decisions had to be made. Daddy's story had previously been about his own life. In his memoir, Daddy has rarely spoken of how his parents got along with each other when he was growing up. Nor does he describe his relationship with his siblings. Choices he made and actions he took affected only himself. Now he had to consider how life's choices affected another—his wife (my mother)—and eventually me.

There is an adage that says, "Nature has a way of making us forget the bad things in life." We tend to remember the good things and, as a means of self-protection, often edit out the bad. Wonderful events remain a joy to return to in our memories, and we relish retelling these stories to our friends, children, and grandchildren. However, the tragic, hurtful events that cut us to the quick of our hearts and souls are another matter. When deciding what information I should share with readers, I was mindful of the "family secrets." I decided mainly to include things that have affected my dad.

Daddy begins his memoir of coming home from New York— where there was no work due to the Great Depression, and people stood in soup lines—to Effingham, South Carolina, where there was poverty but always food. Since home was in a rural part of the country, farmers grew vegetable gardens and kept chickens—and fish were always swimming in the Lynches River.

THE DREAMER AND RENAISSANCE MAN

The Carolina sun was hot in August. My skin was pale. Spring and summer in the New York studios had left their mark. The dried fodder in the cornfield with its serrated edges cut tender hands. They had been cut many times before back through the years. The country boy was home again! The Carolina cornfields! I was not climatized in body or in spirit, but I had always worked the neighbor's fields (my father was not a farmer) during harvesttime. I was confused now and working helped. The week before, I was sitting behind a Mitchel motion picture camera in Universal's studios in New York City. This day I was pulling fodder in a Carolina cornfield. The country boy had debarked from a ship months before onto a New York pier, big-eyed and ready to take on the world. However, after twenty-four hours on the road, through eight states, he debarked from the door of an overland bus into the sandy fields of the Deep South.

It was about here, in this time frame, that realities had to replace dreams. The planning stage was drawing to an end. The actions of life's battle were beginning. Sad to say, at this late date, I really had no plans. Dreams had stayed too long. A trait in my makeup, the "hesitation waltz" it is sometimes called, kept me from reaching too far beyond my homestead gate post. And, too, in that period of time, the grass was no greener in distant pastures.

I can attest to the fact that in all my growing-up years, Daddy did indeed live life as if he were constantly fighting a battle. He always seemed to be to be trying to force the square peg into the round hole. But the battle brewing in Europe began to provide an opportunity for him to get involved in another industry in which he would spend a thirty-year career—shipbuilding.

First, however, he would meet my mother and marry.

About a year after I returned from New York, I met a little big-bosomed girl with honey-blond hair and twinkling blue eyes. I liked what I saw, and a relationship started. Our background was in common because she went to the same high school I had attended. It was at that school auditorium I first saw her—in a play. Things rocked along, light and heavy. At times I was working. At times I wasn't. I built a barn, worked in harvest, and in furniture factories. Through it all the glue of our relationship seemed firm, and Virginia and I were married. All dressed in a blue velvet gown, she came to the altar of the little country church, just across the road from the house which my father had built and brought his bride (my mother) so many years before. This was country—roots. I think it was the right place for a wedding. After the "I dos" and the congratulations, the bridal party left the church. The guests went to the reception, but the bride and groom never showed up.

I am responsible for that, and I have been and will always be scorned for it. I realize a girl's wedding is *her* thing, and that is the way it should be. But for a hothead like me, who was weary of all the pushing and pulling of opinionated aunts and mothers, I felt a need to assert myself in some way. It was the error of my life, and I've never outlived it.

We honeymooned on Lake Waccamaw in eastern North Carolina. The wind blew, the time passed, November days were shortening into winter. Moss hung from the bald cypress tres, festoons of gray matter swinging in the breeze. We were only there a couple of days. Time off was limited, so regrettably we made our way back home.

I've heard that wedding story a thousand times, if I've heard it once. It was indeed the worst way he could have chosen to rebel against Mama's family. But this insistance on attempts at overcoming unwelcome pressure has always been his trademark.

Something to consider when we look at my parents' relation-ship is that he was a full seven years older than she. Today, no parent in his or her right mind would permit their sixteen-year-old daughter to date a twenty-three-year-old man. At least nobody I know. But things were different then. Mother's parents may have been happy that their daughter was marrying a young man from a good family who was more mature. Several years ago, our grandson Peter fell for a sixteen-year-old girl when he was twenty. Poor guy, I think he spent the entire first year of their courtship sitting on her family's couch. Indeed, when they married at ages twenty and twenty-four, her dad made a toast at the reception in which he spoke of Peter: "What a patient soul."

I guess times were different in the 1930s, especially in the coun-try. At any rate, my dad was well experienced with life, had lived and worked away from home, had been independent and decisive, and knew his own mind. My mother was young. Very young. Also, she was joined at the hip to her mother, which Daddy will opine on as his story progresses. In addition, Daddy was the baby in the family of three children; and my mother was the eldest of three children. Her father was somewhat disabled from rheumatoid arthritis, and he was abusive. Perhaps the difference in my parents' ages and experi-ences and their place in their family's structures contributed to their incompatibility.

Then seven years after they were married, things changed. They had tried to have a baby for some time, but Mother's uterus was not in the best position to receive sperm to penetrate her monthly egg and form a new life. But eventually (and with some help from the gynecologist), she conceived.

Nine months later, I was born, and things did not always bode well for Daddy then either in the "mother" department—my mother.

> Perhaps the brightest day of my life was
> June 20, 1945. My lovely wife Virginia gave
> birth to my lovely daughter, Ellen Theresa Stone.
> The miracle of it lasted for days, and the little
> sandy-haired thing was a delight from the start.

117

Problems existed, yes. The major one was feeding. But after the transition from breast to bottle, which Virginia handled so well, everything straightened out.

Many things I remember from those days as this little new life settled into ours. Mr. Nettles, our landlord, who lived in the downstairs flat of the building and who always pronounced his *V*s as *W*s, would smile to everyone who passed and say, "We've got a little *wisiter* upstairs." We called her "Terry," and throughout her "baby years" we joyously watched and helped her grow into a lovely and delightful child.

If there is one part of my life I would like to live over, it would be her formative years—I think I missed a lot there. I was not the companion to her I would have liked to be. I guess it is natural she became a "mama's" child, being female; but still, I could have had a closer role in it. Although I loved her dearly, my firm nature (inborn in me), my positive approach, and somewhat gruff manner did not reveal the love and care that lay beneath. This shortcoming was not aided by my wife's fierce protectiveness and in situations which I more sternly remonstrated the points to be made. Virginia firmly took over, and I was generally ruled out—all of which only emphasized to the child that I was indeed too firm, too demanding, to partake in her guidance. I sincerely hope that she knew my tyrannical moods were a part of me and not an indication of a lack of love, care, or concern for her. Terry has grown into a remarkable woman, an accomplished person in her fields of endeavor. I am very, very proud of her.

I remember one night, shortly after we had moved to Bayfront, I had a stomachache. I often did. I grew up with a nervous stomach, always feeling nauseous. My mother took me to pediatricians and specialists to determine why, but no physical cause could be found.

Mama couldn't soothe me that particular night, and Daddy picked me up and held me, walking the floor with me on his shoulder to try to calm me down. His body felt hard. It was like clinging to a tree, nothing soft about his chest, shoulders, or arms. His inner sternness, as he calls it, manifested itself throughout his physical body. Needless to say, his carrying me around did not stop my yeowling. And no, I did not realize his underlying love for me beneath his gruff exterior. I thought I was a nuisance.

I was indeed my mama's girl. She was soft, loving, and a victim who, even as a little one, I could see was browbeaten by my dad. Maybe I was overly sensitive, but my impression of Daddy was that he was filled with anger toward my mother, and my mother was a victim of his verbal abuse. I never saw anything physical, but she couldn't withstand his bullying. Strangely, later in life, I resented her for that. She should have stood up to him and defended herself.

I finally learned to do that in my twenties, and I still don't take anything much off of anybody. I do realize now that most friends would never intentionally harm friends or hurt their feelings, and I remind myself of that whenever something unpleasant happens. But I usually stand up to anybody that pulls my chain too hard. I'm thinking that being an only child has given me that strength. I was a timid little kid starting school, afraid of the boys in the class, who pulled my hair, hit me, and otherwise frightened me. With no older sibling to defend me, I had to learn to stand my ground. But it was a long time before I could.

Even today, I can't tolerate yelling and harsh talk. I never could. When we first got a television in the late 1950s, I detested that Jackie Gleason show *The Honeymooners*. I don't understand how anybody could think that an angry man verbally abusing his wife was in the least funny. Ralph raged and threatened physical abuse, while Alice was stoic and just stood there quietly with her arms crossed. That stance perhaps suggested her power. But I hated that show and still cannot stand yelling. There has to be a more polite way to talk with someone even if there is something you want to complain about.

Today, I easily make friends and consider myself to be extremely blessed with a loving heart. I hope I come across to others that way, and that they can always depend on me to be a source of encouragement and comfort to them when they need it. However, I'm nobody's doormat. Additionally, I am still sensitive. Maybe I have a touch of PTSD, I don't know. As soon as I feel I'm being manipulated or that somebody with negative energy is trying to drain my positive energy, I bolt. And should I find that I am forced to be around someone who has a short fuse and yells, I try to limit the time I have to tolerate it. A sinking pit in my stomach surfaces, and I go into meetings or whatever the gathering with a dread, which feels oddly familiar.

CHAPTER 17

1946, Passing of an Era

As related before, a significant event occurred in my dad's life the month after my first birthday.

My father died of a heart attack on July 21, 1946 at the age of 79. His passing brought an end to the long existance of the S. J. Stone Mercantile business. The business had existed in symbol only for a number of years, and his principal activity had been sitting in the old store—many of its shelves bare of merchandise—and listening to the battery-powered radio. He would read the daily paper and putter around in his garden. He wore his old, threadbare pants, held up by suspenders, and chewed his tobacco in the twilight of a long and satisfying life. We buried him in Rose Hill Cemetary, Pageland, South Carolina, in the plot he and my mother had bought when they were married. Among the many friends in attendance, one was especially meaningful—the lovely, black-haired girl from the past.

The task of closing up and disposing of the old homestead was at hand. Although my mother wanted to stay there, it simply was not possible. With much of my father's lifetime accumulation worthless to anyone, it was dumped and burned. Some things were burned that should not have been. Two chests of old photographs dating back to the Spanish American War, old manuscripts, bottles—all collector's items—could have been profitably disposed of had we thought twice about it. His old store safe contained hundreds of dollars in old coins; many surely were collectable. These were turned over to the bank. His old ledgers showing thousands of dollars owed the store (my father was always an obliging and trusting man) could have been used to defray the inheritance taxes but were thoughtlessly burned.

We sold the material items: his old shotgun, the iron safe, the radio, and the remaining merchandise. I acquired all of his tools, some of which I use today. I also acquired his old documents: an original land grant from the King of England in 1765, a land grant from South Carolina Governor John Drayton in 1802. My sister took my mother in with her, and the old store and plot were sold. The building burned a couple of years later, and a long chapter in my life ended.

Mother always said that the loss of his father changed Daddy completely. He never was the same. He loved the sweet old man dearly. A light went out of his life when Pa 'Tone passed from his own.

As for the few items Daddy kept from the old house in Effingham, one particularly fitting relic of Pa 'Tone's life was his turn-of-the-twentieth-century camera. He had been the town photographer. Daddy removed the face and camera lens from it and mounted it on a wooden plaque. On the reverse side of the plaque, he etched words to the effect that this must remain in the Stone family. Cousin Billy's granddaughter Charlotte now has it, since she is following in her great-uncle's footsteps. Photography is a big part of her life, and she takes stunning photos.

It pains me to think of the wealth of precious memories and priceless items that were burned in the aftermath of his passing. But some things were saved. Among them was the land grant by King George III to Lynches Creek resident James Keith, which resides now in the South Carolina Historical Society, located in Charleston's Fireproof Building, at 100 Meeting Street. Four times, great-grandfather Austin Stone Sr. purchased the land from Keith in 1774. There were also a couple of wills. Daddy had unwisely stored these priceless and irreplaceable documents in his attic workshop. The land grant originally had a tassle on it, which I saw for years before heat and rot ruined it, and it disappeared. After I donated the documents, I discovered there is a historical society in Lake City, called the Three Rivers Historical Society, which contains similar documents from the area around the Lynches River, where many descendants of Austin Stone still live. It was a huge mistake, one I regret, that I did not donate those documents to them. But I didn't know about them at the time.

1946–1948: Building a Home

During the war years, I dreamed of moving to south Florida after the war was over. However, my job held good here in Charleston although there were frequent changes, so I began thinking of staying in the Charleston area. In 1946, a piece of property on James Island became available. It was the old Presbyterian Parsonage land. My brother had lived with his in-laws in a little house by the creek on this property, and having visited there often, I knew this property well and liked its situation. I bought a small lot on the marsh in the extreme end of the development, 1419 Brookbank Avenue (originally Midland Avenue). As is with all things in my life, the country boy has to do it himself: the clearing of the hedge-row of dense growth and the building of a small house.

I had $4,000, and the whole establishment had to fall within this dollar limitation. It was indeed a labor of love and also involved a lot of sweat and blood. Through the lot's entire length ran the hedgerow mentioned above, all of which I removed by hand. Also, through half of its length, ran an old Civil War redat, a military trench. It was a deep ditch on one side and a bank on the other. This had been built along the creek and was part of a defensive measure to prevent northern troops from landing there from boats in the creek. With a shovel and much labor I filled and leveled the redat.

He was always somehow able to do anything, build anything, repair anything, although we certainly didn't have a forge in our garage! But he was amazingly versatile in the all the trades and crafts, and all that came in handy when he built our home on James Island. He designed and built the little two-bedroom, one-bath house all by himself. I believe my mother said that he hired someone to put in the plumbing. The fact that he physically laid the foundation, framed it up, and finished out the cinder-block house made it very difficult for me to part with. However, the people who own it consider it a treasure and are always grateful to learn some detail about my father's little "empire" on the marsh.

I am still amazed that Daddy didn't photograph the lot as it was when he purchased it so he could continue to take pictures as progress was made clearing, digging, filling, and leveling the property for the house site. The Presbyterian Church had acquired this land after the Civil War, which had been called Bermuda Farms, and later sold it to a developer, who renamed it Bayfront—in my opinion a real comedown in eloquence for this beautiful property along James Island's expansive marsh. Daddy's brother and his wife and son, Billy, had lived in the house Daddy mentions until it burned down, while the farm was still known by its name, Bermuda Farms.

A title problem arose in the deeding of the property which was to hold up loans on the property for two years. Having my own cash, I proceeded to plan building, however. This had to be done around my total wealth of $4,000. I planned two bedrooms, kitchen and bath of the very smallest size possible. The combination

living room/dining room area was more liberal
size-wise. We partied a good bit in those days and
space there was important.

The roof was flat, another cost saver. This
later proved to be a big mistake and was eventually replaced with a large, high-gable roof, creating a large attic. Years later, a utlity room was
added. The building of the house was a one-man
thing. I built it myself and by myself, without
any help from anyone.

Friends asked, "Can you build a house?" I
had one stock answer. "If I can build a ship, I can
certainly build a house." I built the house in one
hundred and twenty working days. I layed it out
and leveled it with a transit I made myself. I dug
the foundation ditches, mixed the concrete from
sand and gravel (saving the cost of ready-mixed
concete) and toted the concrete in buckets and
poured the foundation. I mixed mortar and laid
the blocks (which often didn't dry before nightfall and the mortar froze and the blocks all fell
off). For all sills, joists, sub floor, and roof sheet-
ing, I bought rough (undressed) lumber, which
made leveling and alignment especially hard. But
it saved money.

So soon after the war was a bad time to
build. Certain materials were extremely hard to
get. I drove miles to find nails. I dug up cast-
iron sewage pipe from where the army hospital
had been torn down and then paid them for the
pipe. Switches and electrical recepticals and wiring I pulled out of Army barracks on Marshall
Reservation on Sullivan's Island. Some of this
material is still in my house today after thity-five
years. When I built the walls of the house, doors
and windows were not available, and no one

knew what sizes there would be when they could be bought. So I had to leave the openings to suit myself and have windows and doors specially made. The building of this house surely was one of the many "walls" I've had to climb in my life. This was during the period I worked for the Excess Vessels Stowage, and my schedule gave me three days off per week, at times more.

We still lived in the upstairs flat at 30 Cleveland Street and estimated we could be in our new house by January 1, 1948. So our land-lord rented the flat to someone else as of that date. Then the power of relativity took over. [I assume he means Murphy's Law—"If it can go wrong, it will,"—took over.] The Excess Vessel Stowage was closed, and I had to revert to a five-day-a-week job. This caused a mad scramble to get the house in Bayfront finished to a point we could move in. I worked on the house at night. That is work that could be done at night, such as flooring. I nailed down oak and pine flooring by the light of a kerosene oil lamp (electric power had not yet been brought in), which Virginia moved along as my flooring progressed.

Terry was a little thing and crawled all over the place. I think it was a few days after the January 1 deadline, but the power pole was brought in, and we moved into the new house on unfinished floors. Stacks of concrete blocks served as door steps and no interior painting had been done. Our stove [on Cleveland Street] was for natural gas, so Virginia cooked on a hot plate unil we got an electric range.

Problems continued to plague us. The day after we moved into the new house, the rain began, and it rained every day for three months.

The newly opened streets through the former cabbage and potato fields became rivers of mud. I had to leave my car on the highway a half-mile away and bog in on foot. Groceries, supplies, everything had to be "mushed" in. The first year in Bayfront was a most hectic one. Just one struggle after another.

We gained a few neighbors, but all were up along the highway. A greedy speculator named Grimbel got in on the original land sale and bought twenty-two lots—mostly in the east end around me—and quadrupled the price. Naturally, these didn't sell for years. This was, however, good in a certain way. It let us experience a bit of nature we had long lost the many years that we lived in the city.

Our little corner, with its many acres of brush and sedge, was a haven for local birds and rabbits, and a stopover for thousands of migratory birds on their northward and southward flights—robins, cedar waxwings, bobolinks, and others. We enjoyed a close relationship with raccoons that would come up from the marshes and eat out of our hands. Quail ranged the underbrush of the fields in droves of ten to fifteen or more. All this slowly disappeared as man moved in and took over the wildlife's habitat. This is sad—the encroachment of man into every inch of wildlife's domain. That is why I support movements toward the establishment of federal lands, national parks, and forest and wilderness areas. Without that, wildlife will soon have no place to range, nest, and raise their young.

The Bayfront house quickly became "home" and at this point, we have been here thirty-five years.

I have vague memories of those earliest days on James Island. I remember us being in the dark over there, except for one lantern, and my crawling around trying to stay within reach of the light. I also vividly recall the cinder block steps. The steps were rickety to walk up and down. They were eventually replaced with a set of concrete steps leading up to an open concrete and block stoop, from which you entered the house through the kitchen door—but not right away. One night, we were all going out someplace. Dark had settled in, and my mother was carrying me down the unstable cinder block steps into the yard. She somehow stumbled, or the block rocked, and she lost her footing, falling onto the ground, with me landing on top of her. She skinned her shin rather badly. We went back inside, and Daddy cleaned and dressed her wound. I don't recall if we even went out that night afterward or just stayed home.

1948–1956: Domestic Struggles

M y parents enjoyed the new drive-in theaters, and we often went to those. Seems like I can also recall us going into town to the beautiful old art deco-style movie theaters on King Street. Strangely, I remember that we would go into the movie at any time, during the middle of the movie or whenever. They would watch the feature through to the end and then stay for the rerun. We would leave as the film reached the point where we had arrived. Today, I don't like that. I like to get to the movie theater before the film starts and watch it all the way through from beginning to end. Also, it is the same thing with television shows. It's pretty funny what we remember from our childhood and how it's affected our present habits.

It isn't lost on me that going to the movie theaters helped catch viewers up on the latest news, such as the Korean Conflict or other national information of note. Now I wonder if Daddy ever thought of how he wanted to film the newsreels everybody watched and if he missed not having done so.

The first few years in Bayfront were a long succession of "up and down" events. When I planned writing about my life I decided to deal only with special events, but I suppose the lapse of several years in a new house, a new community, with a lovely growing child, new friends, hurricanes, economic problems, marital discontent, emotional upheavals, and other discords could aptly be considered special events as well. These were good times as well as bad times—a period of adjustment and readjustment, new problems as well as old problems.

Prominent among them was Virginia's everlasting "mother influence." My dear wife, whom I loved, seemed never to be able to escape the entanglement of the apron string. This had always caused much unpleasantness, ofttimes my fault because of my intolerance of this immature trait. Her mother had always dominated. It seemed she always would. Love for a parent is one thing; obsession is quite another.

Grandmama Allen was a complex woman. She was one of nine or ten surviving children of immigrant parents from Germany. They came over to the United States after the Civil War. Owning a cotton farm outside of Augusta, Georgia, my great-grandparents expected their children to work alongside of them harvesting the crop. Grandmama Allen was bright. She loved school and learning. However, one morning as she was dressed and leaving the house, carrying her books, her dad asked her, "Where do you think you're going?"

She answered, "To school."

"No, you're not. It's time to pick the cotton," he stated matter-of-factly. That was the end of her formal education. She was in seventh grade. Many years later, after she had passed away, Mother brought home some of her books. She didn't have many, but at some point, she had bought herself a book on American history. That spoke to me of how much she wanted to be educated. Sadly, she ended up ignorant, nervous, lacking self-confidence, and emotionally needy.

Grandmama Allen is difficult to describe. A combination of needy, highly emotional, and loving—yes, but also manipulative. My mother did, in all honesty, inherit that in spades. It imprinted on me from a young age, especially with all the tension and hostility between my parents. True, Daddy was overbearing. He treated my mother abominably, lacking understanding of mother's kind nature. (He had a kind nature too but in a different way.) As for Grandmama, her nerves grew out of her pores. She couldn't introduce herself to people without crying. However, she was much beloved in her church and successfully drew people to her. She was indeed a piece of work in other ways. Her hold on my mother was one of them.

Terry grew into grade school, and there were social requirements inherant in the fixed mind. Dance lessons—oh yes, the child would not grow up to walk like a lady without dance lessons. I remember the countless recitals: Tip tippy tip, tip tippy tip! Piano and voice followed. Of these, there was more substance, and at both she became very good. And they lasted into adult life.

Virginia expanded her world. She learned to drive a car (and quite well, I might add). Her kind heart and good nature to others soon promoted her to the position of "public taxi" to all who might need to get somewhere at any time. I naturally resented the excessiveness of it. Most of all, the way she permitted people to impose on her. That was a personality trait she had lived with all her life—good perhaps in some respects, but imposition didn't fit into my understanding. Her popularity grew otherwise. She became a pillar of the church. Choir, circles, programs, President of the Woman of the Church—the works. Anything, everything, day and night— zip, zip, zip.

To be honest, I believe Daddy was jealous of my mother's popularity. The pastor's wife in our church even gave my mother a thirtieth birthday party. The love of her friends, the life of the church, and her family made Daddy feel second place. Or looking back, it seems like that to me. His aversion to her giving people a ride had an impact on me that he probably never realized. I had to quit dancing school because there was someone Mama had to pick up on the way into town. I eventually had to quit Girl Scouts because of this same resentment that we picked up another little girl who lived right on the way to the scout leader's house. I never could understand how picking up someone "right on the way" could be an imposition. The dance classes were probably no big loss. However, Girl Scouting is a healthy, informative organization for youngsters to learn a lot of useful skills and experience various aspects of life. That, indeed, was a loss.

As for being a "public taxi," we only had one car. If Mama needed the car, she would have to get me up early and drive Daddy to the shipyard. Then she could use the car until time to return in the late afternoon to bring him home again. That occurred about once a week. She bought groceries and ran additional errands on that day. Later, she took me to piano lessons and eventually voice lessons, both which have benefitted me all my life. I don't play piano anymore, but I can read music. I have sung in various choirs and chorales through the years. A trained voice is always welcome in these groups. I don't see where Mama had a lot of time to be a "public taxi" since she mostly used the car to do things for our family.

Daddy seems to have had two main aversions—government programs to help the poor and being imposed upon. Indeed, he had no interest in the church, which became a third aversion, certainly! However, he always got roped into painting the church sign that stood on the corner of Folly Road and King's Highway (now called Fort Johnson Road). Whenever it got weather-worn or a new pastor came, the sign had to be repainted or modified. It was a white ply-wood sign with black lettering. Daddy's adept skill for detailed per-fection in his work always ensured getting that job foisted onto him when the time came. That corner was the closest he got to the church unless it was for a wedding or funeral that he felt he should attend.

Friends came to dinner. They talked church. Met acquaintenances on the street. They talked church. At a social card table. They talked church. I never got very deep into it. Church was not a hobby of mine.

As time passed we became socially active. Close friends and some not so close shared parties, dances at homes and otherwise. Sometimes we had drinks, sometimes we didn't. There were always temptations. I recall one girl who was especially winsome, who danced especially close. On mornings after a party I could smell her perfume on my pillow. Of course, Victoria kept her firm grip on me. Virginia, though not promiscuous (as far as I know) did also have her adorations.

As for affairs, I'm not sure anything like that happened for Daddy. Shipbuilding was Daddy's career, but photography was his mistress. He wrote about his honeymoon on Lake Waccamaw wishing it could have been extended. Mother's perception of the "magical period" differs from his. She said she spent a lot of the time waiting in the car while Daddy took pictures. From that point on, the camera was almost always around his neck, and he took photos of everybody at every social occasion—family, friends, and young, beautiful women. He spent lots of money on cameras, equipment, and supplies. He handled the household finances, and times were often lean for us. They might not have been if he had been mindful he had a wife and child.

Most of my friends loved him to pieces. He wasn't the run-of-the-mill dad. He lived on the edges of convention in his hobbies. His creative projects were numerous and innovative. In addition to photography, he started a small printing press, located in his attic. He printed business cards, stationery, and other small jobs. The name of his enterprise was "Sea Island Press." Giving in to his inescapable, quirky sense of humor, he also printed up some unique book covers. One was titled "Practical Embalming for the Amateur." Buyers of this bright yellow, glossy cover could clad their own books, resultng in odd looks and many laughs from their friends. Everybody thought that was so cool and that he was too cute. His sense of humor also inspired him to draw funny cartoons.

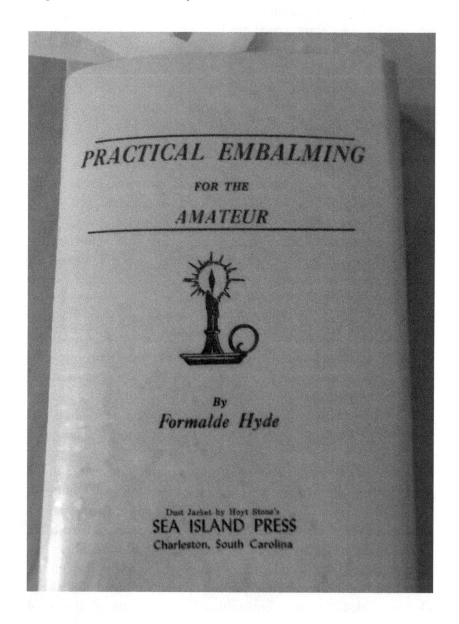

He "doodled" a lot of them both at his job, poking fun at his colleagues, and at home. At times, he entertained me when I was small. There was one in particular I recall. He would draw a dot. Then, he drew a circle around it. A wavy line starting at the top of the circle reached straight up. Two lines, descending from either side of the bottom of the circle, suggested legs. The finished product was the image of a cat from behind.

After retirement from the Shipyard, he launched a line of collages, formed with small sticks of driftwood, shells, and other found objects. He bought little things at craft stores to go along with some of the other materials and formed images of store fronts, sailing ships, and more abstract designs. He called it *trash art*. Somehow, he got a consignment at a gift shop on Seabrook Beach. Tourists from all over the country grabbed up those amazing compositions. Sometimes he would get a call from a person, maybe in Massachusettes or elsewhere, who had seen his art and wanted to order another piece. Some people requested a specific creation. But Daddy didn't work like that. What he created depended on what he saw in the materials he found and had on hand.

Daddy didn't get to follow his dreams, but at his funeral, the minister called him a Renaissance Man. That didn't make me think of the cat's behind. But his various artistic creations were definitely unique and much sought after.

He was an original.

*****

Daddy had other interests, too, besides photography, printing, and creating art from found items.

> In this period I enjoyed other activities. I had boats and loved the outdoors, the rivers, the sea. Virginia never cared for boats. She never learned to swim—the water frightened her. Mostly, I did my boating alone or with others. I revived my interest in photography during this time, buying the first 16mm movie camera that became available in Charleston after the war. I had designed the long living room in our house for the purpose of projecting pictures. During the period, I was finishing out the house and things were going well except perhaps for marital harmony.

I don't recall many films on the motion picture camera. I guess he lost interest in that. We used to invite people to see color slides from our vacations. Honestly! People didn't mind that. They enjoyed it! I have a lot of those pictures. Don't know what will become of them when I'm gone.

Daddy continues his narrative about his and my mother's relationship.

There was peace between us in many ways, but in certain areas there was definitely not. It caused me much worry and my health began to show it. We were losing our compatibility, and there seemed to be no way to stop it. I was firm in my convictions, and Virginia was in hers. Friction over trivia grew into friction over important and very meaningful things. We tried to take our differences as common place, but it took its toll on our relationship. Underlying much of it was the original influence. Her mother taught her early in our marriage that "he ain't like us," and that seemed to be the rule upon which Viginia abandoned any effort at understanding. Compromise has no strength without understanding!

The real "bump" in our up-and-down relatinship came in 1950. I was suddenly terminated from the Navy Yard and, for the first time since 1940, I was walking the street with no income and no prospect of having one in the Charleston area.

The aircraft industry on the West Coast was gearing up to full production of peacetime aircraft. I wrote to Lockheed in Burbank, California, giving my experience history and current unemployment status. Thy responded promptly saying they needed, at once, people like me, offering me a job, offering a salary scale higher than that in the shipbuilding industry. I was ecstatic! Southern California, a challenging new field of work, and most of all a job, an income which at the moment I did not have. What an opportunity for us! For our child! Virginia would have no part of it! She had never had any sense of pioneering. She would have to leave her friends. She would have to leave her church. And, finally, the real reason—it was too far away from her mother. Her childish obsession for her mother completely controlled her total reasoning. I well knew her immaturity in that respect and had always pressured her to get a grip on it, but to no avail.

This is the one time in my life, as I remember, that I could (and should) have bid Virginia goodbye, and I'm sure I would have, but for leaving my little girl, Terry. I passed up the West Coast opportunity and in time did get a job locally in a box factory at minimum wage, eighty-five cents an hour.

In planning to write this book, I had said I would not deal with unpleasant things, but I find that impossible. These unpleasant things are too much a part of my life. At this point my tongue grows short for biting it so often. I will say that from 1949 to 1956 was a period I was at the lowest ebb in my life. In yielding to the incompatibilties between Virginia and myself, I lost my grip on the real meaning of our marriage, lost pleasure and rewards of the developing years of my child (possibly creating in her an image of myself that was not real, not the real me). I lost the dreams I had for things with Virginia and with that went some of the love that once was there. Anyway, she became a changed person in my view. And another thing. Her immature look at realities, which I understood so well but could not get through to her and make her see, caused me much anguish and the sum total of everything, it caused me to lose my health. My anxiety neurosis returned, this time manifesting in quite a different way. I deal with this in an item in a later chapter, "Strange Pastures."

This is one of the most heartbreaking passages in his memoir. I cannot read it without tears welling up from deep within my soul. Between 1949 and 1956 were my grammar school years. These are the years I was taking dancing, going to Brownie and Girl Scouts, and experiencing the constant and escalating battle that raged between my parents, seemingly all the time. I wonder if kids with siblings handle their parents' arguments better than an only child. Siblings have each other for comfort and companionship. Hopefully, they don't take sides and begin fights of their own. I remember one particularl horrrible fight that almost escalated into a physical encounter. Daddy was doing his regular raging at my mother. I was terrified. My mother grabbed a pair of scissors and seemed to be making a motion to stab herself. I lost it. I heard myself screaming at the top of my voice, and I yelled at my dad, "*I hate you!*" He momentarily looked stunned, but it didn't break the rhythm of their conflict.

I wonder if other children are adversely affected by the obvious hatred their parents express toward each other sometimes. Mother told me one time, when I was a little older, that she and Daddy didn't hide their arguments from me. They didn't want me to grow up thinking that marriage was free of discord. Well, they didn't have to worry. I never got that idea for sure! It's a wonder I ever got married at all!

CHAPTER 20

1971: Nobody's Perfect

My mother died at age ninety-four in Miami, Florida, on July 20, 1971, surviving my father by twenty-five years. Her latter years were a long succssion of health problems. She had mumps at age eighty-five, broke her hip shortly after, and had to get around with a walker the rest of her life. She was a dissatisfied person the last twenty years of her life. She could not adapt to the changes fate forced her into. My sister took her in and looked after her after my father died, thus adding much misery to my sister's life also.

My mother could not let go of the past; the old store and some of the old people dominated her mind to the end. I made extended trips to Miami during her final days when she was alternately in and out of hospitals and nursing homes. Those days were quite exasperating. Knowing she would never get better, I think the waiting was the worst. A little towhead girl next door in Miami, Nancy Sierra, was particularly comforting to me during those days; my wife could not be with me as her mother was on an extended visit with her in Charleston.

My mother was buried in Rose Hill Cemetary in Pageland, South Carolina, beside my father. Some members of my wife's family kindly sent flowers; none came to the funeral.

I remember those final days very well. Grandmama Allen was there for a few weeks, staying at my parents' house. I was grown, working, and living on my own. I was twenty-seven years old and had taken a week off from work. I had rented a house on Folly Beach. Mama and Grandmama came down and stayed with me. It was a hot, sunny week. Daddy had gone to Miami to help his sister. Ma 'Tone was not a good patient, always wanting to go home from the hospital or nursing home. Things got so bad that the staff felt like they couldn't meet her needs. Daddy and Aunt Judy spent a lot of time trying to soothe Ma 'Tone and persuade her to stay where she could get the professional care she needed.

For many decades, my mother played bridge in sometimes two different card clubs. That meant she played bridge once a week. I remember that Mama's bridge day fell on one of the days when we were staying at the beach. Grandmama was very sour about that and pouted and silently spread her heavy gloom all over me. But to my mother's credit, she went ahead, which meant that Grandmama had to spend the better part of the day alone with me—her granddaughter. She whined, "This is going to be a long day." That kind of flew all over me. Was I such terrible company? But that was her way. She wanted my mother's attention all the time. Thus was the conflict. Daddy wanted my mother's attention too. By the time this happened, I had certainly come to realize that not all the fault in my parents' marriage was due to Daddy's constant badgering. Grandmama had a toxicity about her, which drove her moods pretty dark when things weren't to her liking. Also, I thought Mama should have postponed Grandmama's visit with her or sent her back early and gone to Florida with Daddy. That was a big mistake on Mama's part, plain and simple. The scales were falling from my eyes like snow on a winter's day.

It was decades later, when I was in my sixties, that I had an epiphany. Mother was living at The Village at Summerville, a little north of Charleston. Not long after she moved in, she met a widower, Hugh Wilson. They became an item, and Mama told me, "Hugh is the love of my life." Bob and I moved to Northeast Georgia during that time, and Mother lived independently at the retirement home. She still drove and had a busy social life there, including her romance with Hugh. Bob and I had upsized when we bought our home in Georgia. The grandchildren were getting bigger, and we wanted to have everybody visit to spend holidays with us. We had enough room for everybody to have a bedroom and easy access to a bathroom.

Bob and I would invite Mother up for a visit. Since she wasn't used to driving that five-hour distance, I drove from Northeast Georgia to Summerville, spent the night, and drove us back to Georgia the next day. We wanted her to stay a couple of weeks. After all, she had her hooks into me just like Grandmama Allen had hers into Mama. She often didn't seem to be able to draw breath without me. However, once Hugh was in the picture, that changed dramatically. The day after she and I arrived back at my house, Hugh would call her. The next day, she would tell me she wanted to go back home. I had begun to be unnecessary for her happiness. It finally dawned on me.

Wow!

She loved me with a smothering, cloying kind of love. She was an emotional vampire. And my purpose in her life was to make her happy! When she had somebody else to do that, well, she wanted to be with him. So we'd pack her up in the car, and I would retrace my route to Summerville, spend the night (she insisted I wasn't to turn around and drive back home the same day), and drive the five-hour journey back home the following day. Honestly, it irked me. But I didn't say anything. Mama was happy.

*****

I also did not know the extent of Daddy's emotional problems—the anxiety that had started during the grueling ten-hour-a-day, seven-day-a-week war schedule, building ships to send out and help our allies defeat the Evil Axis of Germany, Italy, and Japan.

Looking back on all of this, from my seventy-three years, I can see much more objectively where the faults lay. It was apparent how my parents' conflicts affected their marriage and who I became as a result of growing up in the shadow of their overwhelming discord. I bit my nails down to the quick and picked at the skin around my cuticles. I sought solace in cigarettes and daydreaming of a nebulous future. The pieces of my parents' difficult marriage and its causes were falling into place, revealing the whole picture.

The basic incompatibility existing between Virginia and me is in thought, opinion, and interest and has been permanent throughout our married life. It is something we have had to live with. Neither of us has converted to the other's ideologies. This is not to say that our conflict of thought has destroyed the whole insitution of our unity—only that our marriage has been denied its full potential.

There have been many good times. We have done many things together that have been fun—rewarding. Some things would have been even better had we been capable of thinking as a unit. One thing in which there has been almost complete compatibility is camping. It is an activity we share with the least friction from conflict of thought. It seems that in the forest and field, travel there is a quality that promotes harmony, that makes room for unity. We are doing something that has the approval of us both. At times we spend the months of January and February in the Florida Everglades in the little oasis of Ochopee. We made friends there and experience the nomadic life they live. Some are from northern states and are called "snowbirds." Most are from the upper midwest and are solid people with a love for the outdoors, with its freedom and other special quaities the outdoors has to offer. As in anything else, a few whose basic nature is unlikeable are there too.

The nomadic lifestyle is not for us, however. We agree on that. We prefer a home base of our own, not someone else's yard as we migrate to follow the sun. Yet it is not easy to maintain a home at home and a home on the road also. Virginia and I do find a closeness on the road that we seem not to find at home. Perhaps it is because it is a little different. Back at home, we seem to revert back to our basic selves. References of differences throughout this book are not to imply that there are not or have not been good things between us. Virginia is perhaps the best wife I could have found, and in many ways, my life would have been less fulfilled without her and the projection of her attributes into our unity. One can always visualize other roads through life that might have been traveled, but a person can only travel one road, and the road I chose to travel with Virginia has been good. Our basic incompatibility is just an imperfection.

I ran across a snapshot that Daddy took of Mama one time when they were on a trip. They were staying in a motel that night (sometimes they camped along the route to a destination for a particular event and then stayed in a hotel while there). She was sitting on the bed looking at him with the most radiant smile I had ever seen on her face. It was arresting! I had to try to figure it out. I'm thinking they must have been heading into a romantic moment, and she was expressing a joy I had never seen on her face.

Good and bad. That was life with my parents. But like the title of this chapter says, these things are the realities of life. Nobody is perfect.

C H A P T E R   2 1

1950s, '60s, and '70s: Thirty Years of Shipbuilding

The Charleston Naval Shipyard was one of eight United States Naval shipyards, strategically located along the Atlantic and Pacific coastlines and Hawaii. Under the Department of Defense, their operations spanned the great part of the twentieth century. All shipyards' way of doing things were standardized, eventually, and they all worked from the same manuals, procedures, organizational structures, and instructions. There were some variances between shipyards, it turns out, but the efficiency of them all being basically alike tremendously saved costs. They all supported the same mission—to provide naval presence to fight and win a war or, during peacetime, to ensure the United States' superior naval presence around the world as a deterrent to future attacks by enemy nations.

The first dry dock at Charleston was built at the turn of the twentieth century, in 1902, as America was coming out of the Spanish-American War. The shipyard, as well as other Naval fleets and commands in Charleston, grew over time and became known collectively as the Naval Base. During World Wars I and II, a total of 256 ships were built there. A twenty-five-thousand-member workforce supported the effort during World War II—many of them women, who mastered all the building trades that kept the United States Navy afloat and fighting. Following the war, most of the women went back home to resume household duties, and returning soldiers and sailors picked up the tools and administrative duties that the women had so capably performed. The workforce dwindled to around five or six thousand and maintained that level until its closure in 1996. The shipyard had been the major employer in the greater Charleston area. Those of us who worked there just said we worked at the Navy Yard.

My dad was an integral part of actually building ships during World War II. He received a reduction in force following the war, but when the Korean Conflict started in early 1950s, he was called back. He continued there for thirty years until his retirement. He begins writing of his career from its beginning.

> The first ships I was involved with in the Charleston Navy Yard were the building of destroyers. The title "ship fitter" is really a mis-nomer. It is really "shipbuilder," which in fact it is. The action *is* shipbuilding, the taking of blue prints (plans) and the steel materials, cutting out the ship's hull parts and pieces, and putting them together to form a ship, a steel ship itself. Not the machinery part of it or the wiring part of it, not the piping part of it, but the ship itself. The hull—the keel, the frames, the shell plating, the decks, the superstructure, deck houses, mast poles, boat davits, engine foundations, shaft tunnels, rudder, etc.

> I first worked with a very capable ship fitter, John Langley. Next was Bill Brant. Both knew their trade and taught me well, from blue print reading to the special skill of handling heavy steel. Numerous good shipbuilders helped in giving the country boy his start. Some were Scotsmen from the shipyards on the River Clyde. To name two, Scotty Sinclair and Scotty McCullough. At this point I must say there are no better steel shipbuilders than those who learned their trade

on the River Clyde, Scotland. Many years later, I had the pleasure of seeing some of the Clyde shipyards in Scotland, where many of my ship-building friends started out as twelve- and four-teen-year-old boy apprentices in the shipbuilding trade.

Throughout my thirty-year career in ship-building, I was involved in the building and repair of all types of ships, including subma-rines. I liked the sleek, fast destroyers best. My last ten years in the shipbuilding industry were in the design division and principally the subma-rine field in the modernization and conversion of the old fleet and guppy classes. I also worked with the missile-packing nuclear-powered classes, whose building and adaptation was headed by the tyrant Admiral Hyman Rickover, the father of the Nuclear Power Navy.

I had been in shipbuilding for a year and a half when the Japs attacked Pearl Harbor. Actually, I had been considering transferring to Pearl Harbor Naval Shipyard several months before this world-shattering event. Also, I had thought of the Naval Base at Cavite in the Philippines. I could envision the tropics and ship-building as two elements of desire wrapped in one, but the Japanese overrun of both Pearl and Cavite left other things out, so staying was what to think about. I stayed in Charleston. I worked swing shift and that left days for the beaches, the sea, and the old historic town of Charleston. Ship launchings were gala affairs with all the pomp and pageantry one could expect. Watching the sleek 1,600-ton, 360-foot-long destroyers slide backward on the "ways" was the moment of life added to these giant steel creatures of the sea we had created.

With the coming of World War II, the mood of the shipyard changed from gaited productivity to a mad tempo of drive, drive, drive. A day's work increased from eight hours to ten hours, shifts extended from two to three, or work around the clock—a clock that changed from Eastern Standard Time to Daylight Savings Time to War Time. A workweek became seven days long. The shipyard facility was expanded to six times its original size and capacity. Instead of launching one ship at a time, we began launching two to four ships at a time.

Of the sleek 6,000- and 2,000-ton destroyers (DDs), we built twenty during the first two years of the war. Following the destroyer, when invasion landings were in order in the Pacific and appropriate ships were needed, we at the Charleston Navy Yard were assigned a part of the landing ship to build. These were the landing ship tanks (LSTs). They were mammoth things—four hundred feet long—and capable of running themselves right up on the beach and disgorging out onto the beach, through its big bow doors, three thousand tons of tanks, trucks, and other mechanized equipment. We at the Charleston Navy Yard launched eight of these all-important ships in four months.

As the war progressed and convoys of war materials and men began traversing both oceans, the fast-fighting destroyers were relieved of the slow escort services for more formidable duty and were replaced by an especially designed escort ship called the destroyer escort (DE). Of these three-hundred-foot-long, especially armed for anti-submarine ships, the Charleston Navy Yard built twenty-eight, launching all within a nine-month period between June of 1943 and March of 1944.

Another type of landing ship, smaller than the mammoth LSTs, was used in the latter part of the war. These were called landing ships medium (LSMs) and carried tanks, trucks, jeeps, and other invasion support equipment. Approximately three hundred feet in length, they too were beach-landing types and discharged their cargo through bow doors and ramps. Charleston Naval Shipyard built and launched 121 of these in thirteen months, between March of 1944 and April of 1945.

In a six-month period, we built and launched twenty-four LCCs, a forty-foot landing cover craft similar to the famed torpedo boat but armed with twenty-millimeter anti-aircraft guns. This type of craft was used as cover for the LCMs on their run onto the beaches.

Built also during the time period from 1941 to 1946 in the Charleston Navy Yard were fifteen seaplane wrecking derricks (YSDs), two-yard tugs (YT), and two tenders (Ads). These were giant repair ships of six hundred feet in length and equipped with as many as eighty shops to handle any kind of ship service and repair. Throughout the same period of time, the shipyard converted countless ships—private, commercial, and cargo—for the war service of one kind or another. Cruise ships were converted to hospital ships and troop ships. Some cargo ships were fitted with flight decks and became aircraft carriers. We lengthened ships—cutting them in two, pulling them apart and building in sections

to increase their capacities. We did this to submarines. And throughout the mad pace of all this,
new shipbuilding and conversion were repairing
battle damage to all ships—both of our own and
allied countries that came our way.

I cover this enormous workload handled by
the Charleston Naval Shipyard only in terms of
numbers. I have records, which name all ships
built there, but to list them here would be needless. As shown here, one can see the record of the
Charleston Navy Yard and know what the people
working there did toward the war effort. I know
it needless to wish that the many grossly ignorant people—some friends and some relatives
of mine—who display their stupidity and igno-
rance by referring to the Navy Yard as the "gravy
yard," would ever see these figures, this record of
accomplishment of the dedicated craftsmen and
women of the Navy Yard during World War II.

Not all of the shipyards actually built ships, but several of them
did. Of course, Pearl Harbor was the target of Japan's initial attack
and had to recover and rebuild following December 7, 1941. One
shipyard wasn't even established until the end of the war, 1945.
But they all did repairs on ships damaged during the war, both in
the Atlantic and Pacific theaters. Some yards built more ships than
Charleston, and others fewer. However, they all contributed mightily
to the war effort on the high seas and continued for several decades
after World War II.

Daddy recounts one allied ship that came into the shipyard for
repair during the war:

The British light cruiser *Uganda* limped
into the Charleston Navy Yard with heavy battle
damage. An aircraft's bomb dropped close to her
port side shaft of mid ship and exploded, caving

in the side of the aft engine room and destroying the port engine, the engine foundation, and propeller shaft, as well as much of the ship's interior. She still had use of her starboard engine farther forward and had, with the aid of tugs, made it into the British port of Gibraltar, where all the dead were supposedly removed and emergency temporary repairs were made. She then crossed the Atlantic on one engine. At our yard, we drydocked her, where complete permanent repairs were made. The body of one dead seaman was found as our workmen cut away wreckage.

One of my jobs in the repair of this ship was building a new engine foundation. The original foundation had been cast in one piece, but our foundry didn't have a furnace and ladle large enough for this, so it was decided to fabricate one. We patterned and cut from steel the parts and pieces, fitted it all together and welded it up—the interior welding being done by our two midget [little people] welders. They were, in fact, twins that the yard had hired for working in places a normal size man could not get into. Upon completion, the sixty-thousand-pound foundation was moved into an anneal [Daddy uses the verb *anneal*, meaning "to harden or strengthen," as an adjective here] oven- and stress-relieved by heating to red-hot temperature where all tensions were relaxed. Then it was cooled in measured stages until the entire operation was finished.

This was an example of one of the kinds of repairs the ship fitters made. Creativity and ingenuity were definitely good qualities to possess during this remarkable period in American history.

And then his personal breakdown occurred, which ushered in several decades of difficulties in my dad's health. He recounts the experience.

> Toward the end of the war, a new and very unpleasant experience befell me. It was sometime in 1944 and the pressures of the mad pace and responsibility of three years, ten hours a day, seven days a week, month in and month out, problems and deadlines, began to get to me. This added to pressures at home that surfaced from this time and had gotten me in a bad way. Headaches were endless. I smoked endless cigarettes, became absentminded to an alarming extent. It affected my work. I would go to the store for a loaf of bread and come back with a quart of milk. I'd leave work at the end of a shift, go out and catch the bus home, although my car was in the parking lot. I thought I was losing my mind. I asked for two weeks off—a break from it all to relax, take it easy, a getaway from the crowds. I got the time off, but my wife invited her family over for *my* two weeks off, which added to my stress. I gave up, threw in the towel. That was the mistake of my life!
>
> If one ever gives in to a neurosis, he is crippled for life. He will never be emotionally the same again. Doctors said it was anxiety neurosis due to stress and ordered me to give up my supervisory responsibilities at work. I would not do it. I was afraid of the stigma. I was not a quitter. The neurosis continued. With more consultation with the doctor, I gave in and requested a demotion. I went "back to my tools," as the expression goes.

It worked. Headaches vanished, memory returned, but stigma replaced them. Ignorant fellow workers smirked; wise fellow workers gave me their praise for having the guts to do it. But, as said before, to give in to a neurosis is a sad mistake. It opens a gate through which forever after a strange sensitivity flows. It weakens one's ability to combat stress; a person is never again normal in the sense of emotional control. (I will deal with this metamorphosis of the mind under "Strange Pastures" elsewhere in this book.)

I began my own career at the Charleston Naval Shipyard in 1964. Many World War II veterans were working in the Shops Division of the Public Works Department, where I was employed. None of them ever talked about their experiences in the war. Not one. As a nineteen-year-old, I just saw a group of men my father's age, who were gentlemen—pleasant, gentle, and mostly even-tempered. I enjoyed being around them in the workplace. They enjoyed each other, and we liked the barbecues and other social events they planned. One day, one of the men, a mild-mannered, kind man with twinkling, blue eyes and a ready, easy smile, was in the personnel office where I worked, when a ballpoint pen popped open somehow. It made a sudden, sharp *pop!* sound. He nearly jumped out of his skin! It really undid him. It was "shell shock" that originated when he was in the US Army, fighting in World War II.

We have heard of "shell shock," now called *post-traumatic stress disorder*. It affected soldier and civil service worker alike. All contributed to the war. Soldiers fought the enemy directly, while civil service workers fought a different type of enemy—time limits, short deadlines, endless long, hard days at work, many hours building ships, airplanes, armament, munitions, and doing other supportive work. Stress is stress. Daddy saw himself stigmatized, but we are all vulnerable to it, depending on our own circumstances and the conditions under which we live and work each day. Our genetics play a role in it as well, to which I can personally attest.

Mental illness has begun to be understood now, and most people know that it is a disease just like diabetes, arthritis, or any other chronic illness. It has to be and can be managed. As I recall, it was in the late 1950s that tranquilizers came on the scene on the little island where we lived. We mostly knew women who were prescribed them. Librium. They were universal pills covering everything from depression to anxiety to paranoia. People began to talk about taking them. Today, there are different pharmaceutical therapies for the various manifestations, such as clinical depression, anxiety, bipolar disorder, and schizophrenia. Some hated the stigma of admitting they needed them, and many probably still do. But they are fairly common in today's population, and I thank God that progress has been made in successfully enabling people to manage and even cure some of them.

I'm not sure how seriously my mother took Daddy's neurosis. Obviously, he was either too proud to talk about it with her or she couldn't recognize the signs. He was thirty-one years old, and she was only twenty-four—still fairly young. Perhaps she thought Daddy would enjoy having her family over for a visit. They could go to the beach and tour other sites in the greater Charleston area, like Magnolia Gardens, the Charleston Museum. There obviously was a "disconnect" between my dad's illness and my mother's sensitivity to it.

Recalling my grandmother's visit to Charleston while my dad was in Florida helping Aunt Judy with their mother, I am beginning to see a pattern in my mother's preference for her family over her responsibilities as a wife. Like I said earlier, scales are continuing to fall, and I am grievously disappointed.

Yet Daddy loved his work at the shipyard. After the war things wound down, and no more ships were built. They deactivated many ships. The shipyard would morph into a yard that did repairs and ambitious overhauls. Eventually, they became authorized to work with nuclear-powered submarines. But that was a bit later. Daddy continues his narrative:

World War II ended and the bulk of the 25,000 people working at the Charleston Navy

Yard faded into their respective worlds from whence they came. Many career people struggled with the change—tried to readjust to a prewar level of work. It didn't always work—too much had transpired. The old shipyard was not a peacetime facility anymore. Whole buildings had to be closed, dry docks deactivated, storehouses torn down. Long finger piers stretched forlornly out into the river. Only seagulls found their existence useful. Giant cranes, their long steel necks reaching skyward, set idle and rusting. Little activity prevailed and we shuffled our skills to fill the need where need indeed did exist, working as steel fitter, electrician, boilermaker, sandblaster, painter—anything that was needed.

An excess vessels' stowage center was created in the upper reaches of the Wando River, where the water was free of salt, and I worked there for fourteen months. Duties there were multiple. We policed the ships, which were bunched together in groups, called "nests." Each nest was out in the river and reached only by boat. Daily check of the bilges was made to see if any had sprung a leak. Some did. Before reuse, each was to be scraped and painted.

Since some of the ships were for sale, we acted as guide to prospective buyers that may be brought aboard. My nest of ships consisted of minesweepers. Most were wooden hulls and with their deep draft and big 400 horsepower diesel, direct drive engines, they made excellent tugboats, also good net-towing shrimpers. A Philippine lumber company bought three to be converted to tugs for use in the Philippine mahogany business. They lost all three in a storm in the South Pacific en route to the Philippines.

I had advised the people who were to take them across to pour concrete in the bilge to act as ballast since the Navy had removed the heavy mine sweeping generators prior to sale. They ignored this and lost all three ships. Some of the ships already had concrete ballast in their bilge, put in by the Navy when they were deactivated and placed on the sale list.

There were two ships in my nest that had ballast in their bottom that was worth more than the whole ship itself. I had discovered and realized this while inspecting for leaks. Probably others had seen it too but failed to realize its value. These two ships' ballasts were lead! Pigs of lead. Most buyers had passed these two up because they had composite hulls; i.e., steel frames were bolted over wooden planking. Also, they had superior engines that were not considered as good as Fairbanks-Morse engine, which most sweepers had. When it looked as though I would never sell the lead-laden ships, I leaked the information about the lead to a couple of wealthy-looking buyers, who promptly gave me a fat tip and bought both ships.

Time on the river was long and tiring. We made sixteen-hour shifts three times a week. This was good, however. I had ample time off to build my house on James Island, which I did myself and by myself in one hundred and twenty working days. I left the shipyard briefly about 1949. Did odd jobs, pipe fitting, and a stretch in a wooden box factory. But in four months I was back in the shipyard again when the Korean War became lengthy and it looked like we might be really involved.

I hesitate to include the following narrative, where Daddy lists the names of people he considered a "must" to give credence to during his productive years at the yard. However, I am doing so. These sage people have, like my father, passed from this life. However, this book may be discovered by and prove to be of interest to some of their descendants, and they may enjoy seeing their father/grandfather/uncle's name in print. They each contributed greatly to the war effort in this country, and their patriotic service should be honored, as much as my father's and anybody else's who helped to send our sailors out to fight the Evil Axis in some of the finest naval vessels constructed during the World War II years. They were definitely what Tom Brokaw calls them—The Greatest Generation.

It would be impossible to name the many people whose lives and mine meshed during my years in shipbuilding. Like the days in the CCC (the Anvil Rings) I must refrain from making a roster, but must name some that hold a special place in my mind. In doing this, I do not mean in any way to belittle others that I do not name. George Villaponteau was always in a special category. He was an angle smith in the shipfitter shop and a descendant of the French people who settled the upper reaches of the Cooper River country (a subject I did an extensive article on).

Truman Glenn, a tall Texan who came to the shipyard during the last years of World War II and who worked in my team in later years, worked with me on many jobs. I learned a lot about the Midwest from Truman. He had worked many trades there: in the oil fields, the wheat harvest, technical trades. Years later, Truman was beaten to death by two thugs who broke into his home and robbed him.

J. D. (Harry) Lanier was one of the old timers, like myself. We worked the same "slab" for a time. He became a supervisor (and a very good one) and went on to hold one of the highest positions in the Navy Yard. Master shipfitter.

C. B. Rowland, another old-timer, was my immediate boss for a while. He is still with us at this writing. He is a highly intelligent, interesting individual with a super personality. His talents extend beyond shipbuilding. He is a flyer—has owned at least two airplanes—a musician, and a short-wave radio operator. He built one of the most powerful stations in the country and is on voice around the world. He influenced me to stop smoking after I had smoked for thirty years. For this I shall always be grateful.

Others I must mention are, or were, Woodrow Grooms, who fell forty feet from the side of a ship to the concrete floor of a dry dock. In addition to these were J. U. Russell, William Gist, Lindon Mountain, Hampton Paul, Clyde H. Clark, and Bill Stozier, who lost a leg when a tank he was welding blew up. Also Richard Jackson, "Alabama" Hughes, Earl Hilton, Joe Murphy, Hal Nichols, Jimmy Hughes, Scot Sinclear (another shipbuilder from the River Clyde), and Red Pop, a friend from the CCC days.

Red Pop remained a good friend of my dad's up until they both retired from the Shipyard. Red's son, Ed Pop, worked in the same department in which I worked for a few years, in the early 1970s. Today, Red and my dad's remains rest near each other in graves at Mount Pleasant Memorial Gardens in South Carolina. A poignant reminder of their relationship, to be sure.

My last years in the shipfitter shop were involved in several types of shops, but among them was a new breed of destroyer—the DGLs. These were a larger and more powerful attack vessel, a far cry from the pre-war four stackers and the wartime 1,600-ton and 2,200-ton types. The principal feature of these huge floating warriors was the modern advanced firepower—rockets, etc. I had, in a period following World War II, worked in the "mothball" program, the preserving of the ships for an indefinite period of activity. In this time, I worked in the fire control feature of the fighting ships, the weapon systems, and learned a lot about weapons.

The DLGs and DDGs were guided missile ships with a bristling battery of weapons. These ships, the earlier ones, were not built from scratch but were a conversion of the larger class destroyers. The superstructure, everything topside, was stripped to the deck level. The hull was then fitted with new deckhouses, tripod mast, and other above-deck structures. I built new deckhouses and masts for these conversions, and it was in this time frame that I made several design innovations that were noteworthy and adopted by the Bureau of Ships.

Not all of my "inventions" were confined to surface ships. One particularly outstanding one was a device to alleviate a problem of long standing on submarine hatches. These ideas brought small awards, but most of all, they caught the attention of the Naval Design Division at the Shipyard.

Also during this time period, I became interested in the craft of printing as a sideline occupation. An old man had bought a small-letter press outfit with the same desire, but upon receiving it, without even uncrating it, he became unsure that he wanted to fool with it. I set up a shop in my attic and started a sideline printing business: stationery, cards, invitations, hand bills—the works. I added to the equipment by buying up many fine old typefaces. Some I ordered from England and in the end could and did produce some beautiful work. For several years I was involved with this sideline. In time, I changed jobs in the shipyard and lost interest in printing.

I wrote about this earlier. I remember this well. Daddy had built a large attic, which one could walk in, atop the flat roof of the house. He worked one summer on the graveyard shift and slept up there during the daytime, when Mama and I were about our own business and homemaking. In addition, he operated his printing press up there for a good while.

Later, he would get a promotion into the engineering side of naval shipbuilding. He continues his narrative at this point.

In 1958 I made a major change in the field of steel shipbuilding. It seems to have been the result of relative thinking—a subject prevalent in the scheme of things in life. ["Relative" seems to mean a psychic connection to an object or incident that reoccurs over years, to emerge and play out again in different time settings and places.] It started over a watch Virginia, my wife, gave me. Since I worked in heat, grime, dirt, I always wore cheap watches. They were always subjected to the most severe treatment. When one was damaged, I simply bought another. Virginia, in a surprise move, gave me a very nice, costly watch for my birthday. I was adamant, though I appreciated the gesture. A nice watch was for white-collar people. For some unexplainable reason, I remarked, "I'll have to get a white-collar job so I can wear it." A couple of days later, my senior supervisor came to me and said the head of the Design Division would like me to transfer to that department. My vast experience and knowledge of shipbuilding qualified me for a position in naval design, a position I had been offered during the last years of World War II but had declined. My old blacksmith image clinging to me, I guess.

That was part of the "leveling" system the Design Division had used for years. The man from "the mill" was necessary to balance the deficiency of graduate engineers. The college boys had the "book knowledge" but not the "shop knowledge." They didn't know construction practices and procedures. They didn't know the capabilities of the available steel working machinery. They didn't know how much weight the gantry cranes could lift. They didn't know if a certain size section of a ship's hull could pass through the shop doors. In short, they didn't know "shop."

A good college engineer and a good shipbuilder from the shops made a "level" team. One complemented the other. I carried several titles in the Design Division: engineering draftsman, engineering technician, and naval architect technician. With a course in naval architecture, I qualified for any structural design job with the exception of calculation. Two very fine engineers—and immediate supervisors, Joe Inabinet, and the structural design division head, Rubin Lapin—helped me greatly in my advance to becoming a capable designer.

Young ensigns and second lieutenants came through the Public Works Department, where I worked too. Most were smart and knowledgeable in their fields, but they relied heavily on the shop people and planners in carrying out the work of our department. There were a few "hot dogs" who thought they knew it all and that shop people were beneath them in status. Big mistake. They usually were soon humbled.

I remember when Dad went to work in the Design Division. His office was located in a building across the street from the building where I worked. It marked the beginning of a better relationship between us. I often rode to work with him, and we would pick up coffee and breakfast at one of the canteens and visit together in his workspace until I had to cross the street to the building where I worked. His time in the design division brought a number of interesting opportunities and relationships that he continues to relate.

> The position was white-collar, and I wore tie and coat. Also, and the end product of the whole thing, I could wear my expensive watch! My duty involved travel. An assignment to design a new superstructure on a fleet type submarine (a design that became applicable to all fleet type submarines thereafter) could send me on my way by plane to Key West, Florida, or someplace else. My first major design job was indeed an assignment to Key West for the Charleston Naval Design Division. At the tropical Key West Submarine Base, I did an in-depth study of the ship and worked out the features for the new design. Then armed with notes, sketches, photos, etc., I flew back to the home office (with a quick stopover in Miami for a few hours' visit with my sister and mother), got on the drawing board, and prepared plans (blueprints) for the actual work. Assignments led me at various times to Norfolk, Virginia, to New Orleans, and over the north Atlantic to Scotland. On these trips the job came first, of course. But my own time was my own or our own in case other designers were

166

TERRY STONE

along also, and I, or we, enjoyed the interesting features of the place wherever we were.

Carl Langley and I worked several assignments together, mostly in Key West. Carl was a likeable coworker and good traveling companion. He drank too much—never drunk, but his intake of alcohol was astounding! It finally led to his death, but I never think of him without regressing to the smoke-filled room of Sloppy Joe's Bar in tropical Key West, the whine of a leggy soloist seated atop an upended beer barrel, giving a bad imitation of Marlene Deitrich and the slowly revolving blades of the Casablanca fans overhead, sending back down the smell of humanity that arose from below. Sloppy Joe's was not exclusive. Carl and I warmed a stool in every bar on Duval Street. This was during the old days. Alas, Key West has now lost much of its old charm. But then when I think of it, so has most everything.

I have to interrupt here. I never saw my father drink in his younger days. Never...except when the septic tank backed up. Then he would buy a six-pack of beer, drink every one of them, and then commence digging into the nasty, disgusting septic tank to do whatever was necessary to get things working properly again. So this aspect of my dad's life is totally news to me!

*****

Through the foresight, the ingenuity, the demanding bullwhip efforts of Admiral Hyman Rickover, nuclear power came into the field of shipbuilding. We old-timers, of course, "leaned with the wind." The missile packing submarines were all to be so propelled, so that at this late date in our careers we went to school! Although not of the nuclear group, we would be around it, make and install equipment and compartments to house and contain it. We had to know the basic concepts of this new energy, to understand its nature, to know its dangers. Although the average engineer has some knowledge of this strange power—he knows "heat induction" is the heating of thick metal at the center while not affecting the temperature of its surfaces such as propeller shafts (the same as microwave oven in my lady's kitchen) and rudder post work—this new "wonder ray" was profoundly different.

The nuclear power school introduced the perplexing world of millirhems, the beta and gamma factor, the problems of radiation shielding. That is where I came in: the structures of radiation shielding. To design the lead barriers around all reactor-connected units, tanks, piping, valves, etc., anything that carried the harmful radioactive "glow." In the early days not too much was known about personal protection. We wore yellow suits, the gloves, the boots, the stocking mask when working around the "hot stuff," but still when we came out into the "clean room" the buzzers roared. Our dosimeters registered excessively high contamination. One could get only so many millirhems per lifetime, and then he was declared "burned out." But often, work had to go on and burned-out men had to go back in. Later "limits" were revised to reflect advanced technology. Still it was a dangerous game. The Charleston Naval Shipyard became a major overhaul base for the long missile packers as well as the lesser-length attack submarines that had nuclear power plants for propulsion.

Rickover developed and directly oversaw the construction of nuclear reactors aboard submarines. By the time they were developed, rather than US Naval shipyards, civilian contractors built them. The two major ones were General Electric and Newport News Shipbuilding and Drydock.

Nuclear-powered submarines operated almost silently. There were two types. Fast-attack subs could fire torpedoes out of the tubes that would break through the ocean's surface, fly over a target, and drop either a depth charge or a heat-seeking torpedo, striking and potentially decimating an enemy ship. A nuclear-powered submarine could, and often did, stay underwater for months at a time. It sometimes would sneak into a Soviet harbor or at sea, position itself right next to an enemy submarine out on patrol, drop under it, ride in its wake, and shadow it throughout its entire patrol—a spy submarine, totally undetected. The second type, a Fleet Ballistic Missile (FBM) sub, carried sixteen nuclear missiles. The missiles could be launched from deep underwater. When the missile broke the surface, its rocket engine ignited and carried it into a suborbital pattern, from which it could launch twelve fifty-kilo-ton rockets at multiple different targets around the globe. The boat's mission was usually just three months long. They had two crews who rotated on and off duty every three months—the Blue and Gold crews.

If the reader has an interest in knowing more about these submarines and how and when the Cold War ended, I recommend a book entitled *Blind Man's Bluff: the Untold Story of American Submarine Espionage* by Sherry Sontag and Christopher Drew. A fascinating read, the book provides information on daring exploits of the submarine service during that tense period in American History.

Certification to handle nuclear workloads was awarded the Charleston Naval Shipyard in the early 1960s. This is the environment in which my dad worked, as well as my husband, and finally where I was employed. Due to the stringent requirements of the Naval Sea Systems Command Nuclear Division (NAVSEA 08) and our shipyard's subsequent compliance to the letter, there was never a specific nuclear accident per se. However, there were two disasters that occurred during the early years in the nuclear power age. Daddy picks up his narrative at that point—April 10, 1963.

Seven days after the nuclear-powered, deep-diving submarine SSN *Thresher* disintegrated and scattered over an eight-thousand-foot, deep-sea floor two hundred and twenty miles east of Cape Cod, I was on a plane for the Naval Submarine Operations Terminal in Hampton Roads, Virginia, with orders to conduct a survey on a similar nuclear-powered submarine, the SSN *Scorpion*, for the installation of advanced technology in her antenna systems.

The two incidences were not related except in time frame and perhaps kindred spirit, but the communal effect of the *Thresher* disaster on the Navy community confronted me directly when I arrived aboard the *Scorpion* and made my request to begin the survey. The commanding officer (I forget his name, and it appears nowhere in my papers) was hesitant to permit the survey because it involved removing several access plates to the sail area, the superstructure that houses the antenna mast. "I may have to put to sea any moment," he insisted. "We don't know what we may be called to do." The *Scorpion* was also a deep diving sub, although not as pressure rated as the *Thresher*, which was built out of the new HY-80 steel that was not existent when the *Scorpion* was built.

The visibly concerned skipper was emphatic. The survey would have to wait. The whole navy community was in a state of confusion—Bureau of Ships, the OPNAV (operation of ships, submarine branch), DSSP (Deep Submergence Systems Project), and HPBS (Nuclear Power

Branch of the Bureau of Ships headed by Rear Admiral Hyman G. Rickover's Division of Reactor Development—all scrambling in every direction for answers to the *Thresher's* tragic mishap. I, having been associated with the Navy's shipbuilding for many years, could understand the skipper's position, but I opted to stick around rather than catch an afternoon flight home and thus appeared on board the Scorpion the next morning.

Tension was much the same, but by chance I talked with a burly, redheaded chief torpedo man, a veteran submariner of years service aboard the diesel/electric submarines. After a while, the chief said, "Let me go talk to the "Ol' Man; he likes my opinion sometimes." The "Ol' Man" was definitely younger than the chief, but that often is the handle sailors hang on the CO. After a half hour or more, the chief approached me with two seamen in tow. They carried toolboxes. "Remove any access plates this man wants opened," he directed them. "If you need me, I'll be in the forward torpedo room."

I slipped on my coveralls and began my greasy crawl through the sail—superstructure. My clipboard had as much grease on it as I when I emerged a couple of hours later, but the scribbling and signs and symbols showed through. In the afternoon, I went through again to confirm any questions I had and sketch some structural details I had failed to get on the first tour through the greasy forest of glistening steel shafts (mast) and webs of steel bracing, hanging wires, pipes, and tubing. The fiberglass sail, even after months and years of service in the deep seas of the world, still had the smell of sweet gum. It is inherent in the material the big structure that houses the mast is built from.

The sweet gum smell always carried my thoughts back to my country childhood when we kids gathered the sap of the sweet gum trees for chewing gum. It always stuck to the teeth, but it tasted good. It is funny, but all types of ships have a distinctive odor. Of course, there is the smell of steel. Each type of steel has a different aroma, but you have to have smelled a lot of steel like I have to know that.

Other odors combine to create a ship's special odor. The destroyer smells of chromate paint, burnt fuel oil, and mild steel. The cruiser is similar, but one also finds a hint of pine or fir and pitch tar from her wooden deck. The submarine is distinctive with her high tensile steel, diesel oil, and the blanching effect of battery acid. Cargo ships smell like rats. Just plain, unsanitary rats! No paint, no steel, no oil. Just rats. The rat odor absorbs and overwhelms any other odor. Just rats.

In my young and romantic days, I had the title for a poem I wished to write. It was "As Lonely as the Freighter in the Bay." Pictures of faraway places—always the harbor, palm-fringed, glittering sunset—whatever. But there was always that one lonely ship at anchor out there in the bay. I have worked on freighters (cargo ships) construction and design, and they all stink! All smell like rats. Is that why they are always alone there in the bay? I never did write the poem. Eight-track mind. It has always been with me.

I watched the commander up above me (I wish I could remember his name) on the small bridge. He paced back and forth, but his gaze was out across the roads, toward the Chesapeake, and finally the open sea. He was no more relaxed than he had been the day before. He wasn't interested in what I was doing—a substantial modification was to be done to his ship in her upcoming overhaul. I knew her skipper, her crew—the total of 129 men. I don't think he cared much about ship design at that moment. Foremost in his thought was the great disaster; perhaps the back of his mind, along the inroads that led into the spectrum of pre-vision and telepathy, a similar situation was materializing, involving his own ship. The *Scorpion* was indeed destined to meet such a fate. Some five years later, while crossing the Atlantic, at a point four hundred miles southwest of the Azores, the *Scorpion* plunged to the 10,000-foot sea floor to remain there forever.

I remember both disasters well. I did not begin my employment at the shipyard until August of 1964, a year after the *Thresher* disaster, and the Charleston Naval Shipyard had nothing to do with working on that submarine. Nevertheless, there was a cloud of grief hanging over the whole US Navy. The *Thresher* had gone out on a trial run following repairs at the Portsmouth Naval Shipyard in Kittery, Maine. Grimly ironic was that the current Charleston Naval Shipyard's production officer, Captain John Woolston, had had oversight of that particular shipyard's work at the shipyard in Maine. Normally, he would have been aboard the sub on its trial run, but he had been sick that day and unable to sail. The sub's loss had a devastating impact on him. Within a few years, he was transferred to Charleston and, despite the *Thresher* debacle, was eventually given command of the Charleston Naval Shipyard. That's where I met him.

In 1971, I was working in the Management Engineering Office and serving as their secretary. Our offices were adjacent to and connected with the shipyard commander's office. One of my duties was to fill in for either of his secretaries when she was away. Captain Woolston was a quiet, sort of pudgy man with fair skin, thinning brown hair, thin lips, and beady brown eyes. He was a chain-smoker. I never saw him without one. Sometimes there was a cigarette burning in the ashtray when he lit a new one. His introverted personality conveyed a "Don't get too close" message, but I discovered that he was misunderstood. He was always very kind to me. I had been told of his history with the *Thresher* and felt compassion for what I could only imagine was a deep sense of responsibility for whatever had caused the failure of the sub's propulsion system that resulted in the boat's sinking. They call that "survivor's guilt" today. He wore it as a mantle of concern for everything else under his command. To this day, there are conflicting opinions on exactly what happened to the *Thresher*, but you can read about it in various online and in-print materials.

As it happened, I had a brush with one of the crew on the SSN *Scorpion*. Following separation from my first husband, I rented a duplex apartment on James Island and found myself living next door to one of the *Scorpion's* "off" crew. I had been working at the shipyard for a good while by then, and that heavy pit in our stomachs lingered for a long time. *Scorpion* was lost so deep in the ocean that it was impossible to recover. Ninety-nine souls perished, and their remains rest on the sea floor. One theory was that a torpedo had accidentally launched—a heat-seeking one. And seeking that heat, it turned around and came back to the boat—the source of heat—hitting it and causing it to break up and sink. But since it was on a mission and following a Soviet sub, speculation spread that it was destroyed by the enemy sub. Other theories abound, but none have been proven. Deep-diving submersible cameras photographed the wreckage. As late as 2012, requests for reopening the investigation have been made, and the final one was denied. Survivors of lost crew members have attempted to pursue one privately since the sinking occurred in international waters. There has never been a final conclusion. Whatever the ultimate cause, the SSN *Scorpion* sank below crush depth and imploded ten thousand feet below the ocean's surface, taking its crew and secrets with it.

I must emphasize here that I told you that there had been no terrible nuclear disasters, and these nuclear-powered subs both sunk for different reasons, not due to their nuclear components.

*****

While we are on the subject of submarines, there is one thing I wish my father had lived to see—the raising of the Confederate submarine CSS *Hunley* from the floor of the Charleston harbor. The submarine sank following the successful destruction of the USS *Housatonic*, a Union ship blocking the harbor in the latter part of the Civil War. Due to tidal activity and resulting silting, the exact whereabouts of the *Hunley* remained unknown until 1995, and then plans were laid for its raising, which didn't occur until five years later. My dad was an aficionado of Lowcountry history, and to see the raising of the submarine would have thrilled him. He would have been present on the Charleston Battery that day and photographed the entire event, after which he would have created a photo essay of it.

Back to his narrative.

In a lighter vein, I followed another activity in the design division (strictly nonproductive) because I enjoyed it and the results brought joy to my colleagues. I was the unofficial "rib" cartoonist. Depicting fellow workers in some of their funny and unique mishaps in the performance of their duty and sometimes otherwise usually brought fun to all. My cartoons never created an issue because I followed a rule of never "poking fun" at anyone that I did not like. As a part of my makeup, I feel a few of the situations should find their places herein. [Sadly, none of his cartoons reproduced well enough to include here.]

The creation of the Small Business Administration cost the United States Navy its greatest asset—the government shipyards.

Perhaps I should say, 80 percent of the government shipyards with their reliably high standards, and highly skilled workforce. Their non-profit feature was ready service. Also, it opened the door to widespread graft, corruption, and free-wheeling rip-off of the Federal Government. The Small Business Administration was created in the early 1960s when the government bowed to the pressures of greedy, grabbing, businessmen in the private sector, who saw billions of dollars to be made if they could siphon off work on Navy ships that normally was done in the Navy's own shipyards. The Bureau's yards are non-profit shipyards; the private shipyards would do it and tag on large profits. The administrations imposed a requirement that the Navy "farm out" 80 percent of all its work to "Tom, Dick, and Harry" contractors. With this order, "shipyards" sprang up overnight. Every rotting down pier with a tin building on it on the east, west, and gulf coasts suddenly became a shipyard and applied for contracts on Navy ships.

The Navy had to spend billions of dollars setting up a system for letting contracts, writing specifications, expediting, and policing them. I personally have coordinated a contract with a "penny anti" contractor that cost the Navy (the taxpayer) more to negotiate than it would have cost a Navy shipyard to complete the whole job to start with.

Another outrage in the Small Business Administration's actions was the "aid to contractors" provision. If the contractor had no tools with which to do the work, the government furnished them tools. If the contractor had no personnel with which to plan the work, the government assigned them Naval Architects (at the Navy's expense). The "instant shipyards," of course, had not the facilities for handling the specialized work required in ship repair, so the government bought the machinery and installed it on a rent/lease basis, which of course was never paid, and the government eventually sold (what was left) as surplus.

One contractor, declaring himself a shipyard, got a contract to repair a destroyer, which was three hundred feet long. The contractor's pier was only fifty-five feet long, and the water in the creek on which the pier was located was too shallow to float a shrimp boat! The government (crooks in Washington) had the Navy assign the contractor dock space in the Navy Yard where, of course, the Navy Yard furnished him electricity, steam, water, crane services, and provided an ID system for ingress and egress of his employees. The contractor pocketed big profits for his work for the Navy! This type of thing was/is commonplace. This eighty percent loss of work by the Navy's own yards created such a stink that the administration finally said it would be "fair" if the Navy Yards wanted part of the 80 percent it could bid in competition with the contractors. The Navy Yards had to bid and win to work on its own ships!

Being involved in this, I personally know much of their bid did not reflect profits. To sidestep this disadvantage, the contractor deliberately bid low enough to get the job, knowing he could not do it for that but also knowing the system of cost overrun would make it up. Also, I am in a position to know that 50 percent of contracted work did not meet Navy requirements and had to be reworked in a Navy Shipyard.

Some of these "mud flat" shipyards were quick born and short lived. I personally had the pleasure of shooting down at least two of them. The Triple I Company (III), meaning "Integrity Inspectors Incorporation," came into fat contracts in the field of hull inspection, an activity I worked with for ten or more years. The work involved inspecting the hull of the ship, inside and out (while in dry dock), determining what areas of it were too corroded to pass, and document and define these areas with drawings complete as to size, location, types of material, and method of repair. With this, the repairing shipyard could do the work without additional surveillance. The Triple I inspection reports were a farce. They inspected three ships in Norfolk, Virginia. The reports read, "Looks bad here, looks good there," etc. Such reports had no value at all, and the repairing yard had to do a complete survey before work could be done. Yet Triple got paid for the batch of useless paper. The reports were piled on my desk and I was asked to write an evaluation on Triple I's work. The result of my evaluation was that all Triple I contracts were canceled.

I was in on another "deal" involving a ship's hull integrity. A Navy destroyer used as a training ship by a Naval Reserve Unit down in New Orleans had been declared unfit for service by some Navy official and was to be put on the auction lock (sold for scrap). The commander of the Naval Reserve Unit knew that the official (who promoted this action) and a New Orleans scrap metal dealer were good friends. He also knew his ship was good for many more years of service. Thus, the underhanded deal between the Naval Reserve commander made a formal complaint, and the Hull Integrity Team from Charleston Naval Shipyard Design Division to which I was attached, flew to New Orleans, i.e., Algiers, the Naval base on the Mississippi River at New Orleans and checked out the ship. We found what we had expected. This destroyer, though needing minor work, was completely seaworthy and good for many more years of service. Thus, the underhanded deal between a crooked naval official and a crooked scrap yard was aborted.

Volumes could be written about the deals, grafts, and general crookedness in the bureaucracies and private sectors alike.

Within a bureau, the backstabbing, hedge-hopping, and cutthroat atrocities go on, as well. Although I do not care to write about them, things have work credit, and things have happened to me within my career, especially in the area of promotion, work credit, and things like that. There is one incident I will relate because of the funny ending to it. In it, an idea of two of my "friends" was to make big money (an award) on a piece of information that I supplied them with. Of course, they didn't intend to clue me in on it, so they sneaked around and kept it quiet until it exploded in their faces.

An old fleet-type submarine was slated to be modernized, work I was heavily involved in. I was assigned the designing and flew to Key West, Florida, where the sub was, to do the initial design work. In conference with the commanding officer of the sub, he commented that the Bureau was foolish to spend two million dollars on the ship when the longevity plan called for the ship to be decommissioned in two years. I agreed, but orders were orders, so I spent a week on the sub doing my job. The decommissioning of a ship, taking it out of the fleet, is a secret and is classified thus. The skipper knew that I was cleared for secret information or I would not have been assigned to that job.

Back at the office in Charleston, I mentioned the fact that the sub was on the decommission list to my two friends, who also were cleared for secret information. So I was not out of line in telling them. They, without my knowledge, got the idea to put in a suggestion that the Bureau cancel the modernization job, thus saving the two million dollars. This, if accepted, should win them a fat award. I, of course, was not to be in on it.

They carefully guarded their suggestion from me, getting a girl from another office to type it up. A week later, all hell broke loose. The shipyard commander and Naval Intelligence called my two "friends" on the carpet to ask what the hell they meant putting classified information into unclassified circulation. The breach of secrecy had been noticed by a smart young Naval officer on the evaluation team that was to judge the merit of the "suggestion." He had then brought it to the attention of Naval Intelligence. My "friends" seemed to avoid me for weeks thereafter. The scheduled modernization of the submarine was indeed canceled, but the two "smart engineers" didn't get any reward money.

The Beneficial Suggestion Program (nicknamed "Benny Suggs") was indeed a wonderful program. Smart employees could submit a

"Benny Sugg," and it was evaluated for its merit. Indeed, people did receive monetary awards if theirs was accepted, and countless tax dollars were saved as a result of suggestions through this program. Also, the submitters were noticed by management, which could go a long way in qualifying a clever employee for subsequent promotion.

When I first went to work in the shipyard in 1964, I was a young nineteen-year-old and naïve. I kept hearing the term *Benny Suggs* but thought it was a person. One day when I had a Beneficial Suggestion form in my hand, submitted by one of the shop employees, I was told to send it to Benny Suggs. I asked, "Who is Benny Suggs?" The more seasoned employers laughed their heads off at me. But I survived the embarrassment.

I submitted one myself after years working as a secretary. When my boss was trying to reach someone by telephone, he would have me place the call and get the individual on the telephone, after which he would pick up the call. I had to dial the rotary phone (olden days!) over and over and over again until the call went through. I got kind of weary of that and put in a beneficial suggestion that there should be a "redial" key that would save time. They laughed me out of the office for that one, and I felt pretty dumb. Little did anyone realize that in thirty or forty years, digital phones came into being, and guess what! A "redial" key was on them to do just exactly what I had suggested decades before. The Shipyard was long closed, and I had not worked there in years. Otherwise, I would have produced my rejected suggestion and demanded a reward. But the time had long since passed.

Daddy concludes his narrative on his thirty years of shipbuilding.

As I approached thirty years of service, I began considering retirement, and I retired from the Navy Department on July 31, 1970, under the duty of Rear Admiral C. N. Payne. This was not my final termination of work. That was to come five years later. I had been "moonlighting" as a freelance photographer and writer for several years and was determined to continue in that field on a full-time basis for a few years. The few years became five years, and I retired again to devote my life to complete and unabashed pleasure. But the five years in photojournalism are relative to my life story, so my accounting of it follows under "Camera and Typewriter."

I would like to comment on the shipyard commander, Admiral Payne, of whom Daddy writes. He was a truly lovely man and a fine gentleman. He was married to a wonderful "Southern belle," aptly called "Sunshine." She was as gracious as any woman ever born and reared in the "Old South." I was told that she was so kind and her manners so impeccable that if you had been invited for dinner and showed up on the wrong night, she would graciously invite you in and prepare a meal for you. She never let on that you had come on the wrong date. I personally had no knowledge of that, but she epitomized the Navy officers wives, who played a huge role in service to other Navy families and to the communities in which they lived. They volunteered at the Historic Charleston Foundation's spring Tour of Homes and other local festivals and occasions. In addition, these women (the military was still all male at the time) brought a spirit of admiration and respect to the Charleston community, held fundraisers, and cared for the needy just as fervently as they donned hat, gloves, and high heels to support their men at various social functions, such as change-of-command ceremonies.

Those days were very special in my life, and I treasure the memories. I also treasure the relationship that finally began to grow between my father and me.

C H A P T E R   2 2

Strange Pastures

D uring my grammar school years and continuing several years following, my dad developed a lot of digestive problems. He also had recurring chest pains during stressful times. I tried to insulate myself from all the turmoil and strife between him and my mother. As an adolescent, I began living my own life—a very busy one at that. Into my teens, I got more involved in my studies and participated in several after-school clubs, including glee club, dramatics club, school newspaper staff, and voice lessons. I performed at various high school events, like both the Mr. and Miss James Island High School contests and at our band concert. My mind and time were occupied with those things plus dating. My junior and senior year, I was "going steady" with the boy who would become my first husband right after high school. I'm thinking now I had wanted to get married to escape living at home. What a grim joke that turned out to be!

Daddy started being treated by a new doctor, who had set up an internal medicine practice on James Island. In addition to prescribing mood-altering drugs to people, he practiced a very new (to us) nontraditional therapy—clinical hypnotherapy. I was aware Daddy was going through that, but it was a vague thing that I didn't question or pay a lot of attention to. However, in his autobiographical memoir, he writes of this completely and in no uncertain terms.

> I don't often talk about the amazing experiences in reincarnation I have had. I always

remember the words of the old Chinese mystic Lao Tse. He said, "Why speak of the beautiful expanse of the great blue ocean to a frog that lives in a well?"

In my adventures in the hypnotic state, the frequency of bird involvement is noteworthy. If the bird (birds) is not in the foremost subject, it is comparable with my point of view in the subject matter. Many views in the trance state are from a lofty point looking down upon the setting of the subconscious experience.

In acupuncture, the Chinese use names from nature to identify procedures of treatment for specific health problems, i.e., wood, sand, water, etc. In hypnosis it could likely be that the subconscious mind selects specific life forms as fish, birds, animals as the vehicle for transcendental experiences.

Once, in a light hypnotic trance, I found myself in a flight of geese heading south along the Mississippi flyway. I did not have the physical form of a bird, but I was indeed soaring effortlessly along with the flock. The river, which was obviously the navigation line of the flight, was plainly seen far below, and the green, yellow, and brown checkerboard pattern of forest and farmland spread as far as the eye could reach. My feathered fellow travelers seemed not to be aware of my presence (I was present only in the psychic sense), and my strongest sensation was that I was seeing the landscape below me through the eyes of one of the geese. The duration of this experience was short. The hypnotic state was light, so close to the conscious strata of awareness that I examined it clearly from the objective mind.

West Central Florida has a special fascination for me. I never pass through the area without this strong, strange feeling that I am on home ground. Once in a natural dream, I was driving through the area, a trip, which in reality I was to make the very next day. In the dream, as I neared the little town of Hawthorne (I had never been there in real life), I passed a small garden with a chicken wire fence around it on the outskirts of town. As I was passing this garden, a speckled hawk hovered over it as if about to dive on a snake or rodent in the ground foliage. The next day, in reality, as I drove through Hawthorne, on the outskirts, I passed the garden I had seen in my dream. No hawk hovered there, but a sign on the chicken wire fence read "Trained Hawks for Sale."

Once, in sleep, I was startled awake by the vision of a haggard young man in a soldier's uniform trudging along a sandy road in west central Florida. The vision was brief, but it was near the site of the December 28, 1835, Dade Massacre, near the town of Bushnell. It was the young man's eyes that transfixed me. He stared intently as he passed, as if trying to transcend a century of time. According to Rosicrucian calculations of my reincarnation period, I could well have been a young soldier, one of the soldiers in the Dade battle in which only four of the many survived. The ancient arcane mystery schools say a reincarnation period is precisely one hundred and four years. It also determines that the cosmic mind (spirit) completes that 104-year cycle (fetus) until the 104-year period is up. Statistics here are that the young man in the vision seemed to be in is mid-twenties, say twenty-six. He died at

Dade on December 28, 1835. Subtract his twenty-six years from 1835, and his birthday would be December 1809. Now add the 104-year cycle to that and we get December 1913. I was born on December 21, 1913!

I, too, have gone to therapeutic hypnotherapy sessions. A few years ago, I needed to lose weight and just couldn't seem to make myself disciplined enough to do what was necessary. A local clinical hypnotherapist advertises her services periodically in our local newspaper, *The Northeast Georgian*. My husband suggested I try hypnotherapy, so I made an appointment with her. After a few sessions, I did begin a weight-loss program and eventually achieved my goal. I also spoke with her about my dad's experiences. I never was able to get into a deep enough state to experience the animal totems or past lives. However, sometimes I saw images of Walt Disney characters, including Snow White, Dumbo, the Seven Dwarfs, Bambi, Thumper, and the like. Daddy was a great subject and was able to maneuver through several powerful encounters with birds, animals, and people like the young soldier he speaks of above.

*****

In 1939, James Thurber wrote *The Secret Life of Walter Mitty*, in which protagonist Walter Mitty lives much of his life in daydreams. He is a meek, timid man, but his daydream lives are very exciting and impactful in his secret world—a life-saving surgeon, piloting a flying boat in a storm, flying a suicide mission in war, and assuming the character of an assassin testifying in a trial. Walter Mitty's character has become a persona people who are suffering from depression or other mental illnesses often adopt in order to cope with their infirmity. Daddy expounds on this in his writing.

The Walter Mitty syndrome within me has always rushed me into past or future situations when there was a substantial hint of relativity. [I

am not sure what Daddy means here by "relativity," but reading on helps to put the expression into a context.] There was the Thomas Ince
Affair, for example. My awareness of Thomas
Ince—a former Broadway actor turned movie
producer—was established through the many
earlier-year Western movies his Hollywood studio produced. In the early twenties, Ince was
known as "the King of the Western Movie." Years
later, in the motion picture film processing laboratory at Universal Studios in New York City
(NYI), his name was constantly before me again.
Much of the equipment used in the lab came
from the defunct Thomas Ince movie factory in
Hollywood. "Thomas Ince Studios" was stenciled
on all of it: the big chemical vats that held the
hydroquinone, pyros, and other film-developing
chemicals, the hypo-fixing baths, wash agents,
etc. The name was on the big reels and drying
drums upon which thousands of feet of 35mm
motion picture film were wound and rewound,
as the case may be. The name Thomas Ince was
well-fixed in my mind later.

My background in the design and building
of steel ships during World War II qualified me
for the job of "caretaker" of a hybrid fleet of derelict ships awaiting the auction block after World
War II. The fleet, anchored out in a broad river,
miles from nowhere, with a small communica-
tions radio the only touch with anyone and my
lonely presence aboard them provided the time
and mood to know their physical character, their
past record and to feel the psychic vibrations of
the cosmic minds of the people who sailed on
them, who walked their lonely decks before me.

The yacht *Oneida*, 180 feet long with rak-
ish lines and graceful trim, still carried strongly,
to use simple language, its ghosts from its past.
I am sure my lifelong obsession and brief association with the motion picture industry and
its people accounts for my personal attunement
with the spirit life of the *Oneida*. As I often say,
"It is relative." This now aging ship, formerly the
floating palace of the German Kaiser Wilhelm
II, was more lately the seagoing party ship of
William Randolph Hearst Sr., noted publisher
and builder of the fabulous *San Simian*. Hearst
was the "d-d-d-daddy" paramour of the lovely,
stuttering Marion Davies and grandfather of
Patty Hearst, of the Symbionese Liberation Army
fame, and his ship had been pressed into service as
were many other ships when in the early days of
the war there was an acute shortage of troop-car-
rying vessels. After the war, these private ships
not wanted back by former owners, were put on
the auction block to be sold, along with their real
and imagined ghosts. The *Oneida*, still wearing
her camouflage paint, gracefully dominated the
immobile fleet of which she was a part. Many
lonely days I strolled her mahogany-paneled
pathways, climbed her brass-railed companion-
ways, walked her teak decks, mingling with the
ghosts of past dignitaries that left their mark, her
Mephistophelean quality. But the *Oneida* was
not really a devil ship; only relevant devils had
sometimes sailed aboard her.

I wouldn't want to call all movie personalities devil related. Some yes, some no. I see in
the ship's spacious lounge the still petite Mary
Pickford, certainly not a devil! Impish maybe but
no devil! She chats freely among an assortment

of movie dignitaries. There is Raymond Navarro, Paulette Goddard, a young struggling columnist named Louella Parsons. On the fantail Douglas Fairbanks and William S. Hart are shooting skeet over the azure sea. Buster Keaton, forever the comic on camera or off, has a captive audience on the bridge, including roving-eyed Thomas Ince, Ford Starling, and the blonde-bobbed Marion Davies. Many times I had entered the luxurious cabins feeling for Marion Davies' vibratory essence—maybe too many years had passed; perhaps too many GIs in their passage to war shattered her psychic presence. I never determined which was her private boudoir on the many fun cruises the *Oneida* made along the Baja coast with the proud Hearst in command.

Oneida parties were popular among Hollywood's elite, the star set. The guest list always reached the ship's accommodation capacity. Charlie Chaplin was sometimes aboard, although Hearst disliked him. Hearst mistrusted his lovely Marion in the presence of aggressive men and especially with the notorious Chaplin, who the British authoress Elinor Glyn had publicly proclaimed was "hung like a horse!"

It is the night of November 19, 1924, and the *Oneida* has just dropped the lower Santa Catalina light. Champagne flows above deck as the dark Pacific waters pass underneath. Randolph is troubled. Charlie Chaplin is on board, and he must watch Marion. By midnight he was particularly vexed with the flirtatious Miss Davies and the receptive Charlie. I feel these kinds of vibrations more strongly than the more gentle flow of love and affection. In fact, the giant Hearst still dominated his palatial *Oneida* in cosmic substance more than any other I felt in my several months' exposure to the ship. Hearst's mind was at a breaking point that night, and he tried to control it. However, when his lovely Marion disappeared from the group and Charlie Chaplin also became conspicuously absent, Hearst got a revolver from his cabin and slipped into Marion's stateroom door. From the cabin interior comes sounds of amorous excitement, even above the rumbling of the twin Krupp engines that pushed the graceful *Oneida* through the dark night along the southern California Coast. Opening the door suddenly, Hearst saw the form of a man leap from Marion's bed, and in his rage, he pumped two bullets into Charlie's dark form. Marion Davies screamed and cringed, awaiting the same fate. But no, Hearst could not harm his beloved Marion. It was the dastardly Chaplin that had desecrated his hospitality! Upon turning on the light, Hearst staggered back in surprise. The body on the floor was Thomas Ince! After much urgent crackling of the *Oneida's* radio, the ship puts into a San Diego pier and a "heart patient" on a covered stretcher is transferred to a waiting ambulance to then be put on board a Los Angeles-bound train. Upon departure from the *Oneida*, I lose their vibrations.

The story fades from the *Oneida's* cosmic spectrum. But fact in reality form tells the rest of the story. The "heart patient," Thomas Ince, dies en route to Los Angeles, where the body is promptly cremated. Other things happen shortly thereafter. Nellie Ince, Thomas's widow, became the benefactor of a fat trust fund set up by Randolph Hearst. Certain members of the *Oneida's* crew suddenly became rich, and the young, struggling news reporter, Louella Parsons, received a for-life contract as chief Hollywood columnist with Hearst Publications, Inc. As for the lovely, stuttering Marion, regarding Hearst's personal reaction to her, "h-h-h-he was l-l-like th-th-th-thunder."

*****

Wow! I am really envious of my father's journey into these "Walter Mitty" experiences. He indeed was a dreamer, and I now realize the depth and breadth of his mind's journeys into various scenarios, past and future. The *Oneida's* final home was in the Charleston, South Carolina, area, where it awaited auction—an Atlantic coast resting place rather than its Pacific life under the command of Randolph Hearst. One can only speculate how much of Daddy's daydream is attributed to his imagination and how much is based on history he might have researched to come up with the shooting of Thomas Ince. But the connection between the deceased movie mogul's life and the equipment at the New York Institution of Photography laboratory is physical and solid.

*****

Visions in the subconscious are not dreams. The revealing "vision" and a dream are markedly different in character. Whereas the dream is a rambling, somewhat incoherent sequence of loosely joined episodes that oftentimes go on and on during sleep, the vision is a direct, positive revelation, a sudden, short scene with a pointed impact, with instant clarity. Often, it is just one flash on the screen of the mind. You see it suddenly, plainly, and then it is gone. The vision comes from a deeper realm of the mind— from some past or future experience—and is not always restricted to sleep. A vision can and does often flash on the screen of the wide-awake mind. The dream comes, as Carl Jung has said, from the "dream work," the fabrication of wish and recollection without objective guidance. Visions most often come from past incarnations. Futuristic visions are due to the phenomena of an unconscious "tapping" into the code of the Master Intelligence.

I am not one to have visions. I believe it is safe to say I am a pragmatist. As I wrote earlier, I can't get into a deep enough state to identify totem animals that might help me on my life's journey. Yet I know for certain that I have had one powerful vision. It was a week or so after my mother died in 2011. She lived in Summerville, South Carolina, in The Presbyterian Village at Summerville. We had moved to Northeast Georgia a few years before, and I had just a week or two earlier come back from visiting her. She was definitely in decline then.

The nurse's station at the Village called me and told me that Mama had been taken by ambulance to the hospital emergency room. I immediately called the hospital and was connected with the ER. This had happened before, and I had never had any difficulty talking with an ER nurse and learning what was going on. However, this time, the nurse asked me to come into the hospital. Since I live five and one-half hours away, I couldn't just hop in the car and drive over. She insisted a family member would have to come. I called my daughter-in-law in Mount Pleasant, South Carolina, about an hour away from Summerville and told her that the nurse wouldn't tell me anything. Nancy and my stepson Stan prepared to drive there and check in. But as soon as I hung up from talking with Nancy, the phone rang, and it was the hospital chaplain, telling me that my mother had passed away. They had worked on her for a while trying to get her back, but they were unable to. That part disturbed me greatly since she was ninety years old and had a directive that they not perform any heroics if she should suffer a serious heart attack. It bothered me that they jarred and handled her body roughly, trying to get her to breathe, when she had finally passed. The last number of times I had visited her, she had been ready and looking forward to the next life.

She had a funerary directive too, and she was to be cremated. I spoke with the funeral home and sent them a photo they could use to officially identify her. Then I made arrangements with them, The Presbyterian Village, and her home pastor for a memorial service, which we planned for the following Saturday. The beautiful service was exactly as she had requested it. I had a friend cater a big family meal following the service. The next day, we began the sad duty of disposing of her earthly belongings, which by the time she passed away were pretty meager. Bob and I returned home a few days later and attended our home church's worship service the following Sunday.

The vision happened during the Doxology, following collection of tithes and offerings. We stood and began singing that grand old response, when suddenly before my eyes was a vision of my mother, young and beautiful again (perhaps in her mid-thirties) sharing a radiant smile with God. God's face was turned toward her, and I could only see Him in profile, of course. The vision was stunningly clear, as real as this computer I am typing into now. It was a gift. It had always been my role to make sure my mother was happy—often a very heavy burden. The realization of that had been disturbing to me the few years before when I had the epiphany. Yet this vision was different. I was comforted by that "flash on the screen of the wide-awake mind" and am assured she is in a place we all want to be after we take our last breath here on earth. Why in the world would anyone mourn for someone and wish her to return to a weakened body that no longer functioned, leaving that heavenly place? I have been able to let go and be released from my responsibility to her. That gift is beyond measure. I am grateful for it.

*****

In the mind of man there is a door. Through
this door, man looks out upon eternity. He sees

the physical world around him with its hills, its seas, the sky. Through this door he hears the sounds of this world, smells its odors, and feels its presence. It is through this door that man has an awareness of objectivity. Over this door is a sign labeling it: *The Door of the Objective Senses.*

Through man's five senses he is conscious of the world around him, including his own physical self.

In the mind of man there is another door. This door leads not into the objective world but into the strange, mystical region behind the mind. Through this inner door, man can see the Cosmic Universe. He can attune to its harmony, feel its preservation. This door is man's contact with the homeland of the soul. Over this inner door is a sign labeled *The Door of the Psychic Senses.* Through it, man sees his psychic counterpart. Through it comes the psychic powers that manifest in the being of man, the sense of intuition, the infinite laws to be tapped by the systems of man's physical makeup that establishes his relationship with the Universal Whole. Through this door comes the infusion of spirit and will. Through this door comes man's sense of the infinite. Through it he sees the oneness of all creation and finds his link with his God. The realization of the psychic senses is the key to man's ability to look through this inner door. The recognition of self as a physical and psychic duality opens this door to mystical attunement. Many men seek this attunement. Some have found it. In all men, there is the door.

The thought does come through to me, as a student of metaphysics, that we are a lonely lot, few in numbers, afield in thought, sailing an uncharted sea in search of life's mysteries. But if a lonely course is indeed the way of the mystic, then let me say that within my solitude there exists a world of wonder, lovable people, and beautiful things.

I never saw this in Daddy's personality during this period. I did notice a more philosophical viewpoint in his response to major events in life, such as the failure of my first marriage. He appeared to just let things roll as they would. "Turning the page" was a way he looked at life's unfolding episodes, and that had a positive effect on me. As a young woman, I didn't have the maturity that comes with the many life experiences and lessons I have later learned that helped me form an arsenal of coping strategies to fall back on in times of trouble. I saw this dreamer in him develop more defini- tively. However, paralleling his dreamy self-expressed "solitude," his increasing loss of hearing contributed to his isolation as well. Before he tried hearing aids, as well as often afterward, he was "alone" even in a group of people. Being unable to hear was isolating by itself. Conversations around him didn't penetrate, and he obviously stood back and somehow lived in a world of his own making—a dream world, if you will. His was a neutral personality. Sometimes he had a camera and took photos, depending on the occasion.

Perhaps during these social occasions, he retreated into his Walter Mitty experiences. Perhaps those times, his soul flew with a flock of geese, walked dusty roads carrying a musket, built a great sailing ship, explored ancient ruins. Unfortunately, our communi- cations with each other didn't break through the barrier that would let me even ask him, and he never told me. This autobiographical memoir was written mostly for me. I can now visit him in the mys- tical world he so often occupied right in front of my eyes. Before, he was unable to share his rich life and extraordinary experiences with the one person for whom he could never really demonstrate love in an affectionate way.

My interest in metaphysics, that is, the manipulation of certain metastatic elements of it, came about in the mid-1950s. This was an era in which my mental attitude toward the world around me was out of control, when my family relationship was at a very low ebb, and I was unable to do anything about it. As is common in such cases, a symptom indicating a physical disorder exists where in reality the physical disorder is purely synthetic. My symptom was a super-sensitive stomach at times of stress or moments of resentment or displeasure. At such times, I had to rush to the bathroom! After the attack of diarrhea, the stress subsided, the resentment became less, but the ordeal was always the same.

This condition has been called "Yankee stomach." Mary Astor, the stately but promiscuous novice actress, aptly described it as one's soul trying to tell one something. How right she was, but I was to suffer several years and spend a small fortune before I knew of it. The symptom was the result of a mix-up of signals in the sensory system of man. The wires had gotten crossed, so to speak, and the message to be made or express displeasure didn't go to the emotion center but instead went to the bowel processes, where it manifested in a physical manner rather than in a state of emotions.

In computer language, one would say it was punched into the wrong tape. It was the most damnable malady I have ever experienced! I could compile a list a mile long: doctors, X-rays, GIs, medicines in which I sought relief. I even tried six months of chiropractic. Nothing touched it. Several doctors knew it was psychosomatically promoted, but all they knew to do was recommend a long vacation. It was surprising to see how many seemed happy to get me out of their office.

In time, I learned of a young doctor who had, in England and Germany, studied the use of hypnosis in the diagnosis and treatment of emotionally promoted physical problems. His name is Robert Johnson. I know personally a girl he had helped, so I gave it a try. First was the test to see if I was receptive to mesmerism. The actual hypnotic sessions, singularly and grouped, were held late at night, usually after midnight after the doctor's regular patients' appointments were over. Some hypnotists say the late hour is conducive to the trance state as it has a greater element of fatigue.

I was slow at first. The problem seemed to be a matter of turning loose and going with it. Sessions were twice a week, sometimes with the girl I mentioned earlier. She served as a companion-guide into the trance state. After two or three months, I was being induced easily into a deep, somnambulant-like state, where diagnosis or fact-finding is most easily done. The light sub-surface trance is best for suggestive treatment.

One night, while in this lower-level state, the hypnotist informed me that he was going to separate my two bodies, the spiritual—the mind/soul, the id—from the physical body. The id would be gradually lifted from the clutches of the physical, and I would be able to watch the physical body and observe what it might be doing. In this my mental body would float up in the air above the physical body, and he wanted me to look down at it and observe all I could about it and to remember what I saw so I could tell him what I saw when I was brought back to consciousness. He said, "You can see your body there, I cannot. You must tell me what you see." I was plainly aware of slipping away from the physical me and in a moment I saw myself below me. My body was lying, struggling on the floor of a room in an old house. My body was growing darker (the skin) and the eyes sunken into my head. The floor of the room was covered with tile and pieces of the tile kept curling up, coming loose, and blowing away. I tried to hold them in place with my hands, my feet. I lay on them with my body, but they kept curling up and blowing away. I think the doctor could see I had found my image perhaps by the way I writhed and turned because he soon informed me he was going to put me, the id, back into my body and bring me back to full consciousness. I told him what I had seen, and he explained the symbolism. The body was the house of the soul, and the deteriorating floor tiles represented the sorry state of my emotions, my struggles with the tiles representing my failing efforts to contain my emotional state.

Now we must find out the cause of it all. Under hypnosis, he drew from me things I had refused to talk about in the conscious state. He explored it completely: the history of incompatibility in my marital relations, the in-law conflicts, and the inability to find a common ground in it all. He also explored the forces outside my home—family and community affairs—but always came back to the simple complexities of wife and home.

He asked Virginia to come in for a consultation (not hypnotic), and she went but was not cooperative. In her view, nothing was wrong. No fault lay on her side or her family. Realizing that approach would accomplish nothing, the doctor said we would handle it without her help.

Since the cause couldn't be removed, we would, with hypnosis, remove the symptoms. Under hypnosis, he implanted the suggestion that instead of manifestation of diarrhea, the wild emotion would manifest physically as a paralysis of the little finger on the left hand. To my astonishment and relief, this is exactly what happened for several days. But alas, the diarrhea came back. He suggested the paralysis again. Neither diarrhea or paralysis came back, but it began manifesting in a severe smarting of the eyes. "Good!" Dr. Johnson explained. "We've got it on the run!" But smarting eyes were painful, although preferred to the diarrhea, and we continued with the paralysis approach of transference.

At times it worked, at times it didn't. By the rules it should! The doctor had become quite good with the technique of hypnosis, and his proficiency at hypnotherapy was improving. But my problem stubbornly hung on. I felt that somehow I ran interference, and I think he thought so too. A girl patient with much the same problem as mine was responding remarkably well. Hers was in-law related. Though she could not step from under that in-law domination, she was successfully building a shield behind which she could escape. My main problem was not that in-laws dominated me, but that it was that they totally dominated my wife, and I resented that deeply.

I wanted my wife to be her "own woman," to tailor her mind and thoughts around our marriage, not bring our marriage into her family's ways and wishes. Because of this, I became the "oddball" in the eyes of her family, and in hers too. And, of course, I resented that too.

Dr. Johnson's work in hypnosis was not without its problems to him. People with closed minds avoided him as a medical doctor. Some basically ignorant people called him a "quack." He did not advertise his work in hypnotherapy, and mostly through his patients did knowledge of the magnitude and the benefits of his work spread. Also, he held private (expository) sessions in his home to which only invited participants attended. These were patients, colleagues, and special friends. I have at these sessions seen and participated in some amazing things. Some of these "trips," to use the word *addicts* (and believe me, it had to be along the same inroads of the mind) would put the "Bridie Murphy" adventure on the back page.

Some problems for the good doctor even came from these sessions because once an invited guest, who had no experience or background knowledge of the happenings along the inroads of mesmerism, was so carried away with what he had seen, blabbed it to friends who obviously viewed these things with scorn and created quite a flurry of community flack about the midnight "doings" of Dr. Johnson.

Although Dr. Bob Johnson never seemed able to hit the right "note," so to speak, with my personal malady, I had a major breakthrough with the world-renowned hypnotist, Dr. William Krueger. Dr. Krueger of Chicago was an obstetrician and was widely acclaimed for his "painless" childbirth through the use of hypnosis. Dr. Robert Johnson, in his effort to enlighten his colleagues on the field of hypnotherapy, went to great personal expense to set up a symposium and demonstrated his methods to local members of the medical profession. The guest speaker/demonstrator was none other than Dr. Krueger. The conference was held in Charleston's Fort Sumter Hotel. Attendance, I must say, was profoundly shoddy. Perhaps some Charleston doctors were too busy. Perhaps hadn't crawled from under their rock into modern times.

However, several doctors were there, who had open minds and were interested in expanding their field of knowledge. There were three "specimens" supplied by Dr. Johnson. They were the girl (my friend) who had worked with me in the very beginning. Her problem was sex related. She had regressed back into her past incarnation and revealed that in that life she had been a popular prostitute. The attributes of that incarnation conflicted with her present respectable sex relations with her husband. The other was the girl who wished to retain her individuality and her marriage in spite of domination of her in-laws. The other specimen was me, with the crossed-up computer—emotions transferred to physical manifestations.

Each case was presented individually, the person and case history, by Dr. Johnson. Then the person was turned over to Dr. Krueger, who easily induced the hypnotic trance and began the therapy. My turn was last. Dr. Krueger put me into a deep somnambulant trance. He explained to the doctors the degree of depth the hypnotic state was. It was the same level of unconsciousness that people drift to in natural sleep when they sleepwalk. Through his guidance, he, the hypnotist, would carry my subconscious awareness through my own body, through the sensory systems, the channels of automated action taking place there. It was—is, in fact—like a computer, programmed to perform each automated action. And I could see it all!

There were the channels that commanded the muscles of the heart to beat, the channels that commanded the lungs to expand and contract, that commanded the gastric juices from their respective organs to flow to complete the digestive processes. All these were automatic to do these functions. We don't have to consciously tell our heart to beat; we don't say to ourselves, "I think I'll breathe now." All these commands are given by their own little chip of ingrained intelligence within the cosmic mind. We are born with it. There are other channels, too, that are programmed for their assigned purposes, of course, but to cut straight to the point, there is the channel that commands the bowel to react for the purpose of elimination. This physical function is also automatic and comes from the cosmic state of the mind. There are channels that relate to the emotion aspect of man, to express gladness, sadness, and resentment.

Dr. Krueger carried me through them all so I could see what was happening to me. My emotional state had become so complex that somehow in the maze of metamorphic systems, two systems had become crossed up. There is no layman's language in which to describe this, so simply stated, the wires got crossed. When a situation in which the signal started out to activate my emotion of anger or resentment, it went down the bowel channel and activated the bowel.

After exposing my subconscious mind to the mechanics of my systems, the hypnotist brought me slowly and carefully into the light sub-surface level and begin the "suggestion" phase of the session. He said, "If you can *see* the problem, you can *control* it. When the urge comes, see it on the screen of your mind and know the circuits are crossed. The need is *not* there. If you can see it, you can have it under control. You are in the process of reprogramming it." Then he brought me out of the trance.

From that day on, the malady that had tormented me for years did not exist. I became a different person. When I felt resentment, I expressed it in words. When I felt anger, I "blew my stack!" I astounded some people; I insulted others. My freedom of expression sometimes built fires I had to fight my way out of. But no more diarrhea! Thank God! No more diarrhea!

My interest in metaphysics became really profound after this. I remained in Dr. Johnson's private sessions, and he taught me many things. One was the art of self-hypnosis, and in it I experienced even more fascinating things. To drop into a deep hypnotic trance, withdraw my ID from my physical body and float away over the landscape, into strange and intriguing chasms, through many patterned halls of light and shadows (all completely involuntary), to hear voices in unknown tongues, see faces staring—eerie distortions of familiar features—all an experience beyond description. The author Thomas Wolfe said of it in one of his books, "Beneath the tides of sleep and time strange fish are moving."

I have traveled so deep into the subconscious realm of the mind that only fragments of what was experienced there could be brought back to the conscious level and remembered with any degree of clarity. A most fascinating level of the trance state is the light subconscious level, just under the surface of consciousness. It is an uncontrollable zone, filed with light and frivolous fancy. This is the level of Lao-Tzu's "butterflies." The famous Chinese philosopher who founded Taoism especially enjoyed the light sub-surface trance, where he often found himself to be a butterfly and with other butterflies would flutter from flower to flower, sipping the sweetest nectar, sunning golden yellow wings upon the green of balmy gardens. Never a worry or care. Back in the conscious state, he would sit for hours contemplating what he had just experienced. Was not the delightful world of the butterfly—the real world—the real state of mind and this bitter, cold, demanding world the trance state? He could never be sure.

My quest for knowledge of metaphysics was insatiable. I asked Bob Johnson where I could get more. He said, "Go to the Rosicrucians." I applied for admission into that great and most secret order. In time, I was admitted in their neophyte school. For thirteen years I faithfully digested their teachings, studied deep monographs, attended their demanding pronaoi, struggled through complicated examinations. Then the coveted goal was reached. The plateau of the Illuminati. I received the fellowship and the honor of placing the letters FRC after my name. I was at last a Fellow Rosicrucian in the Ancient Mystical Order Rosae Crucis (The Order of the Red Rose and the Golden Cross). Founded in the arcane mystery schools of ancient Egypt, its members included notable names as Thutmose III, the martyred mystic Lord Raymond VI (Count of Toulouse), the illustrious Fra. Michael Maier, Sir Francis Bacon, Benjamin Franklin, Maybanks-Stay, and H. Spencer Lewis, among others.

I remember the early days of his journey into clinical hypnotherapy. However, I have no recollection of his leaving the house after midnight for late-night sessions. He reports this started in the mid-1950s. That means that I was in grammar school, say fifth or sixth grade. I certainly would have been in bed asleep by midnight, not only on school nights but weekends as well. My bedtime was 8:30 p.m. I am aware of his treatments and the controversial methods of Dr. Johnson, the only medical doctor on James Island during the 1950s and 1960s. People came from conventional societal backgrounds and thus were skeptical of nontraditional medical treatments, such as hypnotherapy, acupuncture, and the like. Even chiropractic was suspect, although that was around. People who did this were said to belong to cults and were (God forbid) heretics or at least kooks.

While he was delving into the Rosicrucian Order, I was growing up in the Presbyterian Church, where I studied the Bible in Sunday school and followed the traditional tenants of John Calvin's viewpoint of God in Three Persons. Anything that diverged from that belief was veering off the straight and narrow road of salvation through Jesus Christ and Him alone. Later, I would venture off the path into a new area that was sweeping the country in the late 1960s and early 1970s—sensitivity training, which involved self-examination and discovery of who our true selves are, how others view us, and ultimately how God sees us. That broadened my horizons considerably, and I came to understand more fully the power of God's love, how we can change people's lives by breaking through the barriers of the invisible protections people build around themselves, such as temper, artificial humor—anything that distracts someone from getting too close. That was in the late 1960s. The birth of the hippie movement was starting then as well, and it was "the Age of Aquarius," "Make love not war," and "mellowing out." I did not join the hippies. Too conventional for that. But I definitely was aware of it. And I loved the music.

I was living on my own by 1969, and my mother and I were still very involved with church. However, we were more open and sensitive to people's conversation and behavior. It was during that time that Mama did go with Daddy to some local Theosophical Society meetings in Charleston. She actually broadened her beliefs a bit too, accepting the view on reincarnation and the possibility of different spirits and maybe alien presences in the world.

I have my dad's Rosicrucian Handbook. I have not read through it. I will probably pick it up at some point and look at it. However, right now, I am focused on sharing Daddy's precious story with anyone who cares to experience vicariously his boyhood and young adulthood adventures.

Daddy continues a bit more on his experience in the realm of the subconscious mind.

Dreams—the jumbled fantasies that take place during sleep—are a product of two levels of mind meeting on common ground, a mixing of wish and recollection without the guidance of objective conscious thought. These brief mental melodramas, be they serious, humorous, or unclassifiable, are indeed little gems of action and events played out on the stage that lies beneath the curtain of man's awareness. Such authorities as Freud and Jung searched for the meaning of dreams and their purpose, but I don't believe their conclusions were satisfying. Dreams, in my view, are experiences—projections of wish and thought back-flowing from the cosmic mind—the reservoir of memory and in fact, all knowledge.

People's minds are appendages of the cosmic mind and have access to material through the process of recollection, voluntary or involuntary. The substance of dreams is drawn from this source, but there is no objective control over its application. So in the dream's scenario, the plot often becomes abstract, fleeting, and disjointed; people long dead are alive; places of yesterday are strange and obscure.

What do dreams mean? Nothing! They are but loose circuits of fact and fantasy, sparking uncontrollably in the receiver of the mind. Don't try to analyze a dream. Remember it, enjoy it (unless it as nightmarish), and appreciate its phantasmagoric nature. Accept dreams as little plays, mini performances acted out especially for you on the stage of your mind. Enjoy their intensity; laugh at their humor; they are yours personally, seen by no one else. Call them your special private theater!

I kind of agree with what he says. There are definitely shades of wish, longing, and sometimes dread in some of my dreams, as well as total nonsense in others. I can't always remember my dreams, and it's just as well. Some are based entirely in fact. Others are pure "phantasmagoria," as he says. He goes on about his otherworldly life.

The entire ethereal phase of my previous incarnation cycle fell within the Victorian era. I think influence therein is even more effective than influence in the material state.

The process of relativity is most interesting, and it is most easily understood, I think, in the simpler trends of life. Suggestion is probably stronger than environment in this process. Environment is definitely in there, but being mentally bent by some fact having the implantation of a subject into the metaphysical whole is like grafting in a permanent influence. Influences, no matter how simple during the formative years especially, create traits, interests, and directions. Example: My intense interest in—or to use the subject *relative connection*—the activities of the FBI, the G-Men/Gangster era and its dramatic history that took place during the 1920s and early 1930s was due to my knowledge that when I was born, I was delivered by the father of the well-known G-man Melvin Purvis. This was to trigger my G-man syndrome. No matter how small the initial relevance, each resultant association with the drama of the era, though long past, fuels the relationship and enhances the mesmerism I find in the sites and symbols of this era.

Sometime in the early 1970s, my dad and his sister had a falling-out with their older brother, my Uncle Golden. Uncle Golden seemed to have a hard time holding a job. The story went that he was always trying to bring to fruition a get-rich-quick scheme. His poor, lovely, long-suffering wife, Aunt Faye, finally had to divorce him when he could no longer pay the bills. She worked hard at Legerton's Book Store in downtown Charleston and lived off her meager earnings until my cousin Billy moved her up to Lexington onto their property. However, before that happened, Golden had tried to persuade his mother, my Ma 'Tone, to give him money. Aunt Judy and my dad knew that she would never see anything returned in the bargain and stepped in to stop her from giving him the last of her few dollars.

Thus began a thirty-year-long rift between my dad and Billy and his family. People don't consider what things like this do to family, especially children. While Billy had three very close first cousins on his mother's side, he and I were the only first cousins on our dads' side. We lost a lot of time together, as I also did with Billy's children. It was a shame really, since I didn't have any children of my own. My family members were estranged from me on Daddy's side. I still had some contact with cousins on my mother's side, but they lived in Augusta, Georgia, and had their own families and lives there. We weren't in touch often at all. I missed having family to be close with.

Fortunately, many years later but not before Uncle Golden was in a nursing home in the last few years of his life, he and Daddy were reconciled. It was a blessing to them, I feel sure—especially my dad, I think. Aunt Judy had passed away, and he was in the same fix as I—no close family. Finally, Billy, his wife, children, and I were reconnected and after a few years, Billy and I swore an oath to contact each other every month or so. If he didn't call me, I called him, and we enjoyed a close relationship until he passed away in April of 2018. I wasn't ready to lose him yet, and I am sure his wife, Reita, his children, and grandchildren weren't either. However, he had a form of cancer that was difficult to check. I still miss him.

I am still in touch with Reita and a couple of his children and his granddaughter Charlotte Jennings on Facebook. That is a blessing to me, and I need them a whole lot more than they need me, I'm sure. But I thank the Good Lord for this chance to once again enjoy relationship. Billy provided some good background material for me in the writing of this book, and I treasure all our conversations. It was too funny. Both of us being only children, we had to ask each other questions like, "Did your dad have diabetes? Do you?" And on and on like that. "Did your dad every say anything about so-and-so? Did your dad ever mention such-and-such?" I think we got all those mysteries solved. I sent him a few of the early chapters of this book for him and his family to read. But sadly, he didn't live long enough to see much of it.

Daddy writes down one last experience that occurred within the subject of this chapter, "Strange Pastures."

> While in a deep hypnotic trance, I found myself in a rainstorm on a Holland dyke. A leaky roofed windmill clattered in the gale, but offered a measure of refuge. Upon entering the structure, I glanced up toward the crossbeams, and upon one sat an old, ragged owl. The owl was

shuttering and shifting itself here and there on the beam, trying to avoid the incoming rain. It turned its yellow eyes downward to look at me, and I saw that the owl was my brother.

Daddy makes no attempt to explain what he believes the dream may mean, and we just have to look back at his description of dreams: a "phantasmagorical" display, which becomes your own private theater.

Camera and Typewriter

A few years before his retirement, about 1966, under President Lyndon B. Johnson's term in office, Medicare was created. Under Title XVIII of the Social Security Act, this single-payer medical insurance system provided health care to all Americans over sixty-five years of age. However, the individuals had to have paid into the Social Security retirement plan during their employment. People working for the Federal Government paid into the Federal Government Retirement system. Daddy had paid some into the Social Security System while working other jobs in the private sector, but the majority of his career was spent working for the federal government. He needed to earn forty quarters in the Social Security System to get social security retirement and qualify for Medicare for himself and my mother. So he began a free-lance business in order to pay into the system and obtain that additional help.

He applied his skills in photography with an acquired skill (writing) and began submitting photojournalism articles to various magazines, especially *Sandlapper Magazine,* a magazine published in South Carolina. There are photos and articles by him in a number of their publications. He has some really fantastic experiences during this period. Other times, not so much! He writes of his experiences during those years.

Problems do arise for the freelance photographer and writer. I once photographed President

Eisenhower. It was a blurred failure! All I got was an unrecognizable figure moving at least a foot along the walkway while my camera shutter was opening and closing. The press and newsreel men were on the church lawn at the designated spot. I, being short (for once an advantage) was down in front. We had waited in the ten-degree cold for half an hour for the motorcade to arrive. It came; the limousine stopped in front of us; Mamie looked out of the window and smiled; flash bulbs popped; I held my shot, waiting for the president. The door opened and he stepped out, not ten feet in front of me. He smiled, waved to us, and started up the walk as I framed him in my viewfinder and pressed the button. *Buzzzzzzzzzzph!* Ye God! At once I knew what had happened. I remembered the old rule: Always snap your shutter a few times in freezing temperatures before your crucial shot. Shutter oil gets stiff and must be limbered up. I had failed to do that. But dragging shutter had given me at last a full-second exposure. The exposure was bad, but the blur was unalterable.

I missed another president once but not because of a dragging shutter. I didn't have a camera at all! Seeing President Roosevelt was not expected, so no soup was on my chin for that. Bonnie Prince Charlie was a target of my lens for half an hour once. I knew of his appearance in advance and was ready in the press box, again, down in front. I shot close-ups of England's future king until I actually got tired of it.

I have photographed only a few dignitaries, and most were grab shots as opposed to prearranged photo sessions. Most of my subjects were motion picture and TV personalities like Pat

Boone, Susan Raye, Clyde Akins, Ed McMahon, Ilene Rogers, and Emmitt Kelly—the grand old clown of Ringling Brothers Circus. I photographed astronaut Pete Conrad, the Earl of Shaftesbury, and congressmen and senators, such as Strom Thurmond, Church, and others. I don't like to photograph political people. Some are nice, but most—especially the younger ones—have a certain amount of nausea.

I have no idea what he means by the younger political people having a "certain amount of nausea." However, this is his story, and I'm letting him tell it in his own words, the way he experienced it.

I had a photo session with General Mark Clark once, an assignment for a magazine. I think the general and Mrs. Clark were the most cordial and cooperative subjects I have ever photographed. His kindness did not stop with the end of the session. He sent a California editor of a magazine to me for pictures, which led to a couple of thousand-dollar sales. And he, the general himself, ordered many reprints of a certain photograph I made of him and his wife during the original session. I think the first dignitaries I ever photographed were the governor of Puerto Rico and his wife, but I do not remember their names.

One of my first personality shots was of Whitey Lockman, a New York Giant star. I followed the flying career of Beverly "Bevo" Howard, world-renowned stunt pilot from his clipped-wing cub days to the end and after. I photographed him and his Bucker Jungmeister in many of his aerobatics that brought him fame and for a time number one in the aerobatic field.

I wrote an extensive article on Howard and his famous aircraft for *Sandlapper Magazine* (March 1974 issue). This article is today a part of the record of Howard's flying career in the Library of Historical Records in the Smithsonian Institution in Washington, DC.

I have made pictures of at least two of the world's greatest ships: the *Queen Mary* on her maiden voyage in New York and the French Liner *Normandie* on her second. I always liked to photograph relative things; and for the freelance photographer and writer, it is a good practice. Whether I had a story idea in mind or not, if it was there, I snapped it. Example: While photographing Washington, DC, I made a picture of the house where Lincoln died after being shot by John Wilkes Booth. I also photographed Booth Memorabilia in the Booth Museum in the basement of Ford Theater. A year or so later, I flew out to the Dry Tortugas to make pictures of old Fort Jefferson on Garden Key. I broke my nose in a little seaplane mishap there, but I went ahead and did my photography anyway. I added another picture to the Lincoln/Booth theme while there by making a photo of the cell where Booth was cornered and killed. Incidentally, I never did get around to doing a story on him.

I know this reminiscence is boring to the reader, and I actually considered omitting it during my first draft. However, it is really the essence of my effort in the field of photojournalism, and since this is *my* book, it is about *me* and the things, big or small, that *I* have been or done. I shall enjoy the bit of nostalgia that it provides me in recalling it and putting it down on paper. I am astounded, though, that doing this I find that what I thought would be few has turned out to be many! I had, at one time, ten thousand photographs, color and black and white, in my files.

I have employed two agencies to sell stock photos for me. Both proved the old saying to be true: "Photo agencies are calculated crooks and the easiest way for a photographer to lose his photos." I sued Leo De Wys of New York, recovering most, but not all, of several hundred photographs. There are, I would think, a few agencies that are honest with the freelance, but the dishonest ones greatly overshadow them.

It is the beginner in photo marketing who usually gets done in by these agencies for one basic reason. Sure, they have heard the saying but somehow feel "it can't happen to me." A photographer from "Boondock," USA, wants to get his fine (and they really are) photographs in the market. He sends hundreds, thousands of dollars worth of them to an agency. The agency acknowledges and promptly reports one sale—usually with the appeal, "Send more pictures!" The delighted lens man goes wild. The chances of the photographer out in the boondocks ever seeing one of his photos in print are few indeed, but if he should and queries the agency, they quickly reply, "Sorry, an oversight in accounting." They then mail him a check. After a time and no sales are reported, the photographer begins wondering why. He writes the agency. They do not answer. Three months later he writes again. No answer. The wall of silence has been erected. He calls. He gets the runaround. "We'll check and get back to you." They never get back. In time the "boondock" boy gives up, his agency continues to sell his pictures. There is no contract, no agreement, no nothing.

I had a smart lawyer. He put the whole case in the Consumer Frauds Department's hands and let them go after the agency. It worked. In my case, since the conclusion we were after was to get my photos back. They got away with about twenty, probably already sold. Some of mine were returned from an agency in Spain who I had never heard of. That agency seemed to specialize in geographical locations.

I have photographed many interesting places. With no effort in categorizing, some are as follows: Scotland, the Highlands, Glasgow, Ayr, Iceland (flew over Labrador and Greenland twice but at night), the North Woods of Ontario and Quebec, Toronto, Nova Scotia, the Maine Coast, Niagara Falls, Luray Caverns, the Great Smoky Mountains, the Serpent Mound in Ohio, New Orleans, the French Quarter, the Florida Keys, Key West, the Dry Tortugas, the Marquesas, New York City, Washington, DC, the Everglades, Miami, Miami Beach, Central Florida Citrus Industry, the Dismal Swamps, Okefenokee, the Shenandoah Valley, Yucatan, Quintana Roo Mexico, Grand Cayman Islands, Ocho Rio, Jamaica, Havana by sea and air. The list goes on and on but is already ridiculous. My much-dreamed-of Quintana Roo photographic expedition fizzled down to a one-man thing (me) but it led me into the Yucatan twice. Later, I declined a travel agency request to head up a photo tour to the Yucatan, which they would sponsor, because cruise ship schedules are too tight and would not

permit time for the kind of tour I would care to
be involved in.

*****

Despite the rip-offs and disappointments of unscrupulous
agents and unsatisfactory assignments Daddy refused, the tide turned
for him when he became acquainted with *Sandlapper Magazine,* published by Sandlapper Press. Working for a locally operated, "home-
town" type publication brought him a client that appreciated his
work and was delighted to publish it in its periodicals. I have every
magazine in which his work was published. He began his association with them in 1969 and regularly contributed photo essays to
them through 1975. Not only did this enable him to build up his
Social Security quarters, but it also afforded him the opportunity to
return to his second chosen dream (following blacksmithing)—photography. He began with black-and-white pictures, which he could
develop himself in his darkroom. But later, the magazines began publishing more in color. He then sent his film off to be developed into
color transparencies. He should have lived to work in this day and
age—where we use digital cameras and can edit and Photoshop our
own pictures on our desktop computers. But he was old school, and
he was good at it.

Another requirement for his work with *Sandlapper* was that he
write about the places and people he photographed. So he taught
himself composition. I have to chuckle, as he has told me that he
failed English in high school, and in his last year he was taking all
three years of high school English in order to graduate. But I found
the book he had studied. Combined with practice and his creative,
daydreamy mind, not only did he learn composition, he excelled.
With a master's degree in English, I should write so well. He never
caught on to spelling and punctuation, much less paragraphing.
But with such colorful figurative language, it's not worth mention-
ing. I can correct his spelling and punctuation. His editor evidently
took care of that, plus paragraphing, and the articles are wonder-

ful. Speaking of editors, he continues with his own narrative talking about them.

> I must mention four editors I have known. Delmar Roberts of *Sandlapper Magazine* gave me my start in journalistic writing and leaned heavily on me for photographs and articles. All editors have little quirks: Del's was rewriting the introductory paragraphs. Diane Crenshaw, who followed Del as editor of *Sandlapper*, liked to rewrite short phrases, which sometimes changed the facts. Hubert Pryor of Modern Maturity was a "solid" editor. He knew exactly what he wanted and didn't want. Bob Rowland, who followed Diane at *Sandlapper*, was a *dog*! He never held the job of editor anywhere and never would again. I could write a page on this SOB, but I won't waste the time. His warped brain thought that only PhDs should be writers and cut off all former contributors. He only published the "four-letter crap" of his college professors and drove the magazine out of business.

Daddy must have gotten in to *Sandlapper* pretty soon after it began publishing in 1968. And as far as the last editor he refers to is concerned, the magazine did shut down under Bob Rowland's leadership in 1971. The magazine enjoyed a revival in 1989 and published again until 2011, when it shut down, and it is still no longer in existence. I hope that it will see another revival in the future. It was a nice periodical on South Carolina. Although there are others being published today, I have an emotional attachment to it.

His articles covered a myriad of subjects from "Fury at Folly," about the Hurricane of 1940, to "A Special Winter," a photo essay about the ice storm in mid-South Carolina of 1974. His photos graced a calendar cover as well as several covers of the *South Carolina Magazine*. He also reported on people, from the "Goat Man," a hermit, who with his wife lived on an island behind Folly Island, to William Gilmore Simms, South Carolina author of the mid-nineteenth century who was on par with famous writers of that period such as Nathaniel Hawthorn and Edgar Allen Poe but faded into near obscurity south of the Mason-Dixon line following the Civil War.

In the editor's introductory article, "From Behind the Palmettos" in October of 1973, *Sandlapper Magazine's* editor called attention to the article Daddy contributed to that issue, "The Bulow Empire—Kingdom in the Wilderness," about South Carolina citizen John Bulow, who carved out a vast sugar plantation in Florida during the 1700s. The editor writes of Daddy's work, "Although Stone is most familiar to readers for his outstanding and highly acclaimed photography, he demonstrates once again, that he can tell a good story when the opportunity arises."

I have a copy of every magazine in which my father's articles and photos appear. The list is pretty long. He does speak about many of his articles in his narrative.

In article writing, I always found research the most intriguing aspect. Putting the manuscript together for publication was always "hard labor." As I look back into the research of my more outstanding articles that were published, I find three or four to be gems in terms of gratifying interest from the research point of view. "The Bulow Empire" kept me in a dream world all the way through. It led me into many interesting places and things, from the east coast scrub country of Florida to the midlands of South Carolina; from the cemeteries of old Charleston to the Florida Indian wars. And, in print, it was exactly staged as I intended it to be. I have been encouraged to do "Bulow" in book form, and I guess it should be done, but I do not care for the "hard labor" of it, and I don't want it ghosted.

"Twenty-Two Miles to Calais," a story of the earliest settlers in the Cooper River country of South Carolina, was probably my most systematic and time-consuming research project, and in print it was a gross disappointment—the end product. It was the result of the butchery of inexperienced editors who tried to fit the article into a new and untried feature format, the result of which trimmed some two thousand words of human interest and left the article a mere documentary skeleton of the original story.

"The Magnificent Man and his Flying Machine" was one of my better articles, and the research was mostly of the "armchair" type. I had photographed Beverly Howard in many of his aerobatic feats for years, but the facts and figures on his famous aircraft was what required book research. A file of many photos on many subjects has helped me on numerous writing projects. The editorial treatment of this article was true and precise (something that writers appreciate). This article on Howard and his Jungmeister became a reference piece itself. It is on file in the library of the Smithsonian Institution in Washington, DC, with other material on the famous flyer.

Except for the photography, much of the research for my article "In Search of Spanish Treasure" was "armchair." Trips to Key West, FL, and Cape Canaveral supplied some detail, however. This article also became "research" material when used (with permission) in a research textbook prepared by Dr. Charles Weingartner of the University of South Carolina. Since retiring from actual writing for market, I find myself still researching stories but only as a hobby. It is something I enjoy doing and something I do well, and without deadlines to meet, it is even more fun.

I have always said, "Make your hobby your profession and then work will be play!" But in practice, I found that to be a big fallacy. When you make your hobby your profession, your hobby becomes just plain hard work. But now I research stories to minute detail and enjoy it because the "hard labor" of putting it into proper form does not lie ahead of me. I have often thought of teaming up with an active writer who is prolific enough to need a story idea source (and not too many are), but as yet I have not made an effort to do so. I have given a few away, however—the idea, not my research.

My biggest handicap in manuscript writing is spelling! The older I get, the more difficult it is for me to spell. I was never a good speller, but as of now, spelling is impossible. The reason I decided on a non-paragraph style in writing this book was to avoid much of the problems in writing, but there is no way to avoid the need for spelling. But for Virginia's proofing, spelling errors would be manifold.

*****

My last major research (as a hobby) was one I call the Ed Watson/Belle Starr Connection. Ed Watson, a character living in the Ten Thousand Island, always claimed that it was he who killed Belle Starr, the outlaw woman of the Indian Territory in the Midwest. Other researchers have explored this legend also. While I was in the Everglades working on this very story, Jim Moore, a hobby researcher and state educa-

tional consultant, was working on the Watson/
Starr affair. Moore has researched such projects
as the actual happenings at the OK Corral at
Tombstone, Arizona, and the last days of Butch
Cassidy and the Sundance Kid. I don't know
the conclusions Watson made on the Watson/
Starr Affair. I had previously interviewed Thelma
Smallwood (who has since died), who witnessed,
while a little girl, the killing of Edgar J. Watson at
the landing by her father's store on Chokoloskee
Bay in the early 1900s. The Smallwoods (the old
store still stands and was operated by Thelma
until her death) were probably the Watson's only
friends in the Ten Thousand Island country, and
Thelma, though very friendly to me, hesitated to
divulge much of what she remembered about the
morning Ed Watson was killed by the posse at
the landing by the Smallwood store.

This particular incident had nothing to do
with Belle Starr, but it brought an end to the
notorious redheaded bully who had indeed killed
many people in his lifetime. He, in his arrogant
way, always boasted that he had killed Belle Starr,
and who, whether they believed him or not, was
going to dispute him? Not to his face anyway.

The object of my research into his claim
was to determine if it were possible that he could
have killed her. My finding was that indeed he
could have done it. The time frame on every
count was right for it. I followed his actions from
his first encounter (double murder) in North
Florida with crime to the Indian Territory and
the Canadian River where Belle Starr lived, his
association with Starr (writer Speer Morgan
mentioned a Crick Watson, who rode with Starr
on one of her raids, but this Watson was killed in

Oklahoma) before her death and his sojourn into the Oregon Territory after her death and also his life and times after he came to the Ten Thousand Islands Country.

My friend Nellie Martin did some research for me in Oklahoma at Eufala, where the Starr homestead stood at the time of her reign as the bandit queen. In fact, research turned up evidence that one Edgar Watson was indeed charged with her death, but charges were dropped. My mission was accomplished, however, in that I did establish that Watson could have killed her.

Around the first of May in 1995, Bob and I set off on a cross-country trip west by car. Our destination was Santa Fe, New Mexico. We had done it before and took I-10 across the country, via Panama City, Florida, and though lower Texas. This time, we took I-40 from Asheville, North Carolina, through Memphis, Tennessee, Oklahoma City, and on across Arkansas. This was the time period when Daddy was researching Belle Starr, and he solicited us to make a detour at Eufala to find and photograph Belle Starr's grave.

(I have to digress a bit about the timing of our trip, however, as it was two weeks after the Oklahoma City bombing. Heading toward Oklahoma City on the highway along with us were trucks from Toccoa Casket Company in Georgia. And I mean there were a number of trucks, obviously transporting many caskets. It was heartbreaking to realize that they were going to Oklahoma City in response to the large death toll at the John W. Murrah Building, now with its front blown out. We felt compelled to drive to the site and pay our respects. Then we continued on to Texas. Driving west on I-40 out of Oklahoma City, we saw the same caravan of casket trucks heading east from another company, delivering more coffins in which to lay the dead. Those images are indelibly printed into my memory, and I'll never forget the eerie feeling I had that in our country, homegrown terrorists could do such a horrendous thing.)

Now back to Belle Starr. We stopped overnight just inside Texas and the next day fulfilled our promise to Daddy to assist him in his research. However, it had rained for two solid weeks in the area, and some roads and bridges were washed out, not to mention land being underwater. We stopped at a country store near the place we expected to find her property. Indeed, said the storekeeper, Belle Starr's home and grave were a few miles away, but it was located on a dirt road. The grave itself was out in a meadow. The current owners would gladly welcome us, he said. However, both the road and the meadow were probably under water and not accessible. I was sorry that we couldn't bring Daddy that one bit of evidence he sought in his research—the photo of Belle Starr's grave, with whatever wording was engraved at the tombstone. Today, you can look up the grave online and read the inscription. Something about the text suggests a tantalizing mystery Daddy might have been curious to follow up on: The engraving reads,

> Shed not for her the bitter tear
> Nor give the heart to vain regret.
> Tis but the casket that lies here,
> The gem that filled it sparkles yet.

The wording vaguely hints that maybe she isn't in the grave. Wow! Wouldn't Daddy have pursued that possibility?

Adventures Here:

Miami, Florida

My parents loved to travel, especially my father. He wasn't the world traveler many people are today, but when he visited somewhere, you can rest assured he got the goody out of it! He researched, usually choosing a destination that had already piqued his interest—some person or natural or manmade wonder that intrigued him. Some of his solo excursions (without my mother) were made in tandem with a business trip. Ahead of the departure date, he did research and outlined places he would visit. If on a business trip, usually most of the other men in his group either worked or went off in their own various pursuits, some of them booze and women. Not my daddy! Chaste and prudish "Queen Victoria" accompanied him at all times, and he put his mind on more lofty quests. He worked too but planned a couple of days off and weekends to travel locally.

He loved to take pictures, of course, and he met a lot of interesting people along the way—often, local women who worked in restaurants and shops. He enjoyed taking pictures of them as well and often incorporated them into his stories. One such is absolutely fascinating—and I never heard a hint about her until I read Daddy's book.

The taxi driver knew her well. "Oh, yes. I remember Madam Sherry," he said. He talked about her as he drove me from the airport to the old Patrician Hotel in downtown Miami.

"I was a trainee with Checker," the cabbie said. "Just starting out. I used to run her girls downtown to shop. They were big tippers and real beauties too," he added.

Of that, I knew! A former Madam Sherry beauty had worked with me in a "my girl Friday" capacity at the shipyard for more than a year during World War II. It was from her that I first heard of the fabulous "Moorish Castle" with its marbleized floors and rich clientele. B——, the ex-prostitute, used to tell me of her experiences as a high-demand girl in Madam's glittering Chez Cherie. She told me other things too. She showed one day (I think just to make a point) a small paper envelope with some white powder in it. She said she slept with a local druggist to get it. Sometimes B—— would throw hints at me, but they went past me. Victoria closed my mind to things she thought I shouldn't fool with.

Later, I read Madam Sherry's book, *Pleasure Was My Business*, by Rose Miller (Madam Sherry's real name). Her book was written with writer S. Robert Traline in the early 1960s, years after Miami bowed to the arm-twisting of the Defense Department and outlawed all houses of prostitution in the city. This sent the girls into private practice or into other lines of work. It was when B—— came into the defense work and I got to know the girl—woman, I should say. B—— had class, if that is the word. She was well-groomed, wore stylish clothes, spoke with poise and intelligence. She would have never worked in the fashionable Chez Cherie had she not possessed these qualities. But it was her wit and charm that rolled back the waters of scorn. I guess it as an art of the trade. B—— had fired my interest in Miami's Moorish Castle, but through the years, it had faded. Now, after reading Madam Sherry's book, I was determined to visit it.

I was on my way to Key West, but in two months, I would be on vacation and definitely would be back to seek out this one famed house of ill repute. And, in time, I was there again.

Madam Sherry had built the fabulous pleasure palace with the intent of excelling such establishments as Polly Adler's in New York and the Everleigh Sisters in Chicago, and to know its history, she did! The cabbie had told me it was on 54th Street, but he didn't remember the number. He had not seen it in years. I got the address from the famous madam's book, and now I was on my way. I have this thing about places of note, be they respectable or not, if they are relative or represent a good story. I like to walk in footprints, the "you were there" fascination.

On 54th Street, I received my shock! The address was a vacant lot! Just a large open place covering half a block, scattered with rubble and overgrown with weeds. Maybe the address was wrong? I had seen pictures of the castle with its silver dome. No, it was nowhere to be seen. I would recognize it. It just was not there.

On a side street an old man dozed in a hammock in the shade of a scarlet-topped Royal Poinsettia. "It was right up there on the corner." He was pointing to a vacant lot. "Oh, they tore it down years ago," he continued. "Was nothing but a rat hovel. Winos slept in it. More of a nuisance than when Rose run it. She did keep it clean and quiet. She did not allow no riffraff around there,

but there were the gangsters that made it dangerous as hell around here. Al Capone had money in
it. I'm glad they tore it down."

I remembered B—— and the things she
told me about the magnificent structure with
its spiraling stairways leading up into its many
rooms, its great dining room where sumptuous
meals were served at any hour, day or night.
Lounges, spacious and inviting and gleaming,
white, marbleized floors in which you could see
your reflection. Full-time cooks and maids took
care of the interior, the girls, and the guests. A
gardener kept the grounds that were ablaze with
flowers.

"Rose got into bad trouble with the law
after the war," the old man continued, climbing
back into his hammock. "She was supposed to
go to jail, but she skipped to Mexico City. Some
said the gangsters helped her get away. I guess the
house went for taxes."

I was too late! I would not see the Moorish
Castle that had hosted the rich, the famous, the
royal, the mob. I walked up to the vacant lot
where it had stood and out in the weeds, among
the rubble, I stood where it had stood. I watched
the red ants that hurried over the white sand. The
hot, tropical sun reflected brightly from an object
in the sand. I thought it to be an opal. Picking
it up I saw a fragment of the marbleized floor.
In my hand, I wondered whose feet had walked
on this lone piece of ceramic. In its heyday the
great house had known the great and famous.
European royalty is said to have been frequent
guests. Business and political figures were prominent in its halls. Such thoughts are pointless.

I have this fragment mounted today in front of me with building fragments from other places of interest: a rock from Mary, Queen of Scots' summer castle in Scotland, a chip of brick from Washington's Mount Vernon, limestone chunks from six of the Yucatan's great Meso-American Mayan temples. Of all these fragments of places that have caught my interest, I suppose the piece of marbleized floor of the Chez Cherie is the only one that is relative. I'm sure of one footstep that has been upon it. That of B——, my "girl Friday."

Daddy loved Miami. He always thought he'd live there. His sister had married a railroad man and moved there in the mid-1950s and had taken her and Daddy's mother there from South Carolina to live with them. Since Daddy was several years younger than Aunt Judy, he envisioned that if she passed away before he did, he would inherit the house and he and Mama would stay there at least part of the year.

Alas, that dream also went up in smoke. Literally! In 1990, I got a call from Aunt Judy's next-door neighbor. The house had burned, and Aunt Judy had perished in the fire. She was a hopeless alcoholic and a smoker. As she lay on her living room sofa smoking a cigarette, she either fell asleep or had a heart attack or just passed out. There was no air-conditioning in the house, and three box fans were pointed in her direction to keep her cool in the humid heat. The fire blazed up, and the wind from the fans accelerated the fire's intensity. At first, the firemen didn't see anybody inside, but the neighbor insisted that an old lady lived in there. The living room couch had fallen through the collapsed floor onto the ground beneath the room, and Aunt Judy had been asleep on it. She probably never saw it coming. I hope not, anyway.

The damage to the house was pretty severe, along with years of termite infestation, which had done a job on the studs in the walls and floors. The house would have to be razed. By that time, Daddy was quite disabled, and it was too late for a big adventure like moving to Miami to take place. They had the house demolished and sold the lot. You can Google "4354 S. W. 12th Street, Miami, Florida," and see a picture of the beautiful home that has been built on the site where Aunt Judy's Florida bungalow stood. All that remains of her existence there is a grapefruit tree in the backyard, that every December blesses the new owners with the sweetest grapefruit I have ever tasted.

Outer Banks, North Carolina

Another destination my parents loved to visit was the Outer Banks of Cape Hatteras, North Carolina. This episode reveals a different side of my mother that I never have seen in action, much like the image of her picking away at a fossil with a geological pick hammer, grinning through the "black freckles" generated by the sooty deposits of a poorly placed kerosene lantern and sleeping in a tent in pouring-down rain. Daddy writes of one of their vacations there.

The North Carolina Outer Banks in the early 1960s were not overrun with tourists. There was a motel at Manteo, one at Buxton, and a restaurant, also one at the village of Hatteras. And there was the big Berkley Manor with its twenty-seven dormers on the island of Okracoke. There was a general store at Nags Head, and I don't remember if accommodations existed in the fishing communities of Avon and Frisco. A surprising number of the old-timers of the Banks still lived there then. Some were retirees from the United States Lifesaving Service, which gave way to the Coast Guard years ago. They were entrapped by the strange charm of the Outer Banks while in service there and upon retirement stayed there or returned to spend their remaining years. I found them comparable to the many old Lifesaving buildings still standing at intervals along the length of the Banks' seemingly endless strip of sand. The buildings' time-weathered, peeling paint and rugged countenance matched the retirees' bent form and wrinkled leather faces.

My first fascination with the Outer Banks came years before I first visited there. A girl from home community, whom I dated a time or two, had been a schoolteacher in the little Banks community of Avon. She had only four or five pupils. She said of the Banks, "It is the wild, unbelievable loneliness that gets you." It seemed to be the basis of its charm. Her description of it had kindled the fire, and now I was there. Virginia and I arrived at Manns Harbor in a downpour of cold March rain. We were not delighted with the weather, and our new Plymouth Fury, on the wet 400-mile drive from Charleston, SC, had developed "square" brake drums. Each application of the breaks was a teeth-chattering experience.

The rain continued all day and we took a motel room in Manteo. Rain continued until noon the next day, and a northeaster began blowing. Imagine the fun setting up a side room tent in a forty-mile gale! To prevent the tent from blowing away in the operation, I tied guy ropes from it to the cook grill and three-foot long stakes I had been advised to bring. Then Virginia and I fought our way under the flapping thing and finally got the pipe frame in place. The weather cleared the third day, but during that time I got Virginia's ultimatum, "No more tents!" If she was to follow me through my world of rough and tumble joy, I would have to get a travel trailer. (This was the last trip in the tent.)

After seeing the Wright Brothers Museum and the site of the first successful powered flight (which was at Kill Devil Hills, not Kitty Hawk as the history books used to say) and the Lost Colony site on Roanoke Island, we got to the real business of finding the many shipwrecks that litter the Banks' shifting sands. Countless wrecks back through time were due to notoriously rough seas and shoals off the banks where the Labrador currents and the Gulf Stream meet, but some wrecks were "man-made" by Bankers who survived by pilfering wrecks for their cargo and equipment. Nags Head and the high sand dunes called Jocky Ridge on the upper banks are names, not without purpose. In the early days, Bankers would tie a lantern on the neck of a nag, an Outer Banks pony, at night and let it roam over the higher elevations of the island. Ships at sea, running before a storm, would think the swaying light was a buoy marking safe harbor and would run for it, thus piling up on the beach to be pounced upon by land pirates.

Searching out shipwrecks was fun. On awakening each morning, the first would cry, "Lets run a wreck!" and after breakfast, cooked outdoors on the Coleman stove of sausage and eggs laced with beach sand, we hit the beaches.

There are many shipwrecks on the Banks, named and unnamed. I compiled a map as the week passed, but maps do not remain totally true. The Banks' shipwreck scene is an ever-changing thing. Some remain permanently visible at one spot if high enough on the beach, but others are covered and uncovered from time to time by tide and storm action and the endless shifting sand. Sometimes a hurricane will uncover a wreck that was never known to exist. Sometimes a storm's flood tide will pick up a wreck from one beach and move it to another. Wrecks have been moved from one island to another by a storm—some buried, not to be seen again for years. A section of the bow of an unidentified ship still wearing its green paint, is called the "migrant." It moves from place to place with storm and tide (being especially buoyant). I photographed it on the beach at Cape Point near the Hatteras Lighthouse in 1966. The larger pieces of some known-named ships that stay more or less in a general location are the *Huron* at Nags Head (wrecked in 1877), the *Laura A. Barnes*, on the beach of Bodie Island just north of Oregon Inlet (wrecked in 1921), the *George A. Kohler* (wrecked in 1933 and later burned) lying just north of the village of Avon on Hatteras Island, *Anna R. Heidritter* (wrecked in 1942) on Okracoke Island.

At the communities of Rodanth and Waves are cemeteries with marked but unnamed graves of mariners, who perished in wrecks on their shores.

Interesting studies in humanity are found among the old timers of the Banks. Some date way back. I talked with a woman who saw Billy Mitchell take off the day he proved that battleships were sitting ducks for airplanes. Some of the old-timers are quiet and non-communicative, while others delightedly spin their oft-told tales, usually based in truth.

I was looking at a hunk of the "ghost ship" that lay on display in front of Balance's Service Station at the village of Hatteras. "Lies! All lies!" a wizened old retiree from the Life Saving Service exclaimed, screwing up his toothless face and shifting his chewing tobacco to another side of his mouth. "She were the *Carroll A. Deering*, a mighty fine five-master built in Bath, Maine, and she were only two year old! She were not a ghost ship as that there sign says. I know, I went out thar that morning (in 1921) where she were a-hung up on Diamond Shoals. Her sails was set an flapping in the gale"—his bony arms made circular motions—"but her boats was gone and rope ladders hanging over the side."

His mouth was full by now, and he rolled his slack lips into the shape of a tube and squirted a stream of tobacco juice at a hound dog that lay sunning himself across the driveway. The dog gave him a dirty look and moved under a truck. "Lack I say, boy!" he exclaimed, wiping his mouth with the back of his hand. "They say hot vittles was a-cooking in the galley and the ship's tomcat meowing around. How'd they know? Nobody could git on the ship for six days. The seas was too high!" He ran out of breath and sat panting for a few moments, then discovered he was still alive.

"Hell! I don't know what happened to them people. I guess their boats swamped in that thar storm and they all went to hell knows where. We went out again and sometime later and dynamited her. She might have floated off the bar some night and become a navigation hazard, don't yuh see?" His mouth was full again. He made a tube out of his stubble-covered lips and looked around for the dog. The dog was gone so he squirted the brown stream into an auto tire that lay by the gas pump. "When we dynamited her, pieces went everywhar—pieces washed up on Ocracoke, some at Whalebone Junction. And thar is a piece of her thar in front of yuh—its foredeck timbers with a capstan still in it. Touch it." He panted for a while and spit the whole cud of tobacco out. "Go ahead and touch it! You can tell your children you touched a ghost ship. But it's be a lie. She warn't no ghost!"

Folklore and commercialization make lies of a lot of stories purely for the sensationalism and promotional value. But as for life on the Outer Banks in the old days, pure drama was there without the need for exaggeration.

I saw a house I wanted to buy on Hatteras Island, an old two-story Banks house of the early twenties with weathered white paint and lightning rods sticking up on top. It stood on a sandy ridge overlooking Diamond Shoals (just outside of the National Seashore). Laughing gulls strutted through the small yard and swallow-tailed kites swooped and dived after wasps that flew out of the attic vent lights in the gable ends. This was par for me. Everywhere I have ever been, I have seen the exact house, on the exact spot that I wanted to buy and move into. It would be all I ever wanted—just to live there and let the rest of the world go by.

Daddy created a map of the Outer Banks area, which shows wrecks and landmarks that existed when he and my mother were there. As he said of the shifting land and wrecks, it probably in no way represents the coast as it is today. In fact, there have been a few significant hurricanes (for which the Outer Banks appears to be a magnet) that have made alterations too. However, I am including the map for Daddy's sake. I guess we can add cartographer to his many skills.

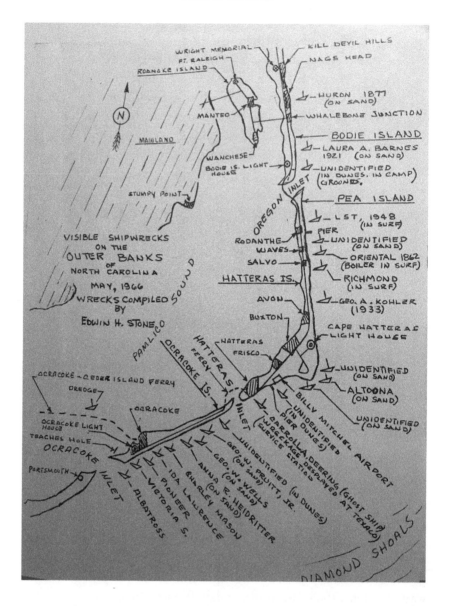

As for Daddy's dream house, I too have the same experience everywhere I travel. A house the perfect color, style, and location beckons me to buy and live in it. But like Daddy, I always return home and eventually put that urge behind me.

Brown Mountain Lights, North Carolina

This story is one about a place I have visited with my parents. Today, one can view TV shows about it within the genre of extraterrestrial and the supernatural. In fact, there have been a couple of episodes that talk about the unknown fate of explorers, who have ventured into this mountain mystery and disappeared. True or not, it makes for a thrilling story.

The Brown Mountain lights puzzled Davy Crockett. The cussed mountain was spooked! His dog agreed and growled each time he saw them. About a century and a half later, long after the dog had chased his last rabbit through a Blue Ridge Mountain hollow and Davy had become immortalized in the dust of the Alamo, I watched the lights on a misty spring night from Jonas Ridge. It was simply perplexing! Brown Mountain—hardly more than a runty hill by mountain standards—has a mysterious display of pyrotechnics that has dumbfounded man from the days of the Indian to modern scientists.

As you watch the low mountain, which starts from nothing on the east end and continues westward as a gradually rising ridge, you see a low dip or pocket in its elevation about two-thirds the way up its length. This pocket is locally called "the saddle." For the rest of is length, its height increases more acutely to its western end, which is a huge butt of solid rock and is the highest point on the mountain. This butt is the only part of the mountain you can see from Lost Cove Cliffs on the Blue Ridge Parkway. You can see some of its lights from there. The best view of the mountain is from Jonas Ridge, Table Rock, or Wiseman's View. My preference is Jonas Ridge.

The entire mountain lies out in front of you as if it were a stage upon which the lights were to perform—and they do perform! The strange lights are more prevalent on damp nights. I've seen the best performance during light rain. Very interesting photos have been made of the lights. But I have been unsuccessful in getting only one picture of one light, maybe because my efforts were made on rainy nights.

A small ball of eerie light will appear along the ridge of the mountain. It will run along the ridge as if someone was running through the trees with a lantern. Sometimes, the light bobs along slowly. It will go down into the saddle and up toward the butt on the west end, then suddenly angle sharply up into the sky, explode, and that would be the end of it. Before you have recovered from the shock of the amazing thing, another ball of light appears on the side of the mountain below the ridge. It runs up the side to the crest, then angles up into the sky for a couple of hundred feet and—*pop!*—it's gone! Sometimes they appear, run along the surface and go out without shooting up into the sky and bursting.

Most reasons given for this phenomenon have been stupid ones. Men from the US Geological Survey studied the mountain in 1913 and again in 1922. Their reports said the lights were from locomotives and autos on the mountain beyond Brown Mountain. These smart men did not say what railroad and autos were around in Davy Crockett's time. Ralph Lael's explanation of the lights may seem far-fetched but certainly leaves the door open for future research along such lines.

Ralph Lael spent a lifetime studying the lights and said he found their source and their purpose. I visited Ralph on two occasions and talked at length with him. He told me what he had experienced during his years on the mountain. He said that this thing—the lights—was beyond understanding of the average man at that time. Juanita Calloway told me, over a cup of coffee in the back room of Lael's Outer Space Rock Shop Museum near the foot of the mountain, that Ralph was neither a liar nor a lunatic, that she personally had seen some of the strange things that take place on the mountain. She said something really frightening had happened to Ralph and she had tried to put his story on paper in rough story form, and it was published.

I have two copies of Lael's strange story, which he gave me on my last visit with him before he died. I have to say that since we have had men going around on the moon, perhaps Ralph really did participate in an early-day "Star Wars!" I refrain from giving details here about Ralph's experiences on Brown Mountain. He tells it all in his book in his own way. After all, it is *his* story.

I watched the Brown Mountain lights that rainy evening with my parents. They really are unusual, to say the least. As for Lael's book, unfortunately, it is not among the books I got from my dad's collection after his death. He collected a number of books in that genre during his foray into the Rosicrucian Order. However, that one did not make it into my possession. Amazon says the book is out of print. A review just relates that it is about alien abduction. Some scientists believe the lights are gas balls that emerge from the ground under the rocks and rise into the air, dissipating after they get so high. Others believe Brown Mountain is a portal for the comings and goings of aliens from outer space.

There are numerous articles available online concerning the strange orbs, and a film was made about them (fiction, I'm sure). Nevertheless, they are still a subject of conversation and speculation among scientists and UFO hunters alike.

Jamestown, Virginia

Daddy writes a very short piece on visiting Jamestown, Virginia, to where our family of Stone immigrants entered this country in the early 1600s.

> Jamestown, Virginia, the site of the first successful English settlement in America, has strong emotional attractions, but I think standing before the 103-foot Tercentenary Monument erected in 1907 evokes the strongest personally, for me. My father stood there before this giant shaft of New Hampshire granite when it was unveiled in 1907.

In 2007, I stood before the same monument in Jamestown at the Quadracentennial celebration. The Fulghums (Bob's mother and his cousin Freddie's dad) hold a reunion of global proportions each year at a different location, but their American roots are all in the Jamestown area. That year, we joined the Fulghum reunion during the four hundredth anniversary of Jamestown's founding. The energy was kinetic, and I indeed experienced some of Daddy's "relative" emotion standing on the same soil on which our ancestor John Stone stood that day in the early 1600s when he debarked the ship that brought him to its shore.

Replicas of the dock and typical ships that brought settlers in were there for visitors to explore, as well as the beautiful James River and the sites where perhaps their ancestors had stood before. Much archeological exploration still continued. A replica of the fort walls was built around the replicated town with buildings and structures our forefathers would have constructed for living, working, and acquiring homemade pottery, glass, and other goods. Outside of the fort, on the bank of the river, graves were being unearthed, containing remains of some of those earliest settlers. A few skeletal remains are on display in the museum, along with artifacts of dinnerware, cookware, muskets, and other tools and trappings commonly made and used in daily life. One of the skeletons was of a man of (to me) undetermined age. Another was similar to it. They had beautiful, perfect teeth. All of them were healthy, with no evidence of decay.

The 1907 Tercentennial and 1807 Bicentennials were also recalled during the 2007 event. Entertainment from those two events was recreated for visitor's enjoyment. I so wanted to experience that, but the Fulghum family's main meeting and meal was being held at the same time, and I had to miss it. I really was pretty angry not to have watched that in order to enjoy what my grandfather experienced upon his 1907 visit. However, I read on a plaque where the Tercentennial in 1907 was not even held at the Jamestown site. It was actually held at Sewell's Point in Hampton Roads. I'm pretty sure my dad didn't know that when he was in Jamestown. He would have mentioned it if he knew. And he had passed away by the time Bob and I went to Jamestown in 2007. So often we come across someone or something we would like to call and tell them about. This was definitely one of those occasions.

My grandfather (Pa 'Tone) went by train to New York a few times each year to buy goods to sell in their general store. He most likely stopped off in Hampton Roads for the event. I have a beautiful wine-colored, cut glass pitcher, which evidently was one of the souvenirs for sale in 1907. It is engraved in gold leaf to my grandmother (Ma 'Tone), "Mrs. E. Stone," and underneath in larger script "Jamestown 1907." My grandmother gave it to me decades ago when we were visiting her in Florida. I hold that pitcher dear. At the same time, it is amusing to note that the souvenirs for sale at the 2007 Celebration were definitely not fine cut glass with gold leaf engraving. They were more of the T-shirt and plastic cup variety. However, there is a still a production pottery shop associated with Jamestown, and we purchased two heavy pottery mugs to remember our weekend there.

Photo of the cut-glass pitcher my grandfather brought my grandmother from the Tercentennial in Jamestown, 1907.

Everglades, Florida

After they acquired their little camper and Daddy was completely retired, they traveled much more often. They met a group of people from other parts of the United States and formed a rather close camping club. Every January, for several years, they all met in the Everglades of Florida. This stoked my parents' need for a warm retreat in cold weather and fed my father's deep inner yearnings for searching out historical cultures and their possible connections with each other.

One remarkable little town they camped near is the southernmost town above Everglades National Park. The town's name is Ochoppee. This was in the early 1980s, mind you, and human population was sparse. Wildlife was plentiful and in good balance, which today is threatened by the careless release of Burmese Pythons, which some people bought as pets but just put out in the jungle when they got too big to care for inside their house. These snakes have multiplied and become a hazard, as they eat many species in the Everglades in huge numbers, disrupting the balance of the area and threatening extinction in some of the native species. I don't know what the camping in or near Ochopee today would be now, in the twenty-first century.

My parents really enjoyed their time down there with the "snow-birds" that stayed much longer during the winter months.

*****

My dad was a prolific photographer. It should be noted that nothing, absolutely nothing short of death, prevented him from getting the shot. He tells of his excursion to the Dry Tortugas in quest of photos. I recall this story very well. I don't remember exactly when it occurred, but it was probably about 1980, when they were wintering in Ochoppee, Florida, in the Everglades.

We landed in a light chop on the west side of the main island in the Dry Tortugas. We had circled too long over the Marquesas, and the wind had picked up. The pilot had been obliging enough to give me a close look on the Marquesas by buzzing the atoll at about two hundred feet. Actually, he circled the formation several times, pointing out points of interest. I had first seen this atoll, strange for the waters other than the south Pacific, several years before while flying in from Central America in a Pan-Am highflying jet. Now, in a rickety little float-plane, I had photographed its circular configuration close up.

Our pilot, Rory Mitchner, taxied the plane toward the beach and came about 180 degrees so the waves would carry us in tail first. The pontoon grounded about six feet from the dry mark. This is where I broke my nose. Debarking procedure was to crawl out onto the pontoon and wait until a wave ran it in. Then as it started back, run to the end of the pontoon and jump! The girl in our party did it successfully. So did the man ahead of me. My turn. Clutching my camera in my right hand (the strap was around my neck) and my twenty-pound gadget bag under my left arm, I ran and jumped. My error was failing to duck under the horizontal tailfin, which I hit with my nose. The impact broke my sunshades, knocked my glasses off, loosened two front teeth, and crushed my nose. I fell back to the beach, and the returning wave wet my backside. However, I saved my equipment. I was stunned but did not pass out. Blood flowed from my nose externally and internally down my throat.

After a brief rest on the beach, I, went ahead and photographed my objective subjects. I dripped blood throughout old Fort Jefferson, on the ramparts, in the bunkers, in Dr. Mudd's prison cell. I don't think I have ever showed such dedication to the pursuit of pictures. We were in the Tortugas two hours, which after my accident seemed much longer.

The trip back home (one hundred fifty miles east) was lengthened also by a stop in Key West. A "hitchhiker" on Garden Key needed a lift to Key West. We had a vacant seat. As is the code of courtesy with Caribbean pilots, we took him along.

He had always suffered sinus trouble, but it was severely exacerbated by banging his nose on the plane's tailfin. His mettle was sorely tested in pursuit of his pictures, and he passed! In retrospect, I'm actually surprised he didn't pass out. When I was a little girl—maybe four or five years old—my mother went out to a church meeting one evening and left me with my dad. I don't recall him doing anything fun with me—he was always working on his own projects. However, I remember that somehow, working with one of his tools, he badly cut his thumb. The blood flowed in rivulets down his hand and onto his wrist. I didn't know it then but quickly realized that my dad can't stand the sight of his own blood.

I remember him going into the bathroom and standing in front of the sink with the water running. I went in there with him since I knew something significant had happened. He began to sway and sag. How I knew to do this I will never know. I grabbed a washcloth off the towel rod, wet it with cold water in the tub, and started rubbing my dad's face with it. He began to revive and eventually got up, and we continued on with the evening. When he told my mother about it, he credited me with keeping him from fainting. That memory is etched deep into my mind. I can still see him, struggling to stay upright but losing the battle. His determination must have been the only thing that got him through that ordeal in the Dry Tortugas. He probably would have fainted dead away otherwise.

Another exploration from the Everglades was not quite as painful.

> Being an amateur archeologist, my fascination for the ruins of the ancient Mayan cities in the Yucatan spilled over into the mysterious shell mound complexes on Florida's west coast. Earlier twentieth century archeologists believed these great elevations, similar to pyramids, were built by American Indians, particularly those of the southwest coast, where artifacts of Calusa Indian origin were found.

Having seen the artifacts from the Cedar Key mounds (mostly destroyed) and the least destroyed mound complex at Crystal River, both on the northwest coast of Florida, I insist that both sites are of Mayan origin. The similarity of the artifacts is unmistakable. Also, having visited the great temple cities of the Yucatan, I find a strong similarity in the layout or arrangement of structures, the difference being the building materials—stone in the Yucatan and shell (the only available material) in the Florida sites. Also, the Florida sites fit into the pattern of location and interrelationship that prevails in the Yucatan. There, the governmental structure seemed to have been a pattern of city complexes within about a thirty-mile radius. In each pattern, there existed one large temple city containing one or more huge pyramids on a central plaza, which was bordered by lesser structures. In this large city dwelt the hierarchy, the lords of the district, the ruling body of government.

Then within a radius of five to twenty miles, smaller satellite cities were built. The working class lived in these, subjects of the lords of the district (the Arkin). They supported the governors and ruling class in the temple city. When one studies the location and arrangement of Florida's west coast shell mound complexes, they see the very same pattern as exists in the Yucatan.

I have put my theory on record with the National Park Service in South Florida and via interview by the *Naples Daily News*, but to my knowledge, no professional archeologist has made a study of it. Many of the great mound complexes in Florida have been destroyed by modern man. Shell, the material of which they

are built, has been much in demand for building roads, drives, and landfill. Some have been
completely leveled for housing. Only two great
temple mounds remain on Marco Island, and
half-million-dollar homes sit atop each of these.
Marco was perhaps the largest mound site on the
south Florida coast. Artifacts found on the island
have been said, by the Smithsonian Institute, to
date from the time of Christ.

Goodland, a fishing village some eight miles
to the east, is built on the site of a satellite city.
All mounds there have been completely leveled,
and artifacts that might have existed have been
bulldozed into the swamps.

North of Marco are several mound complexes. On Mound Key in Estero Bay and on
Captiva and Useppa Islands stand notable
mounds. At least four Maya District patterns
exist on Florida's west coast. I'm sure more have
existed, but they are largely destroyed. Existing
are Crystal River, the center of government with
Cedar Key a satellite; Mound Key, the temple
city, and surrounding satellite cities. Still in evidence are Captiva and Useppa, Marco and its
satellite at Goodland, and another small complex on Dismal Key. Perhaps more exist because
with Marco begins the great maze of the Ten
Thousand Islands that extend almost one hundred miles southward to Cape Sable.

The Ten Thousand Islands, with its laby-
rinth pattern of islands and waterways, contains
secrets not yet discovered by man. To the south of
Marco, the fourth large mound site that indicates
a Mayan state-type center exists, Chokoloskee,
a fishing village in the Ten Thousand Islands.
The island contained five large mounds, accord-

ing to old timers who were there at the turn of the twentieth century. All are leveled today, but the site was surely a temple center in the days of Mayan colonization. About ten miles to the south, on Chatham River, the mound complex that Ed Watson (of the Belle Starr story) built his farm on, was a Chokoloskee satellite.

The Turner River mounds on the river by the same name was an intended Chokoloskee satellite, but it was never completed. After its construction, Mayan colonization started in what is now Florida suddenly stopped. Of all the mound sites in Florida, the Turner River site is probably the most shrouded in mystery and has produced more wild theories among professional archeologists than any other. The "satellite incomplete" theory is mine and mine alone. Because it is a complex of shell mounds up to twenty-six feet, and all lie on the river side of a built-up plateau (the plaza) approximately five feet above swamp level, this indicates that they, the mounds, are stockpiles of shell brought in from the oyster and clam bars on the Gulf coast some four miles away by hundreds of ant-like Mayan workers (the American Indian was never that industrious) and were ready for use in building the pyramids and other mounds into a proper and planned configuration.

The absence of planned configuration in the mounds today prompts some archeologists to say they were not intentionally built by man but instead are Indian shell middens, or natural fortifications of shell cast up by wind and tide in some ancient sea. The fact that Calusa artifacts were found during the few investigations that have been made (mostly in early twentieth century) indicate that they built them. The fact that no artifacts below the surface (and other than the Calusa refuse) has been found in these great shell piles indicate that no one inhabited the site at all, that it was not a completed site, town, village, or whatever. Captain Dick Turner, Indian fighter, discovered the mounds, homesteaded there, and built a farm on them in the early 1870s, thus giving the mound site and the river, by which they are located, his name. Farming on the site ended about 1910, and typical of the Everglades, the site returned to its original jungle state.

My interest in the Turner River shell mounds was an outgrowth of an interest in and the consequent search for a place in the Florida Everglades called the Turner Farm. I had camped in the Everglades for years—that is, in the eastern and southern part—and also visited the western side, but only briefly. I had done some of the obvious things there were to do there but took only a shallow look at its history. I knew that the Black pirate "Black Caesar" (Henri Caesar) used the many waterways of the Ten Thousand Islands and particularly Chokoloskee Bay as a hideout. I visited the village of Chokoloskee first in 1954, the year "the road came in," old-timers would say. The building of the road across Chokoloskee Bay is a benchmark in Chokoloskee history. Prior to that, the community was reached only by boat.

Atlantic Coastline Railroad System's southernmost station was at Everglades City. I have stood on the last cross tie south, quite a way in time and space from the spot in Carolina where I grew up by its tracks. I had fought mosquitoes in Fakahastchee Strand, smelled pine tar stills in Big Cypress, and watched giant oil well pumps like big black birds pecking something out of the ground along the Copeland-Immokalee road. Now that I had decided to make the area a winter waterhole (January, February, and March), found that I had hit a bonanza in projects relative to my favorite hobby.

I established a camp in Big Cypress, just south of the trail, in a campground owned by Evelyn Shealy and her husband Jack. Evelyn was a postmistress of the smallest post office in the USA, Ochopee, Florida. Her building beat out the little post office at Salvo on the North Carolina Outer Banks, by just a few inches. The campground was a level elevation of coral rock just a foot above swamp level, the rock having been blasted out of deep pits and bulldozed flat and smooth. Some ten or twelve "snowbirds" (northerners) wintered there, and there was also some transit in and out most every night. One feature favored by most who wished to get away from it all was its remoteness. We had to drive ninety miles round trip to a supermarket. It was a good place to be when the winter winds howled in Wisconsin and ice choked up the rivers of the northeast. Some of the campers were great fishermen, and for fishing, the rivers of the Everglades cannot be beat.

Things were not as quiet and still as one might think there. If a woman's scream jarred you from your afternoon nap under your favorite coconut tree, you could be sure that an alligator, while strolling across the campground, had decided to rest in the shade in front of her camp.

The area was also a good pot drop, and at night a plane with no lights would fly over, blink a flashlight out of the window, and make his drop in the swamp. A little while later you could hear the airboat crank up and move out into the saw grass prairies and, with searchlights, make the pickup. Also, the great swamp fires provided an interesting panorama. The Park Service fought the fires with fire engines mounted on swamp buggies.

We made acquaintance of Betty and Bill Barron from Ohio, who had been wintering there for a number of years. We were in Ochopee for a short time the first year, but long enough to know the next winter we would be back, and I would pursue two local stories I had heard. One was the Ed Watson-Belle Starr story, which I determined to prove true or false. No one really knew. The other project was to search for the Old Turner Farm somewhere in the jungles of the Turner River. My passion for the old and the lost really came to life. Bill and Betty were bass fishermen, had a boat, and had fished the entire nine-mile length of the Turner River, but they had never seen the old farm. Bill knew of an old, abandoned homestead in the jungles, but he had never heard it called Turner Farm. The information I got that first year was of a Turner Farm site: nothing was left of the buildings, these having been removed by a former owner, the Park Service, or the Miccosukee Indians had torn them down and carried the lumber away. Only an old concrete and tabby cistern remained of the farm, and the site was covered with many ancient shell mounds.

Here, on the upper river, the buildings still stood, house, barn, and there was no cistern. There was a small Indian shell midden and a few Australian pines and orange trees. It definitely was not the old Turner place. (The next year, I led a party to this homestead on the upper river to find the Miccosukee had torn its buildings down and hauled them away.) Books and miscellaneous material I had acquired in the Ochopee/Everglades City area that first year proved fruitful in information I was to use on my second year's search for the farm and also fired me with interest in the great cluster of shell mounds that had existed on the Turner Farm.

From a book, *Man in the Everglades*, by Carlton W. Tebeau, I got my first real clue to the farm's locations. It was on the lower river in the estuarine. The second year, I was ready. Bill was doubtful. He had fished the length of the river for years but had seen nothing of great shell mounds. However, his spirit for adventure was high. He came by my camp one night and announced we were going down the river the next day.

The Turner River is a beguiling waterway. Traveling down its nine-mile length, its features are constantly changing. One passes through wide, grassy prairies with scattered bending palms, through deep, dark tunnels of overlapping vegetation, the jungle growth so dense the river is narrowed to white water flumes barely wider than the boat. We crossed large quiet lakes, from which birds arose in clouds to circle away with wings glistening in the sunlight. Into the estuarine, one wrong turn in its labyrinthine waterways could lead to hours, even days, in the mangrove maze. As the estuarine changes to marine, the big bays start and mosquitoes rise in clouds like smoke on the water. Then, it broadens, and its eeriness becomes less as the jungle's green walls press solidly up to the water's edge. We strain our eyes to penetrate the dense jungle shore on the south side of the river.

Tebeau's book said it was on the south side of the river. Suddenly, up ahead, a break in the vegetation, a small shell-covered beach, a point extending into the river. A few feet back from the river, the foliage thinned out and the white face of the shell mound could be seen rising behind it. Bill had already turned the boat toward shore, and its bottom ground to a stop on the shell-covered landing. We eagerly waded ashore through the shallow water. We had found it!

I think it was at that moment I captioned the landing spot, "Shell Point," a reference that has been used by myself and others ever since. The jungle had so encroached upon and overgrown the mounds that they looked like the wall of the jungle themselves, even though some were as much as twenty feet high. Observations at Shell Point revealed that the river had, through the centuries since this satellite city's construction began, changed course and had eroded into one or more of the large mounds. The remaining mounds—and there were plenty of them—were back from the river's edge from forty to a hundred yards, and the swamp, a prop root jungle, lay in between. This was why the mounds could not be directly seen from the river.

Climbing the first ridge of mounds, we descended upon a plateau of built-up shell four or five feet above swamp level. This raised area covered approximately three acres and was covered with cacti and low thistle. The area was bare of brush in many places, and the white shell, with much sand, glistened in the sunlight. It was inhabited by large, red ants that scurried here and

there, and there was evidence that swamp rabbits lived there, also. This plaza was the intended
plaza, when it was built over a thousand years
before. The cistern was there, partially covered
with shell. Dick Turner's farmhouse had stood
nearby.

Rusted strands of barbed wire lay here and
there, and Bill found an old cast-iron stove leg.
The knobby heart of a rotted post stood near
the cistern. We had indeed found the old Turner
Farm. We climbed to the top of one of the taller
mounds near the farmhouse site, though painful
it was because thorny vegetation grew over it and
jumping cactus covered our legs.

From its summit, we could see through a
break in the Buttonwood and Gumbo Limbo
trees the broad expanse of the river, where it
emptied into Chokoloskee Bay, which lay like
a broad inland sea shimmering in the sunlight.
The first visit to the ancient site was necessarily
short. We must head back up-river to reach the
camp before dark. I would return, however, and
explore the whole site inch by inch—both aspects
of it—a Mayan satellite city in the building and a
pioneer farm in a lonely, isolated world.

I explored the Turner River mound site
extensively one week after I found it. It was an
eyeball survey. The National Park Service didn't
allow digging or other alteration type analysis
of things on park land, so a surface examination
was all I could do and actually all I was qualified
to do. Also, the digging type takes time—weeks,
months—and I didn't have that kind of time.

Walter Panko, another friend (snowbird)
camping at Ochopee for the winter, got interested in the project and offered to take me back

to the site. Bill Barron went along too. Walter had a big boat, and I had also determined from the previous trip that less time would be lost in transit if we took the boat to the Chokoloskee Bay causeway and put in there. From that point, we then followed the Flamingo Waterway route south to the mouth of Turner River, then up river about a mile to Shell Point, which was the beginning of the shell mound complex. Pulling Walt's boat trailer to the launch site with my pickup truck, we made a quick run to the mound site and again waded ashore to the old Mayan satellite city project, a jungle-shrouded gem of prehistoric intrigue.

Walter had planned to go with me on this survey of the site, but after a short distance into the thistle-covered hills, he and Bill decided to go up river fishing instead. As they chugged off up river into the estuarine, I headed into the jungles alone. I climbed the first high mound to its summit, hacking at clinging foliage with my machete.

Taking out compass and mapping pad, I established reference and demarcation lines—the basis for making a rough map of the site as I climbed through the many hills and crevices, and there were many! As I checked my way through the thorny growth to the top of the mounds, some being high enough to look down upon the tops of others, I realized the immensity of the site. It covered at least forty acres and extended up river one-half to three-quarters of a mile.

I found that the entire area had been built up to about five feet above swamp level just as I had noticed the immediate area around the old farmhouse site the week before. It was indeed a plaza upon or around which the town was to be built. Most of the shell mounds, over thirty in all, were on the river side of the plaza, simply stock piles of material bought in from the river and dumped. Although paralleling the river, the piles were not right on the river's edge. Only at the shell point did the mounds lie right up to the river. For the most part, they were some one hundred to two hundred feet from the jungle waterway, and a strip of swamp lay in between. This strip of swamp, typical of the other swamp areas all around, was filled with mangrove trees with their entangled prop roots that made travel through it laborious and, in some places, impossible.

It was a bit odd that the hundreds, perhaps thousands, of human ants so long ago had left the river with their wicker baskets of shells and bogged up to two hundred feet through the swamp before setting them down to be emptied on the slowly growing stock pile. But then, that was centuries ago. Perhaps the river changed course gradually through the last thousand or more years and progressed to its present course. One would like to wonder, too, why the Maya colonizers were to build this city as others, so far inland from the source of supply—the vast oyster and clam beds along the coastal edge of Florida's many west coast islands. But here again, we are looking through a great time span. The Ten Thousand Islands are steadily growing out into the Gulf of Mexico and have been for eons of time.

The devil mangroves drop their spore-like seed, which are washed in clusters out into the shallow limestone sea, where they root in the chalky bottom and grow in great groups as young trees for sand and flotsam to cling to and build new islands. The process is never ending. Perhaps at the time of the Maya colonization of Florida's west coast, the shore of this coast was much closer, but the relentless propagation of the mangrove built it to where it is today.

I orientated myself (a precaution against getting lost) to the river, the lifeline of these trackless Everglades. The mound site was on the south side of the river. All that was needed at any time would be to follow my compass north through the fringe of swamp some two hundred feet, and I would reach the river.

The mounds were all sizes and shapes, I learned as I hacked my way, crisscrossing the site about every fifty yards or so, deviating a little on steep climbs and in exceptionally dense growth. Some mounds were large and towering with steep sides, almost perpendicular and fallen dry foliage made climbing slippery with real danger of falling on my machete. Some large mounds had bases and divided higher up to become two mounds. Some bases ran east and west, then merged with other mounds. Sometimes several linked up together and formed a ridge that rose and fell in height. Some were short and squatty—the sum total of it was complete disorganization! They were stock piles, plain and simple! And over it grew the prickly, dense vegetation—buttonwood, cacti, wild plum, red-skinned gumbo limbo, and mahogany.

South on the plateau or plaza, I could see the old farm fields because that is what it was after Dick Turner came. Then the great swamp again, extending seemingly forever and totally inhospitable to man. Most of the plaza was pleasingly less dense. It had scattered buttonwood and smaller eucalyptus and open places where only short weak-type plants grew. It offered a respite from the mounds' vines and cacti—some cactus, the Tetetzo and Chollo variety, were larger than I have seen on the limestone plains of the Yucatan. Some Sapodillia grew near the mounds, and Spanish Bayonet was plentiful.

I don't recall seeing the Australian Pine, which usually grows around any south Florida homestead. There was an absence of birds. It was noticeable. No birds flitted through, sang, or chirped in the entire expanse of this high place in the swamp. I found an aging fence post that had a strand of rusted barbed wire still clinging to it. How many years? I think the farm was abandoned in about 1910. Near the base of a mound, a piece of mesh fencing was ingrown a foot deep in a giant eucalyptus tree.

Here, in the middle of this ancient plaza, the less ancient field of a long-forgotten farm, I felt that I was trespassing in two areas—three, if one counted the unknown span of time the Calusa camped on these high places before Dick Turner came.

Removing my backpack for a moment of comfort and settling on the leaf covered ground, which was composed of shell lime and black swamp mulch, a combination that grew profusely the big red tomatoes, the starchy cassava—the base for the taste of tapioca—and sugar cane brought to Key West and sold in the tropical market. I visualized life at this time, with the mosquitoes and the heat, the same heat I was experiencing at that moment as I lay in the shade and sipped warm water from my canteen—a veteran of my Yucatan photographic expedition.

Even warm water prevents dehydration. After another hour of hacking, climbing, and slippery descents into the mounds, they suddenly ended. I had reached the end of the site, and more or less happily so! They had grown smaller a way back, but now there were no more. I concluded my map because nothing lay ahead of me now but the eternal swamp.

Mosquitoes had increased in intensity, and my thorn pricks, scratches, and abrasions were paining me something terrible. I decided that, before I started the struggle back to the shell point, I would make my way north to the river and bathe my insect-bitten face, wash my sweat-drenched hair, and maybe take a swim if it looked safe. My pocket compass pointed the way, and I started sloshing half a boot deep in the swamp ooze. Mossy vines festooned from the overhead, and the devil mangroves made progress slow. From one-half to three inches in diameter, the slime-covered prop roots arched from the tree trunk for several feet and intermeshed with roots from other trees forming a formidable bed, spring-like maze. Too high to step over and too low to crawl under, especially with a backpack, I tried chopping my way through. I could cut the smaller ones, but had to go over or slide under the larger ones. I removed my backpack, which helped so by dipping in the ooze going under and painfully straddling going over, I could make better progress.

After twenty minutes or so, I had progressed north about a hundred yards, but there was no sign of the river. I tied an orange tape around a tree at eye level and continued my struggle northward. The orange tape is a rule of the jungle. *Mark the trail!* You may wish to return.

Another half hour in the prop roots but no river. Where the hell was the river? I checked my compass. I could see two orange tapes—right in line. I was going north. I listened for some sound from the river, maybe a boat. No sound. This was a remote river, and probably a boat on the river was rare. The silence was alarming. Silence! Not a frog, not a bird, nothing except the zing of mosquitoes. Nothing in the swamp moved but me. Was I lost? No, I was not lost! The *river* was lost. The river was not where it was supposed to be. I was not lost. One is not lost if he can return to where he came from. Follow my tracks in the ooze—the orange tape. And follow them, I did.

By 3:30 p.m., I dragged myself over the last mound and slid heavily down through the chafing shells on the river side to the water's edge at shell point. I dropped my backpack to the ground and stripped off my sweat-drenched clothes. I'd hang them to dry and then eat my lunch. I had forgotten all about my lunch in the excitement of the day. I opened my pack, got a rope, and made a clothesline, then staggering around in my shorts and boots, I reached back into the pack for my lunch. *Gone!* No lunch! Virginia had made me a peanut-butter-and-jelly sandwich and put it in a yellow bread wrapper along with a banana and several peppermint sticks. It was in the pack a moment before I got the rope! The damned place was spooked! What hungry ghost of Arkin, or more lately of old Dick Turner, lingered still in this bewitched place? Or had a silent Mikasuki followed me in the shadows awaiting the opportune time to steal my lunch?

I stood trembling in my drawers, peering into the dark underbrush. *Calm it, boy! Calm it! You have climbed too many walls not to be able to get through this one.* I washed my face and hands in the river and splashed water all over my aching body. Then I sat down to rationalize. I was a country boy, and I knew that I was the only human being in that section of the Everglades, and no ghost, as thin as they are, would steal my lunch. The only animals I knew with the cunning, the prowess, with the love for people food that could have gotten a whiff of my lunch (I bet it was the banana!) when I opened the pack and tippy-toed up there when my back was turned was the raccoon!

He couldn't have gone too far. I climbed down the path up the big mound. Nothing there. Back down to the landing and along a small path by the river to the base of a small mound. There, a peppermint stick lay in the sand. Up to the top of that mound and another peppermint stick. Then a bit farther, another peppermint. The culprit didn't know it, but he had marked his trail with peppermint sticks like I marked mine with orange tape. A few steps on, and there he was! About a twenty-pound raccoon sitting calmly on his launches eating my peanut butter and jelly sandwich. With peanut butter around his mouth and jelly clinging to his mustache, he eyed me out of the corner of his eyes, but he kept on eating. The bread wrapper lay close by with the banana and two peppermint sticks still in it. I retrieved that and trudged back to the point. Banana and peppermint candy aren't really bad, if it's all you have got.

Before I leave the subject of the Turner River Mounds, I should explain the mystery of the "lost river" that so completely baffled me that day in the mangrove jungle. A few days after the event, a park ranger, who I found to be most likeable and also efficient (most of the Everglades rangers were not real happy about the publicity I was drawing to this gem of history in their great sanctuary), told me of the existence of a contour map somewhere in their archives that showed the site complete with its boundaries and elevations. He found the map, which had been drawn at a survey by a man named Thomasson for a company called the Turner River Shell Company in the 1950s—a commercial enterprise that planned to dig out all the mounds and sell the shells.

Fortunately, the Park Service acquired the site before this project destroyed more than two or three mounds. Looking at this map revealed why I could not find the river. About halfway up river in the mound site, the river suddenly turned north, a fact that I did not know, and a condition that from that point on destroyed my original orientation. The shell mounds also turned north with the river, making the river lie to my left or west of the mounds at that point, and no matter how far I might have struggled on a northward course from the mounds, I would not have reached it. In my back-and-forth transit across the mounds, I had failed to use my compass. Thus, I failed to notice the change in the direction the mounds were running.

My dad includes a map he drew of the Turner River Shell Mound site in his manuscript. Many may find this an interesting interlude in Daddy's story. I myself have never heard him speak of this. By the early 1980s, he and Mother spent their winter vacations in the Everglades; I was married, working full time, and no longer living at home. I'm sure some of their friends heard him talk about it. I was beginning to see more and more why Daddy's minister called him a Renaissance man in his eulogy at the memorial. Beginning as a blacksmith in the Civilian Conservation Corps then moving to photography, then shipbuilding, photojournalism, and amateur archeology, Daddy seemed to reinvent himself along the way in the different stages of his life.

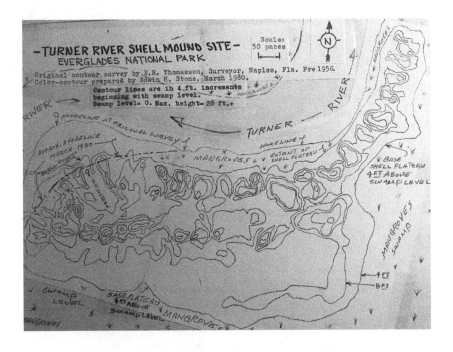

*****

While my parents were wintering in the Everglades, their precious cat was at home being cared for by a loving neighbor who visited every day with Fluffy, prepared her meal of raw beef kidney, and even took a nap with her on my parents' bed. Mama and Daddy called me about once a week. When I answered the phone, the first words out of their mouths were, "How's Fluffy?" Never mind how I was. They loved that cat, who made her home with them for nineteen years. It was sweet and kind of funny, their devotion to this little feline. My dad writes of her, and this is a good place to let him tell about her in his own words.

> Fluffy was a little calico cat. She was one of a litter of four. Friendly was a black, white, and gray tabby—a shorthair male. His name describes his disposition well. Blacky was a solid black male, temperamentally mean. Calico was a small shorthair, female of course, with a kitten's disposition. Fluffy, mentioned above, was long-haired. Virginia called her "the little princess." She was quiet and reserved. As a kitten, she stayed apart from the others. While the others pushed and shoved around their milk bowl, Fluffy held back. She was definitely not one of the pack. In her breeding, somewhere back in time, there was ancestry definitely not from the alley.
>
> Fluffy was the survivor and lived with us a long, long nineteen years. The others were disposed of through normal processes. Fluffy was Virginia's cat, and in time she learned about us better than we knew ourselves. The cat devised little schemes to have us do her bidding. A housebroken cat (she was too coy for litter boxes), she knew her cue to go outdoors was to go to the door and look up. This, of course, put someone promptly on their feet across the room to the door. She also knew that when she came to us and mewed for food, no one was in a hurry to get up and go to the kitchen to feed her. So she devised a system. When hungry and wanting to be fed, she would go to the door and look up as though she wanted to go outside. When one of

us got up to let her out, she whirled around and led us to the kitchen!

Fluffy was one of the family—slept on our bed, on a lap before TV. A book or magazine in the lap was an invasion of her territory, and she promptly rooted it out and claimed her spot. She knew when we were happy and when we were sad.

She loved the yard outside. It was her territory, and she defended it fiercely. When we were away for days or weeks, we always made arrangements for someone to come down and feed her, but that was food for the body, not for the soul. No matter how long we were away, Fluffy would sit in the driveway by the street every day waiting for us to return. When we did at last return, she went into her pouting act and showed her resentment. When preparing to leave on a trip, the world's greatest "sit-down" protest would be pulled. When the suitcases came out of the attic, she knew what it meant, and her protest began. Into the open suitcase she would hop and sit there to prevent its being packed.

The dear little cat brought us much joy. She is missed where she always sat and enjoyed the morning sun. The spot is unmarked, but we who cared about her know where it is.

My parents made an attempt to acclimate her to camping once. She was in her elder years then. They took her on a short camping trip in their travel trailer to Edisto Beach. She was terrified and mewed and complained the whole time. Cats travel as easily as dogs if they are taken as a kitten and become used to it.

Or she may have felt that living that way was far beneath her dignity!

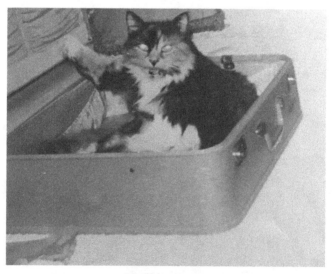

Fluffy's protest

Southwestern United States

Daddy made one last trip in the final year of his life, but it wasn't by automobile, airplane, or any other means of transport. Just in his mind. His earlier chapter in *Stranger Pastures* explains how he did this, and I must tell this bizarre story in my own words.

Daddy was hospitalized for an entire month in the winter of 1997. He was taken in an ambulance and admited under an emergency, and since the Medical University of South Carolina didn't have much available bed space on the medical/surgery floor, they put him into a room on the transplant floor. Daddy was confused about where he was. He insisted he wasn't in Charleston but rather was in Charlotte, North Carolina. To my knowledge, he had never spent any time in Charlotte, so where this idea came from is a big question. Confusion reigned almost the entire month. He was experiencing breakdown in most of his body systems. Unable to walk, he had a mysterious interior bleed, the source of which was difficult to find, and he seemed to be slipping away. Indeed one evening, my mother and I were told it didn't look like he would live through the night.

Initially, Mother had called EMS to transport him to the hospital from home the night he was admitted, and the meager belongings they took included a pair of worn-out bedroom shoes. We started gathering up his other belongings in preparation to probably remove them the next day, and my mother decided to just throw out those old shoes. The hospital care staff had insisted that we go home, and they would call if we needed to come back in. We each went to our own homes that night, prepared for the worst.

The next morning, my mother called me from the hospital and said that Daddy had awakened and asked for breakfast. Then he looked around and asked what happened to his bedroom shoes. I don't know what she told him!

Since he had rallied, the hospital's treatment plan changed, and the goal became to get him into rehabilitation with a view to coming back home.

He was still incoherant and delusional, and things got even more bizaare as the weeks went by. Kidney transplant patients came and went for four weeks on the floor, yet Daddy remained in the hospital.

One afternoon, a nurse called me. Her voice was very hesitant; she spoke with uncertainty when I answered her call. "Um, I am in your dad's room. Um, uh. He asked me to call you and, um, tell you, uh uh, that his car broke down in Jacksonboro and he wants, um, you to come and get him." I immediately recognized that he was, in his mind, returning home from somewhere, perhaps Savannah or Beaufort, and the journey and breakdown were very real to him.

A few days later, my mother said she walked into his room, and he was sitting up in the bed with his hands in front of him grasping something invisible—the steering wheel of a car!

Eventually, he was released from the hospital and admitted to a nursing home west of the Ashley River. Rehab began. After a month or so, Daddy was very much more present in the moment, and he talked about the mysterious journey he took. His success at self-hypnosis permitted him to leave his broken and declining body and take a trip he had always wanted to take to the Southwestern United States. He had always been facinated with the vast difference of the environment between the Southwest and the Southeast. Cacti, tumbleweed, cowboys, ranches, Native American cultures, and mysterious sites like Chaco Canyon beckoned him to trade the hot, humid air on the Southeastern coastline for the hot, arid weather of the desert. He maintained that he had driven all the way out to Arizona and back during his hospital stay.

I had not appreciated this nearly as much until I read his account of traveling absent from his body into any world he cared to visit.

CHAPTER 25

Adventures There:

Canada

I'll never forget the late summer when my parents went to Canada, camping. In a tent! I was not living at home by then. Daddy was involved in a Theosophical Society that met in Charleston, and my mother had gotten somewhat interested in it too. Their ultimate destination was Toronto, Ontario, Canada, to an International Rosicrucian Convention in Quebec. They had booked a hotel for the few days they would be there, since they would be required to dress more formally for some of the events. Throwing caution to the wind, they set out with the tent and camping paraphernalia in their car. There was no backup plan as they took off on this big adventure. In my wildest dreams, I could not imagine my mother consenting to such an excursion. I know Daddy said that when they were camping, their life together was companionable, not stressful at all. But this was on a whole different level. It just baffled me.

They loved the leisurely trip they took through Ontario and onward to Quebec. Daddy tells the story in his own colorful words.

> The gentle glow of the waters of Lake Nipissing against the Precambrian granite shore had a soothing effect on the senses. The air in our yellow Sears Roebuck tent was growing cooler as the weak rays of the August sun slanted less

obtusely, and the long days of the Huron summer were on the wane. We hoped our thin blankets, brought from home in South Carolina, would be sufficient. There had been a thin frost on the tent that morning. Perhaps we should let the kerosene oil lantern burn all night. It had been a long day, and we had ranged far and wide in the deep north woods—all the way to the Ottawa River and up its western bank to the Temiscaming dam and across the province of Quebec.

Tourists had not found Temiscaming (Te-mis-ca-ming), a north woods logging town that draped itself over a prominent hill in the Kipawa Highlands. Motels were nonexistent. We lunched in a little café down on the river along with loggers and mill hands—most who spoke French. The town was French, right up to the fountain on the town's square.

The little bronze boy, principal object of the statuary art, was naked except for the draping of grayish white pigeon excrement that covered his head and shoulders like a shawl. He stood boldly on his pedestal with one hand flung skyward, the other hand grasping his penis from which a stream of water under high pressure spurted up into the air and formed rainbows in the mist that drifted through the sunlight against a shadowy backdrop of hemlock and spruce. Au Marche on signs was easy to translate. French was not my favorite subject in school, although the petite little teacher was.

We watched for moose in the bogs, watched the loggers on the river—acres and acres of logs rafted to drift downstream to the mills. Through the country pictured by James Oliver Curwood, across the great northwest portage, but now by car, we had returned to Nipissing Junction. Fatigue fosters sleep. Chill tugs one back to awareness. Tossing and turning on the folding cots worked the tent's sewed-in floor, the working floor tipped the kerosene lantern, which then burned abnormally producing a ribbon of black carbon that filled the tent's interior with a storm of sooty "snowflakes." Virginia ran snowy fingers through her hair. They came out black. Tags of carbon clung to the ceiling, to every conceivable perch. I said, "Today, we buy sleeping bags!" Virginia grinned through black freckles.

Proudfoot, the tall Hudson Bay Indian who ran the campground, told us where to go: Northland Outfitters, Ltd. in North Bay. They had manufactured snowshoes, tents, sleeping bags—everything for loggers and trappers in the bush. Our two bags were a good investment, and we used them for years of cold weather throughout the Great Smokey Mountains and elsewhere.

While traveling north the week before, we had stopped in Toronto and made reservations at the Royal York Hotel for the following weekend to attend the International Rosicrucian Convention. After the week in Northern Ontario and Quebec, we drove down from Lake Nipissing for that event. An episode on the Toronto Convention is included in this book under the category "Strange Pastures" (Chapter 22), so I will not review it here in this sequence of activities. However, to pick up this story line, at Toronto the evening following the convention, we were packing to leave the hotel and head south toward home. However, we kept looking northward out of the window toward the vast green northland we had left three days ago, and the realization came through to us that we had not had enough of it. "Let's go back!" There was another week left of our vacation.

Back north we went. This time, to the Georgian Bay region with its tongue-twisting names: Nottawasaga Bay, Michamilinac and Penetanguishene (No-ta-was-a-ga, Mich-a-mil-i-nac, Pen-e-tan-gui-she-ne). Not as deep as the north woods as Nipissing Junction, we found a more congested humanity. Collingwood, a small shipbuilding town on the south shore of Nottawasaga Bay, was the place an old friend at the Charleston Naval Shipyard had learned the shipbuilding trade. He was French-Canadian—Patrick Archambault. His son, Pat Jr., was even closer to me as we worked together for most of our shipbuilding careers. Both of them have now passed over the threshold into another dimension.

Camping at Craigleith Provincial Park added a new experience, looking through a window of time to an age in the forming world. The Ordovician era when life on this planet was little more than invertebrate forms swimming in the slime of ever-changing seas. The Niagara Escarpment, a sedimentary rock formation on the south shore of Georgian Bay, is the same escarpment, ridge of Cambrian rock over which the Niagara River flows forming the Niagara Falls in the northwestern corner of New York State. Sitting on this rock formation, which has long cracks running as true as if cut by man (said to have been caused by the weight of the ice during the last Ice Age), one can chip out fossilized tribolites that have been sealed therein for more than three-hundred seventy-five million years. Paleontologists from all over the world come to

Craigleith to study this rare window into the visible beginnings of life on this planet. Only micropaleontology comes before it. Virginia found a strange fascination sitting in the pale northland sun, picking away in this ancient sea bottom with a geological pick hammer.

A Great Lake storm gave us a wet farewell to Craigleith. It blew up during the night; high waves pounded the escarpment; driving rain soaked the tent to its thickest seams. Time was short for us, so we packed up in the rain. Two of the wettest, muddiest people the town of Meaford, Ontario, ever saw stopped at the café for a breakfast of Canadian bacon, hash brown potatoes, and hot coffee. We looked like we had crawled from under a Pecambrian rock. A bright sun dried our tent after an overnight at Ipperwash on Lake Huron at Kettle Point, and from there, we left Ontario for our two-day homeward run.

Scotland

My dad always romanticized the places where he traveled. Sometimes it wasn't necessary to use much imagination, as the romantic energy of a location's setting in history envelops you and seeps into your pores. I tend to do the same.

In the summer of 1999, I attended Oxford University's Programme of English Literature. During my six-week stay, I made it my business to take in as much of the aura of the place as I could. I took two courses for credit, so that meant I had to produce researched essays with a critique of some aspect of the book with which I was working. That was rewarding. Exeter College, the college hosting the program, backed to the ancient Bodlean Library. Stone walls surrounded many of the colleges we went to for plays, concerts, and the like. Even doing laundry took us into an area where we passed under a medieval stone arch.

J. R. R. Tolkien and a few other famous people attended Exeter College. Perhaps I was sleeping in his bed. We drank beer at the pub he and the other two "Inklings," C. S. Lewis, and Lewis Carroll frequented, and walked in the footsteps of ancients who were burned alive at the stake for being Catholic when Protestantism ruled and vice versa.

We enjoyed tours of famous places such as Stonehenge and Salisbury. We also took a bus ride to the edge of Wales to see Tintern Abbey, written about by Romantic poet William Wordsworth of the late eighteenth century and early nineteenth century. One's mind can't help but be transported to an earlier time, one, two or more centuries ago and even millennia in the past.

However, Daddy is not quite done with Scotland, and his story continues.

There was something about Joan Murray that captivated me. A handsome Scottish lassie with the complexion of chilled cream, the reddest lips, the bluest eyes and the blackest hair was not it. It had to do with the inborn substance. She was a living product of the Western Isles, from the town of Stornoway in the far Hebrides. These Gaelic Isles, considered foreign by many mainland Scots, could be considered the real Scotland. Only recent years have seen change in centuries of language and customs. Today, the propensity is toward the old. Gaelic is still the oral language, English a begrudged written one.

Joan Murray had recently graduated from the Stornoway Business School and had crossed Minch to the mainland to work as a clerk in a Dunoon hotel—McCalls, it was. Miss Bea, owner and operator of the hotel, was warm and pleasant and implored all the guests to be tolerant of the lassie from the out islands and help her all we could. She was lonely and homesick, but her main problem was her speech. Her strong Gaelic tongue was a real handicap. She knew English words on sight but had to master the pronunciation of many. She quickly grew to rely on me for words relatively American.

One morning, she was struggling with the word *hurricane*. After much effort to follow my syllabication, she exclaimed in despair, "Gail force winds! I say that, aye?" As she so strongly associated herself with her homeland, she associated those she met with theirs. Her "hurricane" project came from my being from the South Atlantic coast. One morning, she was very disturbed. "How do I...? How do?" She was pointing to the word *Canaveral* in the headlines of the newspaper. It was the morning after the tragic accident at Cape Canaveral, Florida, that took the lives of three American astronauts. Everything was very personal with her, and sometimes she was impatient. We made some pictures, and in an extension of the mood, she asked each morning, "Where are my pictures, Master Stone?" The word was *Mister*!

The sun rises in January, if at all, about 10:30 a.m. in Scotland and sets about 3:30 p.m., so many daily functions take place in the dark. The postman is there before we go to work, and Joan always had each hotel guest's mail stacked neatly by the register. Into the third week, she asked me timidly, "Why doesn't your wife write to you?" That was indeed a mystery. In the entire twenty-eight days I spent in Scotland, I received not one letter from her. "She and her mother are probably on the go and don't have time to write."

I was back at home several days when this mystery was cleared up. All of a sudden, all of my wife's missives came back. She had been using domestic postage, so they never left the states. *A stamp is a stamp*, she thought.

The hotel bar had two sides. One was for the hotel guests and special invitations, and the other was for the street people. Like any Scottish pub, both sides are often lively. Just in front of the door, on the street-people side stood Castle Hill. It stood some sixty feet above the street level with a summit overlooking the east bay, the harbor streets, and across the Firth of Clyde to the burghs of Gourock and Greenock. Atop Castle Hill, fragments of the crumbling foundation of Mary, Queen of Scots, summer castle are seen. It was burned in 1685 by invading Athol Clans.

Today, another Mary graces the top of the hill—the bronze statue of Robert Burns's Scottish beauty, Highland Mary. I pursued Mary Campbell's personal and tragic story, which led from her birthplace somewhere in Bishop's Glen, above town at the end of Auchamore Road to the pubs of Greenock, where she died somewhat mysteriously on October 20, 1789. In the wrought-iron impalement on Castle Hill, her statue gazes across the Clyde to the homeland of her lover.

Another time (I was in Robert Burns's country twice), I was in the town of Ayr, walked the River Ayr's ancient horse bridge, built in the year 1235, and each time in the rain—Scotland's perpetual winter rain—"Caledonian dew." Mary, Queen of Scots, also frequented Toward Castle down the Cowal Coast from Dunoon. This mighty castle still stands in all its original grandeur. It is now a school for Glasgow's retarded children. Toward Castle was visited by Queen Victoria (ugh!) on her tour of the Western Isles. That woman again! And to think I have stood in her tracks on the stone steps where she stood, looking across Rothesay Bay.

The real live Scottish lassie, Joan Murray, is my personal touch with feminine Scottish charm and her endeared Western Isles. I don't know which was more luxuriant, maybe both were one and one was both. "You must love Stornoway!" she always insisted. She wanted her love for her homeland to be shared by all—a kind of "love me, love my islands thing." I remember a fragment of a poem by an unknown Hebridian, and it could well have been written by or for her.

> From the lone shieling in the
> Misty island
> Mountains divide us and the
> Waste of seas—
> But still the blood is strong, the
> Heart is Highland,
> And, we in dreams behold the
> Hebrides.

One can access this poem online through the web site scottish-poetrylibrary.org/uk. It is by an anonymous Scottish author.

The Scottish interlude was short lived. Once came a letter to the states written on blue stationery, urging again that I visit "lovely Stornoway." To her, no place could compare with her Stornoway. A friend flew to Scotland a year or two later on assignment and enquired of Joan Murray for me. She had indeed left Argyll. Someone thought she had married. No one knew where she had gone. She had not made any friends. But I know where she went and where she is. One could not know her without knowing. I hear her talking in her native Gaelic tongue in her beloved Hebrides. I see her on the Mince with wild wind in her hair. I see her backed by a red sunset on an Oban quay. I see her walking the painted shores of the Isle of Skye.

Not all of Daddy's Scottish experiences were that poetic.

The waiter brought Johnny and me drinks we had not ordered. "Compliments of the party over there." He indicated a table occupied by a uniformed navy chief with a tall blonde that looked English and a Scottish brunette who was with a tall Norse-looking man, who obviously wore an artificial leg. We looked, got their attention, and raised the drinks in salute. All exchanged smiles, and we proceeded to drink our drinks. The place was the Chief's Club at Ardnadam, overlooking the Holy Loch in Scotland's western highlands. The season was winter—January's gales bring the thunder of giant waves crashing against ancient Caledonian sea walls. This was not audible inside. Inside was cozy and a loud orchestra was driving all foreigners mad with repeated renditions of the new hit "Winchester Cathedral."

A girl came toward us from the table that had sent the drinks. I was her target. I reminded her of an old and very dear friend, she said.

"That's nice, who?"

She didn't say but continued, "I just had to speak to you. May I touch you?" She wasn't drunk, just delightfully aggressive.

I answered, "Only if you give me the next long, slow dance."

She pulled me to my feet. "This one is slow." She was indeed Scottish and married to an Icelander—the one-legged one—from Iceland. "He doesn't dance. The leg, you know."

I asked, "What does he do?" as we danced slowly across the large un-crowded floor.

"He's a butcher."

Oh, God!

"Not to worry," she assured me. "He's a good man and wants me to have a good time. Hold me closer!" Formalities over, our unity lost its stiffness. She was delightful. We danced again and again. Her husband just sat and drank drink after drink.

Funny, I thought afterward. She never mentioned the old and very dear friend again.

My first thought was that I wondered if her husband was some kind of pervert who enjoyed watching his wife with other men. I knew those types exist, along with a number of other fetishes. I'm thinking I'll close the book on this one. Very interesting encounter, for sure. However, there are other experiences he had that demand to be known.

One significant trip Daddy made was when he worked at the Charleston Naval Shipyard in the Design Division. His specialty was hull integrity, and when ships were being fitted for renovation, he and engineers in other fields traveled to the port where that particular ship was based and do a "ship check," to investigate the present condition and configuration of the ship and then work toward a design that would refit the ship for the needs of the US Navy. Most of Daddy's years in Design Division were focused on submarines, and there were two main homeports outside of the United States. One was in Rota, Spain. The other was in Holy Loch, Scotland. Below is Daddy's account of his travels in Scotland during his trip there.

The man with the beard had an International
Driver's License, so he drove the Cortina. I didn't
want to drive the thing with the steering wheel on
the wrong side. Jerry could have driven because
he had had duty in Scotland and was familiar
with driving on the wrong side of the road, but
he wanted to take pictures from the car. This
Sunday excursion into Scotland's western highlands was unexpected. Work had been suspended
on the missile-packing submarine where our
design team was doing pre-arrival overhaul planning and designing, because the crew was taking
on missiles. No one is unnecessarily exposed to
that operation.

Most of our people had left the day before
for Glasgow and Edinburgh, but I stayed and visited with the captain of the supply ship. A meeting his wife, a friend of mine, had been arranged
before we left the states. It had been a pleasant
visit, and he offered to take back to the states
any items I might wish "smuggled" in such as
scotch whiskey, silverware, tartans, and that sort
of thing. I declined his offer, however, because
it really wasn't necessary. I didn't plan to have a
lot of things going back, and I carried an official passport, the green one, and customs was not
permitted to search my luggage.

I had been to Glasgow the week before and
with no special interest in Edinburgh, I started to
get up a trip into the Highlands. My friend Jerry
wanted to go, as well as an engineer from the
Woods Hole Test Laboratory in Massachusetts.
He had the international driver's license.

We rented the Cortina and split the cost
three ways. I do not plan to relate the trip in
detail. That would be outside the purpose of this

book. I covered it all pretty well in a magazine article published in *Sandlapper*, the magazine of South Carolina, September 24 issue entitled "Scotland—A Travelogue." I will say, however, that in a few short hours in the highlands, one passed through more Scottish history and legend than he might expect.

Scotland in January is cold, but the breath of the Gulf Stream that begins in the Gulf of Mexico melts the snows along the western coast lowlands pretty fast. However, in the highlands, it is usually white with the peaks glistening with ice and sleet when the wind blows. Working on top of the superstructure of a submarine in a Holy Loch gale in January is an experience not to be forgotten nor desired. The driving sleet, coming off the mountains through Glen Massan and the channel formed by the rise of Ardnadam and the hills of Kilmun and Strone, pelts the face in the stinging gust and builds up on one's glasses, which have to be constantly wiped off. It makes more desirable the worm-like crawl through the "bowels" of the vessel amid the maze of piping, wiring, machinery, and the like. But both displeasures must be done if one is to design ways and means for installing new or alternate equipment and prepare blueprints for the job. This is done often. Modern technology changes fast. I have seen a system change and become obsolete while still on the drawing board.

The road into Dunoon follows the Holy Loch through the hamlets of Ardnadam and Sandbank, by Robertson's boat yard where Britain' famous racing yachts *Scepture, Solverign, Kurrewa,* and others were built. The stately Blairmore Inn rises beyond the moors of Glen

Lean and fades into the forest of Ardentinny. One knows that there are castles in Scotland. They are everywhere. Their condition varies. Some are occupied and well-kept like Castle Dunderave on the north shore of Loch Fyne. Dunderave is the "Doom Castle" in Neil Munro's love story. Some are mere standing walls without roofs, said to hold the ghosts of a glorious past; some sleeping, crumbled ruins. Inveraray Castle, seat of the Duke of Argyll, is on Loch Fyne at the head of Glen Aray and under the shadow of the watch tower on Dunniquich Hill. Inveraray Castle and the town holds much Scottish history. Sir Walter Scott wrote of Dunniqiuch Hill and its watch tower in his Legend of Montrose.

The Gaelic tongue is so strong in the highlands it is hard to communicate there. Lunch at MacBrides Inn in Inveraray was a disaster. I thought the tassie meant "hot steak and gravy." How nice after riding all morning in a car that had no heater. The girl brought cold cuts with potatoes that looked like polar bears locked in a frozen sea of congealed mutton fat. It added to the natural chill of the establishment. The view to the window of the icy two-thousand-foot Cruach Nan Capull (Gaelic) across the Loch Fyne completed my misery. I drank the tea. It was warm.

The absence of heat in this great and beautiful land is amazing. No public buildings are heated—post office, city hall—and if you go to the theater, you wear your overcoat and earmuffs.

As I travel through these indescribable highlands, I find there is no end to their awesome splendor. Through the green mansions of Glen Etive to Dunstaffnage—the site of the ancient Scottish monarchy where the Stone of Destiny, upon which forty Scottish Kings were crowned, first stood before its removal to Scone in the ninth century and then taken to Westminster Abby in the thirteenth century, where it became the base of the present Coronation Chair. This is the land of the ancient Celts whose far-flung culture is responsible for many blank pages on modern studies of ancient civilizations. Iona is the island birthplace of Scottish Christianity and the habitat of the ghosts of Scotland's kings, including Duncan and Macbeth.

The snow-capped high Grampains make one fall victim to Scotland's most colorful legend. As we drive through them, we wonder, could this be the right day of the year, the right year of the century, and if out there in some hidden valley, is there really Brigadoon?

Yucatan

For years, my dad nurtured a fascination for the Mayan culture. He traveled there a couple of times. His earlier searches in western Florida uncovered ziggurats, similar in structure to the ones found in Central America, and he sought to identify a connection between them. In story form, he tells of some of his adventures.

I had planned on driving to Dzilam de Bravo to search for Jean Lafitte's grave, but the aging Nash Rambler I had rented had a dying battery, and I didn't trust it off the main road. In gathering material on the irate Jean Lafitte in New Orleans a few years ago, I had heard two stories as to his resting place. They conflicted greatly. One account is that the pirate had died in Campeche on the Yucatan peninsula and while on the way back to New Orleans, it decomposed so rapidly it was rolled over the side. Another report, equally unconfirmed, told of a grave marker in a cemetery in the pueblo Dzilam de Bravo, on the north coast of the Yucatan, with a faded inscription that reads, "Jean Lafitte."

Since I was in Merida, the capital of the Yucatan, I decided to go to Dzilam de Bravo and see what I could find. Considering the Nash Rambler, the only vehicle I could find for rent, and the 120-degree heat out on the vast Yucatan plain, I decided to urge the ailing car over the thirty kilometers to the resort town of Progreso on the Gulf of Mexico for a breath of cooler air. Dehydration comes fast in this land south of the Tropic of Cancer, and a familiar sign, "Coca-Cola," brought me in off the road at a little rock hut named "Casa Pochco." Built of native stone with a dirt floor and a sheet iron roof—typical of Yucatecan structures out on the plain—the little shack also sported the sign "El Correo" (post office) and Estacion de Autobus, if the second-class bus ever came.

It was there that I ran into the language barrier so often encountered out on the plain where Maya, the native half-stuttered, half-gurgled language is more often spoken than Spanish. I requested, "Una Coca-Cola, por favor." The man behind the counter reached into a tub of water and fished out a bottle, popped the cap off, and sat it before me. Taking a handful of coins from my pocket, I inquired, not knowing the cost, "Dos pasos?" (two pasos was the normal price). Apparently, the "dos" (two) was all that registered with him. He reached into the tub over my protest, pulled out another bottle, popped the top, and sat it beside the first bottle. He became confused at my expression, I guess, and stuttered something. I paid him for the two drinks, but he kept on babbling. "No comprendo," I said.

He slammed his fist down on the counter exclaiming, "Maya! Maya!" A teenage mestizo standing near came to my rescue. He said something to the irritated old man in Maya then turned to me and said something in Spanish. I understood neither, but the storm cleared, and I no longer received the wrath of "Kukulcan."

I gave the boy the second Coke and as we drank he indicated to me that he was waiting for the bus to Progreso. I invited him to ride there with me. Conversation was in bits and pieces, his English being as sketchy as my Spanish. I frequently had to remind him, "No hablo Espaniol!"

In Progreso, I let him off on the Playa del Azure and drove around to see and photograph the town. Progreso was/is the Yucatan's only north coast seaport. Oddly, ocean-going ships do not come into the shore. A mile-long pier was built out across the shallow limestone shelf to deep water.

I observed my first Yucatan siesta in Progreso. The town simply closed up beneath me. I think I was the only living person there for an hour or two. It is an active town—business and resort. Rancheros from out on the plain bring their carts, pulled by bony donkeys, in with fruit and vegetables. The second-class bus arrived now and then bringing an amazing assortment of humanity that spills out on the streets. Some carried live chickens. I saw one bus delayed for half an hour while a fat Mayan woman tried to retrieve a suckling pig that had gotten loose under the bus seats.

I had come to the Yucatan for the purpose of photographing the Mayan antiquities and the Yucatan culture. It was a place that had fascinated me from my days in grade school when maps of Middle America showed a yellow void marked simply "Yucatan." My book, *The Yucatan Traveler*, was never published. I submitted it to Crown Publishers, Inc., who plagiarized it, subject for subject, photograph for photograph, and published it under their Crescent Books list.

A search of Crown's Crescent Books section online reveals a number of books published by them on the Yucatan. A couple were published in the early 1940s. Others are more recent, and some are in Spanish, apparently, for a university textbook. I did not find one that met his description.

Daddy picks up an account of his first trip to Yucatan.

The fat man in the white suit seated behind the huge mahogany desk was Senor Arturo Dias Solis, Generante General of the Colon Hotel on Calle 62. He spoke almost perfect English. "As I say, Mr. Stone, use great care out on the plain. Carry agua (water), should your automobile fail and no one comes along for two days." He shifted his immense weight from one side of the big, padded chair to the other and, with subtle pride, told me the story of his hotel.

His father had built the fabulous, old Moorish-style hotel in the early 1920s during the days of the sisal barons. World War I had so increased the demand for hemp, for rope making, and other needs that the old henequen plantations found new life, and their owners made fortunes, his father being one of them. Merida was the oasis to which the affluent from the steamy plains flocked, and few good hostelries existed then. The family fortune went into the grand hotel, with its ballroom, restaurant Ora y Azul, its *bano de vapors*, Merida's rooftops, and hundreds of lazily turning windmills. By the time the hotel was finished and the family sold the hacienda and moved in, the boom ended, the free-spending clientele faded, and the hotel fell into disrepair. The family fortune was gone, and they scattered to survive. A brother left the peninsula. I think he settled in San Cristobal da Las Casas. Others went elsewhere. Sisters hastily married awaiting suitors, "equally as poor!" Solis added with a sweep of his hands. But Senior Arturo had clung to his father's dream and had managed.

It became and is now a commercial hotel, not the resort hotel it was intended to be—businesspeople, the expense-account crowd—sometimes honeymooners. I had taken a suite to the left at the top of the stairs (there was an elevator, but it was mostly used by the cleaning maids with their carts and for foodstuffs for the kitchen of the still fabulous Restaureante Ora y Azul, which has live organ music breakfast, lunch, and dinner).

The suite was not my choice. The smartass desk clerk with the crooked smile, who let me make a fool out of myself with my sketchy Spanish then answered in perfect English, had assigned me the suite until a single room became available. I only paid room rates, so I didn't complain as days passed and no one told me to move. The hotel guests I met were few. Three, not counting doubles. And a diversified group they—we—were. A retired flyer, a college professor, and young honeymooners from Tampa, Florida. Our base in common was that we all spoke English. Most hotel guests were Yucatecan/Mexican businesspeople. All spoke Spanish and came and went like their pants were on fire. The honeymooners stayed to themselves mostly.

The flyer—or ex-flyer, I should say—Mr. DeWitt, was a retired Eastman Kodak man. He sat around in the cool lobby most of the time. He was congenial and talked freely, but the country, the Maya, everything, was old stuff to him. He had been coming to the Yucatan for years. His story is wild, but so is this country. Many years before, he had come to Merida on his honeymoon. His love for flying and the rickety old airplane he owned must have been as great as his love for his bride because the trip from New York State to the Yucatan was quite unusual. His bride went by train to Mexico City, and he flew his old biplane—hop, skip, and jump—by way of Florida, Cuba, and across the Yucatan peninsula. He arrived in Merida without incident, but his bride didn't.

It seems, as he told it, that floods on the Usumacinta River at Tenosique in Tabasco state had so weakened the bridges that the passengers had to derail and walk across the shaky structures to be picked up on the other side by the narrow-gauge train from Campeche. During this ordeal, his bride was kidnapped, along with others, and robbed of their belongings and held for ransom by a group of Chiapas bandits. The railroad, responsible for its passengers, took action (Mexican-style), and in time the bride and her flying husband were reunited. They had been guests of the Hotel Colon that trip and each year thereafter returned to Merida on vacations without the airplane. His wife had since died, but DeWitt alone returned each year to Merida. I thought it was kind of sad.

The college professor was from Delaware. He, his wife, and their leggy teenage daughter had arrived the day after I flew in from Miami and took a suite across the court from mine. I had seen the girl running on the patio the day before I met them. Mr. and Mrs. Sundett and daughter, of course, spoke English and that entitled their spot in my and DeWitt's corner of the lounge. Mrs. Sundett never seemed to be sure who was who. My phone rang one evening, and a female voice addressed me as Mr. DeWitt. I quickly advised that she had a wrong number. The next evening, Mrs. Sundett said that she had called me the evening before to ask me to join them for dinner at Los Tulipanes but hadn't gotten through to me. It was then she learned I was Stone, not Dewitt.

The big La Plaza de la Independencia is the hub of Merida. La Ciudad Blanca, formally, before the Spanish came, was the Mayan city called Ho. Some old natives on the plains today refer to the capitol of Yucatan as "Ho." At the Plaza, the Cathedral of Merida stands dominant on the east side. La Palacio Municipal stands on the west, and the Executive Palace is on the north. On the south, there is the great Casa de Montejo. Built in 1549, sixty years before the *Mayflower* dropped anchor in Massachusetts Bay, it was home of Francisco de Montejo, conqueror of the Yucantesian Maya and founder of modern Merida. The pink limestone building, with its golden doors and balcony, has ornamentation depicting helmeted Spanish conquistadors standing on the heads of Mayan subjects.

The giant laurel trees in the plaza itself came to Merida by chance. On a ship bound for Havana, the plantings were to grace that city's plaza. A driving hurricane drove the ship past Havana and wrecked it on Yucatan's shores, so the plantings were salvaged and planted in Merida's plaza.

The Parisian influence in Merida is strong. I don't think it came from the brief reign of Emperor Maximillin and his wife Carlotta. On the streets, one can ride the tour circuit in horse-drawn carriages that were once rolled on the streets of Paris. When Yucatan and Mexico got their independence from Spain in 1820, Yucatan was reluctant but did join Mexico as a state in the federation. Meridans, by far the center of

Yucatan's population, snubbed Mexico socially and turned their interest toward Paris. The aristocracy sent their children to school in Paris, not in Mexico City. Fashions from Paris were the dress of the day, not fashions of Mexico City. In a section of Paris, where the affluent from Merida owned property and sometimes lived, the people were called Meridans, not Mexicans.

I had lunch in the open cloistered Restaurante de Reforma on the corner of Calle 59 and 62 with a Mexican gentleman from the high central plateau north of Mexico City. It was his first trip to Merida also. "Si, Senior"—he chewed vigorously as he talked—"thees dry land produces the toughest beef I have ever eaten, but oh! This Merida! She ees the cleanest city in all May-hee-coh!"

Looking back, my Meridan interlude seems a bit ridiculous—in part, at least. The Colon suite was one of those parts. One lone, skinny, country boy sitting in a big cavernous suite built for millionaire land barons. The hired help resented me; I could tell by their look. A fat little Yucatecian maid, every inch of forty inches tall, even "bossed" me around. If my shoes—boots—were not under the bed, the one I slept in (I had three) when she came around to collect shoes for shining, she would waddle to me and, with a stiff finger, repeatedly point to my feet demanding, "Zapatos! Zapatos?" Need it or not, the shoes came off.

I don't recall reading this section years ago. However, I do recall the way Daddy protected himself from getting "Montezuma's Revenge." The stomach upset is from a microbe in the water, *E. coli*, and the "revenge" is called "travelers' diarrhea." Native Mexicans have flora in their intestines that eradicate the bug, but most visitors do not.

My husband and I went on a Caribbean cruise with a group of friends years ago. One of our ports of call was Playa Del Carmen in the Yucatan peninsula. We were cautioned about this malady and urged not to eat fresh salads and other produce. And for heaven's sake, don't drink any of the water.

We took a tour bus to Tulum to investigate the Mayan ruins there. Our tour guide had a cooler full of soft drinks and beer, immersed in crushed ice. He liberally passed them around. It was February, but the temperature was maybe one hundred degrees in the shade! The bus was not air-conditioned either, and our throats quickly became parched. When he pulled a Coke out of the ice chest, he cautioned that we should be very careful to wipe off all water droplets from around the mouth of the bottle, lest we ingest the horrid bug, which can totally disable someone. *E. coli* isn't prevalent in the United States where most of us live. But it can be ingested in undercooked ground beef and other meats. Mexicans sometimes fertilize their produce and fruit with human excrement. Since the native people tolerate *E. coli*, it doesn't affect them. But if we eat food grown in their soil, we are definitely at risk. It can be deadly, as cases that have sprung up periodically in the United States have proven. Food scientists and microbiologists must be able to identify it in testing meats before shipping them out to restaurants and food markets.

My father, pretty smart actually, determined how he could keep from accidently swallowing it through shaving and brushing his teeth. He bought a cheap bottle of whiskey. Keeping it on the sink, he would run water into the sink and pour a bit of the alcohol in. After a minute of swishing the water around, the microbe was essentially killed. He brushed his teeth and washed without having to worry about Montezuma's Revenge.

The previous stories were told concerning his first trip to the Yucatan. He went alone. Well before cell phones, he was literally off the grid for weeks, making my mother and me very nervous. He was exploring the Mayan ruins in the jungle on his own. God knows anything could have happened to him—he could have fallen into a pit;

an animal could have attacked him; he could have been bitten by an insect or a snake. Let your imagination think of it, and he was completely vulnerable. But there was no need to worry. He wasn't worried, and he came home safe and sound. That was just his first trip.

He continues his narrative about another trip to the Yucatan.

My wife, Virginia, was with me on my second visit to the Yucatan. On this trip, I visited the large Mayan centers like Tulum on the wild Caribe coast of Quintana Roo.

Standing on the high platform of the Castillo in Tulum, one's view is twofold. Toward the south the blue-green waters of the Caribbean lead one's mind on to the Gulf of Honduras. Toward the west, over the old city's wall, is the pea soup-green expanse of the jungle coat of Quintana Roo. Tulum, ancient Zamna, the largest Mayan center on the Caribe coast, was the last stronghold of the Maya in the Yucatan. In a way, the area is still a "holdout" from the days of the Spanish Conquest.

First a territory, then a state (it obtained statehood the year before my first visit there), it is said to still, in its dense jungle, harbor bands of dreaded Chan Santa Cruz Indians that recognize no government. Quintana Roo, as a territory, was a Mexican Siberia. Undesirables, political enemies, crooks were sent to these jungles to get them out of Mexican society. Some of their descendants live there today. The inhabitants of these jungles engage in (other than robbery and murder) bee keeping. The best honey in the world is said to come from the Quintana Roo jungles. Some engage in the chicle trade—the gathering of white milky juice of the sapodilla tree for the chewing gum industry. This sparsely

settled Caribe coast is the wildest stretch of coastline in Middle America.

Quintana Roo achieved statehood in 1974. So Daddy's visit
occurred in 1975. Daddy loved to say the names of these exotic places,
like Quintana Roo. He would say them in a singsong voice. He was
obviously romanticizing these places and daydreamed of them often.

Cayman Island

The trip where Daddy and my mother visited Tulum was a cruise to the Caribbean. They went with a group of friends and saw several of the Caribbean Islands.

The song "Cayman Woman" came to mind the moment I saw her. I had walked into the little white, weather-beaten store in George Town, Grand Cayman Island. I was looking for a camera, a certain camera that would cost me $300.00 in the States. The girl didn't have one. She had Minaltas, yes, but no Rollies. I momentarily forgot the camera, however. "The soft voice and warm skin." I forget the rest of the song's words except each stanza ended with emphasis, "Cayman Woman!" And there she stood in front of me. Virginia was looking at clothes in a shop down the street. I was glad of that. I didn't make my thoughts known to the girl. There was no point. But I browsed longer than necessary. I bought a book, a trinket or two, other things, just to enjoy the sight of her.

In another George Town shop, I found the camera I was looking for. Another attractive girl ran that shop too, but she was not a Cayman woman. She was a transplanted Canadian girl from Toronto. She had visited the Caymans two years before and refused to live anywhere else again. I bought the camera for $150.00, ending a search through the upper Caribbean for it.

The Cayman Islands, consisting of three separate islands, remain a part of the old British Empire, though they have self-government in the old English custom. Barristers wear white wigs. They identify their location: British West Indies.

Grand Cayman, the big island, sits by the Cayman Trench, a crack in the continental plate, that a few miles offshore, plunges to a depth of 24,720 feet. The other two islands, Little Cayman Brac, lie seventy miles northeast of Grand Cayman. I wonder why they are considered a part of Grand Cayman. It has to do with the chain, I guess.

Virginia and I attended a turtle burger party at the Galleon Beach Hotel for the cruise ship passengers. The burgers were good, but I felt odd eating them. I'd rather spent the time touring more of the island or looking at the "Cayman Woman."

I'm glad I visited Grand Cayman when I did. Much of the rapidly disappearing old charm still existed, although the flux of high-rise, tourist-oriented buildings was rapidly overshadowing the quaint old wooden structures.

The "money laundry" business, with its enormous clusters of towering bank buildings, is swallowing up the old original town of George Town. It was a former shipbuilding town, where Scottish craftsmen in five individual shipyards built for the south-seas market, the famous Cayman Island schooners. No shipyard exists there today. Living is easy on Grand Cayman for its permanent people. Two factors, one old and one new, take care of that.

Back in history, a British fleet was wrecked by a hurricane on the shores of Grand Cayman. The islanders saved many lives and nursed many injured back to health. The Crown, in appreciation, declared Grand Cayman free of taxation forever. No native of the Caymans pays taxes today. That takes care of state taxes. City and other local governmental taxes do not exist either. The mammoth banking industry (there were 196 individual banks in George Town in 1976), in exchange for the privilege of operating in the island, pays for all municipal functions. Government officials, workers' salaries, road and street building, police and firemen—all. The only thing native residents have to do is provide for personal needs.

Most buildings on Grand Cayman stand a few feet off ground. The land mass rises an average of about four feet above sea level. The island is overrun by hurricanes so often it is referred to as "Hurricane Road." The Cayman dialect of English is as distinctive as their driving on the left side of the street. The "yes mon, no mon" has a soothing tone to it. Ask a Cayman policeman (dressed like a London "Bobby") for a direction, and he responds, "Dis way mon, tree block an' tick a right mon. Yes mon, tank ye mon!"

Hog Sty Bay is losing its original rocky quay to modern concrete piers. The old streets are losing their quaint old wooden buildings; the duty-free gift shops that open when a cruise ship comes and closes when it sails away are beginning to stay open all day. Will the soothing native tongue pass away too? "Yeah, mon! Too soon, mon!"

It is important to remember that Daddy's autobiographical memoir was written in the late 1970s or early 1980s, and his descriptions reflect that period.

Jamaica

Another stopover in the Caribbean cruise my parents took was Ocho Rios. Daddy picks up his narrative here.

The barefooted Jamaican boys, sixty feet up in the tall coconut palm of Prospect Plantation, were throwing down the huge nuts to the group below. The boys on the ground were shucking them out and throwing them into the large cart that was pulled by a tractor. Sir Cameron Mitchell's plantation is located near Oracabessa, or Gold Head, where Columbus first saw Jamaica in 1494. It is self-sufficient, exporting as well as coconuts, bananas, sugarcane, and other tropical fruits.

On the high bluff on Jamaica's north coast, overlooking the Spanish Main, Sir Cameron had built the great plantation. There, too, he had built his Cadet School, where they get an excellent education, leading to college degrees. It seemed like a great arrangement for many of the youth of Jamaica. The old bauxite shipping terminal on Ocho Rios Bay, owned by Henry J. Kaiser, of World War II shipbuilding/liberty ship fame (and after a brief interlude in auto manufacture—the cars that bore his name) was overshadowed by high rise hotels and apartment complexes.

The small town of quaint huts with rusting sheet-iron roofs was yielding to the pressures of tourism. Ocho Rios is crowded between the gleaming white sands of the crescent-like bay and the dark green jungle-covered mountain backdrop. This newer tourist mecca on Jamaica's north shore approaches Montego Bay in popularity. Montego Bay lies some fifty kilometers west. In its Spanish translation, Ocho Rios means "eight rivers," That is wrong. There are rivers, but not eight. The words are a corruption of the words "Las Chorreras," which means "waterfalls," of which there are many on the rivers that cascade down from the mountains to the sea.

Probably the most noted is Dunn's River Falls, which forms a cascade stairway up a wooded hill. Black Jamaican girls in bright red and yellow bikinis pose out on the rocks for gratuities, but I missed them. They were on their "break," as one late-leaving girl put it. She promised me she would come back in five minutes if I would give her "an extra dollar," but she didn't. I photographed the white falls without the black beauty. The most beautiful waterfall near Ocho Rios is the Shaw Park, the old resort high on a hill behind the town. With a fast shutter to freeze the action, it looks like white lace spread over the black rocks. The result is spectacular!

Although Virginia bought handcrafts in support of the eager natives, she found shopper's heaven in the fashionable boutiques outside the straw market. A tour of the black coral industry in St. Ann's Bay, where Columbus beached and repaired two leaking ships in 1503 (his last voyage to the western world he had discovered) was interesting.

Jamaican roots entwine many cultures, from the indigenous Arawak Indians, Negroes, Spanish, English, to pirates. The Jamaican State motto befits this cosmopolitan race: "Out of Many One People."

Although Jamaicans have parted company with the Empire—Great Britain—even dropping the word "British" from the geographical expression "British West Indies," they are still very much "English" in certain ways. Most noticeable perhaps is in their speech. Their English is very sharp and precise.

In the mountains of western Jamaica lies the Cockpit Country. In the Cockpit Country are strange and eerie people, the Maroons. These long interbred native and runaway slaves live in these forbidden hills on 1,500 acres of land granted them in the eighteenth century, complete with autonomy. They have their own rules, their own religion, their own music. From their music comes the basic "reggae." Tourists avoid the Cockpit Country.

Tourism is big in Jamaica, and the craftsmen are unshakable salesmen. You can drag a hand carver several blocks before he will turn your coat sleeve loose, if you don't buy his ducks.

Jamaica has, hidden in the vast coves and rolling mountains, many relics of its past splendors. Unlike Sir Cameron Mitchell's Great Prospect Plantation, the ghosts of other plantations still stand but are in crumbling ruins. Near Ocho Rios, at Discovery Bay, stand the magnificent arches and walls of a Spanish hacienda, where pimiento plant native to Jamaica was found and developed into a highly desirable spice. Many food and medicinal plants were grown and developed in Jamaica under the rule of Diego, Christopher Columbus's son, who was made governor general of the island in 1509.

Xayamaca, native name of Jamaica, did not fare well under the Spanish and not until the English were well seated in the island did its potential really be fully realized. Jamaica is a land of mystery and voodoo. In the dark hills paralleling the coast, the culture is strong and said to equal Haitian practices. The cult often leads to bizarre happenings. Mrs. Annie Palmer, mistress of the great Rose Hall Plantation on the north

shore near Montego Bay, was a master of voodoo. It is said she learned of its powers while a
child living in Haiti. Though now renovated,
the giant plantation house is said to sometimes
echo through its mammoth halls the screams of
her dying lovers she killed there. Annie herself
was murdered in her bed in Rose Hall. Some say
a slave, whom she had had whipped, did it. A
movie has been made of her life based, I think,
on the historical novel by the Jamaican writer
George de Lisser, entitled *The White Witch of Rose
Hall.*

The folk arts are prominent in Jamaican
culture: music, whose distinctive "reggae" accom-
panies all art forms; the pageants, carnivals, and
dances that are mandatory on all holidays; the
"wild people," called "Rastas"; a semi-religious,
semi-political cult, and the Pocomanina crowd
all add their individual flavor. Come to Jamaica.
There could be a "thing" for you. Its Koo Koos
and Boonoonoonoos are festivities not to be
missed when visiting this strange, strange island.

The cruise Bob and I took did not go to Jamaica, and I am
utterly fascinated by my father's description of the island, with all
its oddities and serendipitous facets. My mother bought a beautiful
aqua-blue outfit in Ocho Rios, which she wore to a party on the
cruise ship.

CHAPTER 26

Rubbing Shoulders and Noteworthy Encounters

Throughout his almost eighty-five years of life, Daddy bumped into people who were famous or who had connections with the famous, the not so famous, and the infamous!

Back through time, the country boy has met some interesting people. A few were notable; many were not. I think the most impressive person I ever met was during the dark years of World War II. I worked for the Navy Department in the massive shipbuilding program at the Charleston Naval Shipyard. The person was not really a big man, and his name was hardly a household word, although a movie has been made about him—a documentary move, that is. But then, who cares about a documentary movie, even those cast with big-name stars?

I had heard the story, and when I saw the movie, I was intrigued by the person. The movie was *The Story of Dr. Wassell*, produced by Cecil B. DeMille at Paramount Studios and starred the great Gary Cooper as the legendary Dr. Wassell in his epic experiences in the New Guinea jungles during the Japanese overrun of the South Pacific. I never met Gary Cooper, but I did meet and shake the trembling hand of the real Dr. Wassell, whom the story was about.

Rear Admiral Cornydon McAlmont Wassell, as a young physician, was a medical missionary to China in 1914. He later joined the United States Naval Reserve and as a lieutenant was sent to Java in December 1941, following the Japanese bombing of Pearl Harbor. He was assigned to a cadre of Dutch physicians and cared for the wounded servicemen stationed there. After the Japanese invaded and conquered the area, a medical ship was dispatched to pick up and transport the most ambulatory of the wounded Naval personnel. Dr. Wassell was unpersuasive in trying to also include the more severely wounded sailors and insisted on remaining with them in hospital to tend to their care. When it seemed too dangerous for them all, he managed to influence a British army convoy to transport even these non-ambulatory patients to a ship, where they were transported to safety. He took a vote of the dozen or so patients, and they all agreed to try as best they could to hang on and endure the one hundred and fifty-mile trip on rough, jungle roads. All but one was rescued and saved.

Dr. Wassell was awarded the Navy Cross for bravery. His citation reads, "By his courage, determination, and untiring devotion to duty, Lieutenant Commander Wassell saved many lives." He retired from the Navy as a rear admiral and spent his last years in Key West, Florida, moving later back to his home state of Arkansas, where he passed away in 1958. He is buried in Arlington National Cemetery. At the time of his courageous acts, he became an instant celebrity, and President Franklin Delano Roosevelt's praise of him inspired Cecil B. DeMille to make a film of his story.

*****

My parents began camping after I moved out on my own and enjoyed that mode of travel for years afterward. They loved the Smoky and Blue Ridge Mountains, and on one of their trips, they spent a week or two in Cades Cove, Tennessee. It was on that trip that Daddy "rubbed shoulders" with a well-known celebrity. He tells of it in his own inimitable way.

> Ingrid Bergman smiled a quick smile of recognition and turned back to the card rack. The chance meeting was in a card shop in Gatlinburg, Tennessee, in the Great Smoky Mountains where she was filming the summer scenes of the movie *A Walk in Spring Rain*. I wanted to speak to her but didn't, not just for the pleasure and experience of it but because of something relative (relativity is a pet subject with me)—this being a mutual friend from the past. A former classmate of mine in the New York Institute of Photography, Bob Capa, and Ingrid Bergman had a relationship that experienced some degree of fulfillment before his untimely death by a land mine in Indo-China. She spoke of him fondly in her book, *Stromboli*.

I have not read Bergman's book, and I don't know her history with Bob Capa, but Daddy has been faithful to drop these little tantalizing nuggets without much (if any) embellishment. I'll leave you to tease this one out. I researched Dr. Wassell, and I think he might have been more important, anyway.

*****

He tells us earlier in his memoirs about a trip to Quebec to attend a Rosicrucian Conference. He and my mother traveled around Ontario a bit before and after the meeting. Following is one of the experiences he had.

Tension was high in the modest Corbeil homestead that night. Smoke curled from the chimney and drifted on the night air on the Ontario highlands. Mrs. Dionne was in labor, and Dr. Defoe had not yet arrived. Madame La Gros did what she had to do—boil lots of hot water. That was the prime requisite in midwifery. Twins, maybe triplets, were expected. But *five!* Heaven forbid! They kept coming: one, two, three, maybe four were delivered before the doctor arrived, but Madame La Gros had done well, laying the tiny premature infants in a softly-lined wicker hamper. Of course, the press gave Dr. Defoe all the credit. Madame Le Gros was never mentioned.

I saw Madame La Gros and her wicker hamper years later. A veiled old lady silhouetted by window light in the back room of her store in Callander, Ontario. She looked very much like Whistler's Mother. "She talks to no one," her niece store clerk and cousin of the five girls said. "Please don't take any pictures." Of course, I would buy postcards. I respected the privacy of the old French lady. It seemed to be the right thing to do.

There are numerous articles available on the Dionne quintuplets. Madame La Gros's souvenir shop is mentioned also, along with another midwife who was called in to help with the unusual birth.

*****

My parents' trip to Canada for the Rosicrucian Convention was filled with interesting, funny, and, well, strange encounters. I don't know where my mother was during this experience, but my dad definitely felt it worth relating.

William Vernon-Brown of Brampton grinned as he seesawed by with the big Negro gal from Detroit. I was dancing with the big White girl from North Battleford, Saskatchewan. She was light on her feet for such a big girl, but trouble was I just could not reach around her. It was like waltzing with a wall! "Where is Johnny?" I asked, eager to get loose. "Somewhere," she mumbled, her eyes closed. Cheek to cheek, she kept whirling. I kept up with her by hooking my thumb in her belt loop.

On the ballroom floor, deep in the bowels of the cavernous Royal York Hotel, you didn't feel the chill of the pre-autumn, Ontario night that engulfed the city of Toronto. The music stopped and, thankfully, William Vernon-Brown took my arm and led me to the bar. We had talked briefly in the afternoon after the medi-transmittal experiments. I had told him I definitely believed in "flying saucers," and now he felt that he considered me a confidant. He said it was his job. He was a working member of the information force. He called it The Reception Project. "This saucer thing," he said seriously, "they are here to help us! Their planet is a million light years ahead of us." Quoting after twenty years isn't exact. However, he told me "they" knew we had nuclear fission, and they knew we would destroy our civilization with it because we had not advanced enough to handle it. We had, in fact, split the atom too soon. A civilization must first reach "oneness" before they were right for such a deadly force. Our factions must first achieve a state of international love and understanding. We must first eliminate all causes for war.

We must discontinue its development, postpone all use of it in both war and peace projects. In short, ban all nuclear energy on this planet! Sure, the "saucers" were nuclear-powered, but they, the outer spacemen, were inertial. They had accomplished complete "oneness." He would show me proof, take me tomorrow to Barrie, in the hills, and show me the scorched earth!

Interesting, yes. But, sorry, "I don't have the time."

*****

I don't know why my father didn't write about this infamous family, but he certainly told me about them years ago. He was only a little boy when the incident occurred, but it is significant in the history of the community in which my dad grew up.

There was something about that Bigham family! Living in nearby Pamplico, the family seemed to have more than its share of murders. Daddy was a little boy in Effingham in 1921 when a group of men came by the store and picked up his father. They drove down to the Bigham place to see about a reported disturbing occurrence. Turns out the whole family had been shot to death!

Years before, Smiley Bigham Sr. had been accused of beating to death a neighbor's slave, and he was known for the severe mistreatment of his own servants. Later, in 1906, State Senator Smiley Bigham Jr.'s obituary reveals that *he* was suspected of having poisoned his father. Further, Smiley's wife, Dora, was suspected of poisoning *him*. In 1908, Smiley Bigham III reportedly drove a nail through the ear of a servant boy! He was arrested on the charge of murder. Then a month before Smiley's trial, the senator's daughter-in-law, Ruth Bigham, was murdered by her own husband, Dr. G. Cleveland Bigham, supposedly to prevent her from testifying against Smiley. Blood is thicker than the marriage bond, apparently. Cleveland orchestrated the murder of Ruth by telling a simple-minded youngster that he should be on the lookout for a ghost. Ruth habitually wore pastel and pale colors and walked in the evening along the river's edge. The boy, William Avant, saw Ruth and, frightened at the otherworldly vision, shot and killed her. Although Dr. Cleveland Bigham was charged with being the mastermind behind her murder, justice was never served in her case. He was charged merely with manslaughter and sentenced to three years. He appealed, and the judge released him on his own recognizance, during which time he fled the state without serving a day of his sentence.

Then there was the big day of which I wrote earlier. January 15, 1921, the neighborhood was alerted to a disturbing situation at the Bigham house. Upon their arrival, the men found only Edmund Bigham alive, while his brother, Smiley III, his mother, sister, and her two children had been shot dead. Edmond maintained that Smiley shot them all and then shot himself in the head. Further, Edmund asserted that before his mother died of her wounds, she told him that Smiley had done the mass shooting before shooting himself. I have no idea what could have been the motive for such a thing, but it appears that murder was in the Bigham blood!

The authorities did not believe Edmund, and he was arrested. Then things began to get really weird. Edmund was tried, convicted, and sentenced to death *twice* before appeals enabled him to be retried a third time, hoping for a better outcome. The case was a sensation, and members of the community packed into the courthouse, prickling with excitement. The court performance became a theatrical masterpiece. Edmund loudly prophesied that all the witnesses and the officials had lied about him, and they would, every one of them, die before he did! Whether it was from fear or the actual power of Edmund's witchcraft, one of the witnesses promptly had a heart attack and fell dead in the witness box. Also, a subsequent flood nearly wiped from the map the town of Conway, where the trial took place. The "Bigham flood" or "freshet" was an eerie reminder of the curse Edmund had cast upon them. To further fire up the drama, his mother's skull was shoved in his face, hoping to shame him into confessing to her murder, which spurred the opposing attorneys to get into a fistfight over the gruesome stunt.

After Edmund was convicted at this trial, a new trial was ordered based on the subsequent appeal. Shortly before this trial was to begin, the court announced that due to a "delicate and temporary condition," again *this* trial would be postponed. Seemed Edmund's wife was pregnant, and that justified a delay.

These country people were caught up in the irresistible spookiness of the situation and felt jinxed by Edmund's curses and his powerful legend. Edmund's cool, level calm provoked a spine-chilling feeling in the crowd of men, aghast at the spectacle unfolding in front of them. The county's Black residents were equally enthralled and packed the balcony to watch the event. The judge announced the trial's postponement, and the courthouse emptied for the short adjournment before resuming. Spectators' anticipation escalated, and then the judge announced there had been a plea deal. Edmund pleaded guilty and was given a life sentence. The courthouse drama ended, but the Bigham drama continued. The prosecuting attorney and jury all died before he did, another fulfillment of Edmund's prophesy!

In 1960, Senator Ralph Gasque of Marion was able to get Bigham paroled into his custody. He lived his final two years with him.

*****

Daddy's fascination with the Yucatan followed him through the latter years of his life. Here is another vignette of an encounter there.

The little archeology coed lost her pen at Kabah and asked to borrow mine. I had several pens in my gadget bag, so I gave her one. Kabah was our first stop in the one-day tour of two important Mayan ruins (cities) in western Yucatan. The girl was a student at some western university—in New Mexico, I think. Here again, I was true to form by not getting names of people I meet. Our encounter was short, consisting mostly of asking favors. She took notes mostly, but on occasion filmed a structure with her eight-millimeter movie camera. I was working in thirty-five-millimeter stills, color and black and white.

In Uxmal (oosh-mal), which is the most beautiful Maya center in the Yucatan, the girl and I met again. It was at the toppled phallic monument. The mighty symbol of the male organ lay broken, wrong end up in front of the Governor's Palace, where Fray Diego de Landa had pulled it down from its pedestal and half buried in sand. Fran de Landa did more than any other person to destroy records of the ancient Maya's culture. He burned all their books (codices; only three escaped the Fray's fires at Ticul) and vowed to Christianize these heathens if he had to chop the heads off all of them in the doing!

The student asked me to take her movie camera and shoot a scene of her by the monument. She blushed deeply when she did, but I saw a naughty twinkle in her eye. After a short burst of frames, I stopped the camera and said, "You know what you are standing by. Let's have a little endearment!"

As I began shooting again, she threw her arms around the great stone idol, snuggled rapturously against it, kissing it several times. She took my Leica and made a shot of me there and on the steps of the Governor's Palace. She said, "Girls in the dorm will be shocked when they see that scene of me standing by that…thing over there. I'm really very square." She returned my Leica and with a quick wave, said, "Thanks and thanks for the pen."

I wanted to see her again, and did—in the
lunchroom at the Lapalapa. She squeezed in at a
crowded table across the room from me. On the
bus back to Merida, she chose a seat on the oppo-
site end. I presumed she felt she had opened a
door and panicked. I did not pursue her further.

A picture of the young student standing at the base of the steps
of the Governor's Palace is in Daddy's book, as well as a picture she
took of my dad leaning against the same fallen monument. There
is a certain creep factor involved in considering the Maya's obsession with the penis. Of course, fertility was an important process to
those who lived off of the success of crops and other cultivated living
things. As with many ancient cultures, the gods of fertility must be
appeased and honored in order to grow successful crops and raise
herds of goats and other livestock. Plus, since it was a male-dominant
society, that could also explain the obsession with the penis!

*****

Mike Burke's wife (I don't remember her
name) invited me aboard the *Fantome*, which
was being fitted out on a Miami pier in Biscayne
for service in the Windjammer Cruises. Captain
Burke had spoken to me earlier about doing some
work on her, after one of employees had mentioned to him, "that fellow out there on the dock
has thirty years' experience in steel shipbuilding."
Regrettably, I was not available to work on his
ship, but I wished I had been.

The *Fantome* was an interesting ship with
quite a history of derogation, and I hate to see
a ship of any kind neglected and junked. This
made me glad Captain Burke was putting her
into service following its long and mostly idle
existence. Built in Italy as a training ship for the

Italian Navy, the three hundred foot, four-mast, steel-hulled *Fantome* served several functions before being sold to private interests. Sold several times, it seems she never suited the purpose intended and spent much of her time lying derelict in some obscure port.

Eventually, the Greek shipping magnate Aristotle Onassis bought the rusting *Fantome* with a definite purpose in mind. She was cleaned, painted, and put in glittering array fit for a princess. For, indeed, she was thus intended. The cruddy little Greek with the covetous red eye for beautiful, important women intended to give the beautiful *Fantome* to Princess Grace (to be) as a wedding present upon her marriage to Prince Rainier of Monaco. The gift was never given, however, and the *Fantome* went back into idleness until Mike Burke bought her. The reason she was not given to Princess Grace? Onassis did not get an invitation to the wedding!

*****

One of the most gripping stories was originally told to me by my mother. This story reveals the inner strength and character of the man who sired me. I would hope to be as brave and clever and to apply whatever knowledge and ability I have to help someone. Thankfully, Daddy included it in his memoir.

The truck was upside down in the water. Only the rear wheels and the bottom structure of the chassis were above water and one corner of the floor pan (floorboard). Two or three cars had stopped and some men were standing on the bridge by the broken rail where the vehicle had gone over.

My wife stayed in our car. I asked the man where the driver was. No one knew. "In the wreck," one person suggested. I climbed down the embankment and across the rocks to a point where I could get out on the upturned truck. It wobbled as if it would settle even deeper in the water.

Leaning close to the floor pan, I called, "Anyone in there?"

A low voice replied.

"Can you get the door open?" I asked. He couldn't. The truck wobbled again as I moved. I realized the small air space the man was breathing in could quickly vanish should the truck sink more. I called to the men on the bridge to go to my car and tell my wife to open the trunk for my toolbox.

With the proper wrench, I removed the thin metal floor plate and pulled it up far enough for the Negro driver to crawl up through. The truck rocked again as we both scrambled for the rocks.

The man was stunned and confused—wet, but otherwise he was all right.

I love this story. It conveys that deep below his gruff exterior, his heart beat with compassion for anyone in such a predicament as the truck driver. Daddy saved his life. His quick action and ingenuity had made all the difference in the outcome of the truck driver's story.

I am very proud to call him my dad.

*****

To live in such a rural area as Effingham during the early 1900s, you wouldn't think anyone this famous would ever find her way there, but Daddy rubbed shoulders with this woman when he was a young boy, and it would resonate with him in his later years.

Research reveals that Aimee Semple McPherson lay in a hospital bed, hovering between life and death. It was 1913, and she was only twenty-three years old. Instead of dying, a voice told her to "go," which she realized was a call into ministry. She got up and did so, and in a scant decade, she skyrocketed to international fame as an evangelist. She toured the United States speaking in tongues and healing people, who flocked into the tent where she was preaching. Never mind she was a woman in a man's role. She was beautiful, charismatic, and took the world by storm. In 1923, she dedicated the Church of the Four-Square Gospel, and thousands entered the temple's doors to be blessed by her. She had Hollywood star quality, and everybody loved her.

Apparently, she came to the close proximity of Effingham, South Carolina, and Daddy had an encounter with her as a small boy.

> Aimee Semple McPherson once put her hand on my head and said something to the effect that this country lad would grow up to be a very great man. At this point (age 70) I'd like to speak to her through the live telephone that was buried in her coffin with her in 1944 and say, "Aimee, I am still waiting?"

From the contents of Daddy's autobiographical memoir, I am overwhelmed at his diverse talents, determination, and accomplishments. It is true that he didn't reach his dream of being a motion picture photographer. Also, he was held back from working in the airplane industry. He is not nationally recognized. However, he fulfilled important roles in many places where he found himself. One of the "Greatest Generation," he contributed greatly to the World War II effort. He played a key role, which nobody else could do, as the company blacksmith in building Myrtle Beach State Park. His name doesn't appear on buildings or movie screens, but it does appear on a magazine article in the Smithsonian Institution's records. He also penned and photographed numerous articles for *Sandlapper*

Magazine and provided photos for a more nationally known one, *Modern Maturity.* His research contributed to an archeological textbook. He developed a few inventions that were put into play in the building of naval ships. He was an enigma and a phenomenon in his surrounding area and somebody whose creations were sought after.

I have heard it said, "Be careful not to step on the gems at your feet while reaching for the stars."

I hope my dad came to recognize the gems at his feet and the accomplishments he achieved while longing to touch the star of cinematography. Life didn't bring him all he wanted. He wasn't perfect, and he had a turbulent marriage. He was anathema to some of my mother's relatives and sometimes couldn't always get along well with his own.

Yet perhaps we will think of him when we view a photo of a navy submarine or catch a glimpse of his essence in one of his still-life Lowcountry marsh pictures. We can perceive his anguish at his father's passing, his disappointment in not becoming a world-class cinematographer, or sense his anxiety from the unrelenting stresses during World War II. Perhaps we will chuckle at his quirky sense of humor or become awe struck at his archeological achievements. I will always remember him if I catch a whiff of English Leather Cologne. We definitely can thrill at his out-of-body experiences in the realm of phantasmagoria he relates and think of him when we see a flock of Canada geese soaring overhead. There is no doubt that he was a dreamer, as he describes himself time and again. He made his mark on the world. And we ultimately understand why the minister, in his eulogy of my father, called him a Renaissance Man.

In 1985, my father took my mother and me to Pamplico to spend one summer day with his first cousin and his two children. We visited Effingham too, and he pointed out the site where the general store had been located. A pecan grove is situated on land there now. It must have been that same day that he discovered the remnants of the rusty chain in the tree, from which his swing hung and propelled him into his imaginary airplane. Then we drove to the site of Austin Stone's land on the Lynches River that he had purchased from James Keith in 1774. My dad photographed a number of grave markers in the old family cemetery, as well as his beloved Lynches River. He scooped up some sandy soil from where the river has kissed that land for centuries. That bottle of soil is labeled and rested on my dad's desk the rest of his life. Now it is a fixture on mine.

Edwin Hoyt Stone was my dad—the only dad I had—and looking closely at him through his autobiographical memoir, he may not have achieved "fame," but it's obvious that he was truly extraordinary!

AFTERWORD

I frequently dream of going home, back to the little flat-roofed cottage my dad built on the marshy banks of James Island Creek. Built of cinder block and roughly finished, I would call it "home" for all my childhood and a couple of years of young adulthood.

My roots were deeply imbedded in the pluff mud of that marsh. From the terrace, the house boasted a 180-degree view of James Island Creek and the Holy City of Charleston, South Carolina, beyond. As a child, at low tide I would go to the edge of the property and play with the fiddler crabs that emerged from holes in the mud. Often, I could sit on the terrace and watch herons and egrets fly over the marsh. Mama and Daddy would tie chicken necks to a string and lower them into the creek off the dock, scooping up the caught crabs with a dip net. We had to be careful not to let them pinch us when we dropped them into a bucket of salt creek water. At other times, we would navigate the creek in a boat, breathing in the pungent aroma of the marsh. I can still feel the sticky air that blanketed us during sultry summer days.

The house itself holds memories—oh, so many memories of years of my growing up. It holds the echoes of the uneasy relationship I had with my dad and his and my mom's stormy marriage. In my room, as an only child, I played with my dolls and my cat Butch, did homework after I was in school, and finally as a teenager awaited my boyfriend's arrival to take me out on dates. After I was married, many Thanksgivings, Christmases, and other occasions saw us gather with family and friends to enjoy my mother's cooking. When she invited my husband and me to dinner, Bob would always say, "Great! We're going to have something good for a change."

319

Daddy's interest was focused more in the darkroom, that magical closet where, with the application of special chemicals, blank paper would turn into black-and-white photographs. It was one of only a few places where I could interact with him—always in his world, never the world of a little girl.

I always figured I would return in my senior years and grow old in that house. Being their only child, I took for granted that one day I would live out my final years in that unique cottage on the marsh. Sadly, that did not come about.

Daddy died in 1998, and then a few years later, my mother moved to the Presbyterian Home in Summerville, now called "The Village." She felt she must sell the house. That may be the worst period in my entire life. It was like a death—no, two deaths. As long as I had that house, my parents' spirits would somehow remain in that space. In retrospect, it was a sacred space for me. And then it was gone. My roots bled from being violently plucked out of the origins of my life.

Mother spent her last night of moving at our house. The day of moving Mother to The Village, Bob took her to Summerville in our car, while I drove her car over to the house very early, arriving just as the sun was coming up. I sat out on the terrace one last time, sipping coffee I had brought—a beautiful day in January was dawning, pink and purple light. I watched the egrets and herons on their early morning flight. The familiar and unforgettable aroma of the marsh was strong. I listened to the birds sing, as they arrived for the seeds that my parents had always fed them so faithfully. Then I went into the house to await the movers, who would move the few remaining pieces of furniture, which my mother had chosen for her room at The Village. The leftover odds and ends from the yard sale were packed into my mother's car for me to drop off at the nearest Goodwill box.

I pulled down the disappearing stairway in the hall and climbed into the attic to look around one last time. Still there was the photo enlarger that Daddy had moved up into the attic after he built the pitched roof on the house and anchored onto a workbench. Neither hell nor high water would enable us remove it. When Daddy secured something somewhere, it could never be undone, like when he wrapped Christmas presents. He used almost a roll of tape for each box. You needed a secret code to get into them. I also explored the cubbies my dad had built and the other now empty spaces that had held his books, negatives, and other paraphernalia—his life's work, really.

Then I descended the stairs and walked into the room that had been mine—empty now. My parents' room was also bare—not even a coat hanger remained in the closet.

When I dream of returning, the house usually appears in one of two different scenarios: either people are living there (which is true) or the house has been abandoned and is being overtaken by the rising sea level (which may happen at some distant time). But the sleep fairies will never let me reclaim it. It is always out of my reach, and I wake up with that same numb, crushing grief that overwhelmed me on that last morning.

Maybe someday my ashes will be scattered there and become a part of the pluff mud. I will return to my roots. Until then, I'm not truly anchored.

ACKNOWLEDGMENTS

This book has been a very long time in the making, many years thinking about how to publish his original memoir, which contained adages and quips of his personal opinions on society, all irrelevant to the grand stories he told.

First of all, I have to give credit to the Cornelia Company of Writers, a group of brilliant, creative, and delightfully eccentric people, who write everything from children's make-believe, serious novels, memoirs, poetry, nonfiction, and whimsical and poignant stories told in the vernacular of the people of their setting. The idea of publishing Daddy's book "as was" was definitely a no-go. Plus, since I was in the writer's group, they wanted to read *my* writing and not just his. Collaboration and brain storming gave birth to the dialogue, where Daddy would tell his stories and I would provide comment, historical background on the location, and sometimes the personalities of the people with which he interacted.

When I began to read portions of my manuscript, one of the writers said, "I've never seen anything like this!" I kept going and ended up with a four-hundred-page book that chased preverbal rabbits down, not only rabbit holes, but also into weeds and forests.

That's where my editor Nancy Addison came in. We met at a solar eclipse party in 2017 at a mutual friend's home—one of our writers' group. Later, Nancy told me she normally wouldn't go to a party where she only knew the hostess, but since the setting was ideal for observing the total eclipse, she came. Nancy began to come to the library to our meetings and read some of my manuscript as I shared with the group. As we began to know each other, it began to dawn on me that I might actually publish my book, I asked her if she would like to edit it. She expressed delight, and this wonderful friendship and adventure began.

My deep thanks go to her for her dedication and devotion to this task. She literally turned a four-hundred-page sow's ear into a silk purse. One could not ask for a better and more thorough editor.

Thanks also goes to my late husband, Bob, who read much of it and commented and supported my efforts. He recently passed. I miss him so very much.

Most of all, I must thank my father for writing his memoir for me. Not only did I gather a lot of knowledge and respect for his diversity and skills, but also through reading the personal, I gained more insight into our family dynamics. Working sections of his manuscript, I began to know more about myself. I realized, after seventy-something years, that our strained relationship affected me in a number of ways—mainly in my relationships with men. I discovered why I have always been so needy, craving constant reassurance that I was loved and cherished. It's sad, really, but I can go forward now, feeling secure within myself. I am quite content living a life unencumbered by the drama and complications that often come with a relationship.

I feel whole. Thank you, Daddy, for helping me realize who you are, who I am, and how I've developed.

ABOUT THE AUTHOR

 Terry Stone was born in Charleston, South Carolina, and grew up on beautiful James Island. She fell in love with the English language as a child and always enjoyed opportunities to write. After high school, she attended Palmer Business College and then went to work for the US government, where she worked in various positions. Like her dad, she seemed to reinvent herself along the way—starting out as a clerk typist, becoming a department head secretary, then going into management analysis, and finally becoming a computer systems programmer and analyst. She left civil service when her husband retired and spent a few years volunteering, working a short time in retail home sales, and eventually deciding to return to college to finish her degree. She persevered part-time and earned a BA and MA in English. Following that, she and her husband moved from Charleston to Northeast Georgia, where she taught freshman English at Piedmont College (now a university).

CPSIA information can be obtained
at www.ICGtesting.com
Printed in the USA
JSHW021922170123
36389JS00001B/5

9 781639 858293